A Guidebook for Teaching PHYSICS

A Guidebook for Teaching PHYSICS

William Yurkewicz, Jr.

Allyn and Bacon, Inc.   **Boston • London • Sydney • Toronto**

This book is part of A GUIDEBOOK FOR TEACHING Series

Copyright © 1985 by Allyn and Bacon, Inc., 7 Wells Avenue, Newton, Massachusetts 02159.

Library of Congress Cataloging in Publication Data

Yurkewicz, William.
  A guidebook for teaching physics.

  (A Guidebook for teaching series)
  1. Physics—Study and teaching—Handbooks, manuals, etc.
2. Curriculum development—Handbooks, manuals, etc.
I. Title. II. Series.
QC30.Y87 1985   530'.07'1   84-28436
ISBN 0-205-08355-2

Printed in the United States of America

10 9 8 7 6 5 4   90 89 88

Dedication

For Diane,
Susan, and Michael

Contents

Preface

This book provides the physics teacher with so many specific ideas and resources for teaching physics that he or she will not be able to use them all in one course. Many books are available that outline, in a general way, what high school students need to know about physics. Others convey the content of physics without providing specific suggestions for how to help students learn that content. This book is different.

I have tried to produce a comprehensive handbook with an emphasis on practicality. For each concept in physics that a teacher might wish students to learn, *A Guidebook for Teaching Physics* provides instructional objectives, a summary of content related to the basic concept, classroom activities, discussion questions, group activities, laboratory work, projects, individual assignments, annotated lists of materials, and evaluation activities. Perhaps the most valuable feature of the book is the section of Reproduction Pages, which can be used to make masters for spirit duplication, transparencies for the overhead projector, or student copies with a duplicating machine—saving you, the teacher, hours of preparation time.

Although the book suggests a sequence of activities that might be used to teach a particular concept, the teacher chooses the materials and strategies that he or she wants to use without being locked into prescribed lesson plans. The order of topics may also be varied to supplement available textbooks or prescribed syllabi.

In general, for each topic the book provides:

1. A brief introduction to the several concepts presented, along with a discussion of why these concepts might be important to students, and an outline of choices the teacher may want to make in the organization of the instruction.

2. A list of objectives to be attained through use of the methods and materials in the chapter. This saves the teacher the tedium of writing behavioral objectives for lesson plans.

3. A content overview that serves a dual purpose: first to remind the teacher of the basic ideas in the chapter; and second to provide material for brief introductory lectures if the teacher wishes to employ this instructional method.

4. A wealth of learning experiences to employ in teaching concepts in the chapter.

5. Evaluation items to determine how well the student has achieved the objectives of the chapter.

6. Annotated lists of materials useful for teaching topics in the chapter. The lists include films, film loops, filmstrips, books, and articles.

Rather than promote a single teaching approach, the goal of this book has been to suggest activities and materials that teachers with a wide variety of styles and approaches will find useful. Thus, for example, numerous activities for small groups of students are included, but additional lessons involve individual work as well as large-group instruction. The teacher is encouraged to understand the rationale for each approach and choose those which are most consistent with his or her own goals and students' needs and preferences.

Several biases, however, will be evident throughout the book. These are based on my own ideas of physics instruction and educational philosophy developed over many years of study and teaching in several different settings. I believe that the study of physics can enhance people's perceptions of their environment and thus enrich their lives. Therefore, I think that all students should take physics. Instruction should involve physical objects or models whenever possible, and the concepts will be learned more effectively when students can relate them to their own experiences. An atmosphere free from threat and opened to inquiry is preferred for physics instruction and, finally, the instructional materials themselves should not be so complex as to obliterate the concept they are supposed to illustrate—the simpler the example the better.

Most of the activities and approaches in this book were used successfully in my own classes or in those of colleagues. I feel confident, therefore, that many other teachers will find them practical and useful, but I will have no way of knowing this without feedback from those who use *A Guidebook for Teaching Physics*. I invite you to write your comments about the book using the Feedback Form that appears at the end. It can be torn out and mailed with a minimum of inconvenience. I promise a personal reply and will sincerely appreciate your suggestions. They will help me to decide what changes to make when revising this book.

A number of lessons that I have developed with my class are based on ideas presented in a publication by the New York State Education Department, Bureau of Curriculum Development, *Physics Handbook*. I appreciate the Department's permission to include them in this work.

I am grateful to Fran Fariello who typed the manuscript and to Mimi and Ralph Ciancio who helped with the composition. The following producers of educational materials supplied review copies of books listed in the resources sections: Atheneum, F. W. Faxton Co., Inc., Hayden Book Co., John Wiley and Sons, Inc., D. C. Heath and Co., and Allyn and Bacon.

William Yurkewicz, Jr.

1

Considerations for Organizing a Physics Course

An advanced, industrialized society has some degree of control over Mother Nature. Less advanced societies, on the other hand, are at her mercy. Even today people in some parts of the world stop their activities when darkness comes, starve when food becomes scarce, freeze in cold weather, and die from a myriad of diseases. We simply turn the lights on, take food from our freezer and pop it into a microwave oven, check the setting of the thermostat for our central heating system, and enjoy some of the most advanced medical care in the history of mankind. We have control over our environment because we have studied the natural world over many years, methodically recorded descriptions of its behavior, and observed that there is some order in the universe. Our knowledge of the universe has produced a quality of life inconceivable to our predecessors.

The development of our civilization is, to a large degree, dependent on the history of science and our growing knowledge of the behavior of nature. Physics as a science represents a large portion of this knowledge.

Despite our advantageous position, our civilization suffers some drawbacks. Most people involved in a technological way of life do not understand the applied science central to their existence. Eric Fromm, in *The Art of Loving*,[1] describes this state as an alienation from nature. Similarly, in the prologue to *Personality Dynamics and Effective Behavior*,[2] James Coleman maintains that our age, the Golden Age of Technology, has fostered a profound anxiety. Both authors speak of fears that derive from our ignorance. In short, our society enjoys simultaneously the advantages of great technology and the disadvantages of our not understanding its basis in nature. The main goal in teaching physics is to begin to bridge the intellectual gap between our daily, practical lives and their roots in natural phenomena.

---

1. Eric Fromm, *The Art of Loving* (Harper and Row, 1974), Chapter 2.
2. James Coleman, *Personality Dynamics and Effective Behavior* (Scott, Foresman and Company, 1960), 2-4.

ASSESSING STUDENT NEEDS

It is safe to assume that your students will have other reasons for undertaking the study of physics. Most of them will not, at this point, intend to become physicists; most will not even know what a physicist does. Several will be interested in various engineering careers, some in technical fields, some in related sciences. The majority will be completing a sequence in science and not have any special interest in physics. It is important that you become aware of their different interests and needs in order to determine appropriate kinds of instruction. Discussions with your Guidance Department at the outset will provide some background information on student needs. Additional information can be obtained by using Reproduction Page 1 to survey your classes.

An evaluation of this survey will help you determine the general level of instruction required, curricular choices, and specific student assignments. The responses to the career question (Item 2) are an aid to discussing specific occupations related to physics. Any teacher of a particular subject does some career education simply by introducing students to problems relevant to his discipline. Much more can be done by including comments about particular jobs in class discussions. Several books on what a physicist does are included in the references at the end of this chapter. They are appropriate reading for both teachers and students considering a career or further study in physics. Some coordination with your Guidance Department and local industries will provide ample information related to careers in physics and may encourage interested students to pursue them.

TYPES OF PHYSICS PROGRAMS

There are two major complete physics programs on the market: The Physical Science Study Committee (P.S.S.C.) and Project Physics. They both include text books, films, lab work and student activities. Each represents a complete high school physics course, the result of many years of work by a variety of contributors, extensive field testing, and revision. P.S.S.C. is geared to students having strong interests and abilities in physics. Project Physics uses a humanities-related story line in its presentation. Both present a mathematical treatment of good, solid physics. The National Science Foundation has sponsored summer institutes for training teachers in these programs throughout the United States. Both P.S.S.C. and Project Physics recommend that teachers attend a training session before using either program.

Prior to initiating either program in its entirety, you should consider your students' and school's various and particular needs and how well they would be met by one or the other program. Also, depending on the extent of your current instructional hardware and software, a considerable financial expenditure may be required to do either program in its entirety.

Many textbook publishers offer programs in physics that are less extensive than the P.S.S.C. or Project Physics in books with accompanying manuals. Each has its own emphasis and mode of presentation. Many of these books are listed in the references. It is a good idea to have one copy of each in your professional library; consult them for appropriate material as instructional needs arise.

Recently many physics text programs have been developed for non-science majors. Generally, they deal with standard concepts but do not require extensive mathematics. Attempts have been made to make these programs something more than just a watered-down physics course. They, too, should be included in your reference library as sources of some good instructional ideas.

In selecting any text program for your course, be sure to assess the reading level of your students and choose materials that are appropriate. Several references at the end of this chapter will aid you in managing the selection.

CURRICULUM SELECTION

There is much more material available for a physics course than can be covered in one year. Therefore, you must be selective. When one item is selected, another will need to be omitted, and the teacher should establish a rationale for his choices. Reproduction Page 2 is a modification of the Johnson Model of Curriculum Development and represents a rational approach to the selection process. You may wish to use this page for presentations to your Board of Education, supervisor, or colleagues. A detailed description of this model follows.

- Cultural Content. The source of all things that people can learn in school is our culture. If something is not known, it obviously cannot be taught to a student. It seems unnecessary to state this, but some people have actually tried to teach the unknown, as in a course entitled "A Quick, Simple Solution to World Pollution Problems." Cultural content includes facts and concepts, of course, but processes and attitudes make up a large portion of what we would like our students to learn. Don't overlook these when using the model.

- Screens. These are your selection criteria. They represent a rational selection procedure, the basis for the items to be included in your physics course. The first screen, "Is it teachable?", applies to all subjects. Many things are known, but we do not know how to teach them to others. For example, we know some people love a particular type of music, but we do not know how to teach other people to love that type of music. Each item in your course should also meet the "related to physics" criterion. Following the arrows in the diagram, we come to a series of options. From this point, an item is included by passing through one of several additional screens. If this process still produces more material than can be covered in your course, you will have to arrange priorities for your final selection. You can include different screens in your selection process. What is important is that you follow a rational procedure.

- Curriculum. The result of the screening is your curriculum—what you intend your students to learn in the physics course, your course objectives. As used above, the word "curriculum" means simply *what* you want students to learn. It does not denote how they will be taught, the type of "instruction" employed. If this distinction is not made, teachers run the risk of engaging in classroom activities for the sake of the activity rather than for what the student can learn from them.

- Instruction. These are classroom activities that have a high probability of producing the learning stated in the objectives. Since a variety of student needs and interests is involved, a corresponding group of instructional techniques should be employed. The following chapters in this book are directed to that task.

- Evaluation. As shown on the diagram, evaluation involves a comparison between learning objectives and what the students have actually learned. Unfortunately, the outcome is not always a perfect match, but appropriate instruction can improve the results.

ORGANIZATION OF THE PHYSICS COURSE

Organization is important in any course. If done properly, it insures that sufficient time is allowed to cover all of the curriculum adequately. Several options are available as the basis for arrangement. Project Physics uses a historical approach which organizes the subject matter according to a time line corresponding to the development of major concepts in science. In a biographical approach, topics can be arranged in clusters related to the work of famous physicists, or on the basis of cultural development. Many texts arrange curricula according to major concepts; the subject matter is clustered according to such ideas as motion, energy, and so forth. You may prefer to organize your curriculum according to the degree of abstraction involved and proceed from very concrete studies to less tangible concepts. The majority of textbooks on the market arrange physics by topic. (The following chapters in this guidebook are similarly arranged.) Many texts listed in the references illustrate each of these approaches. Regardless of what arrangement you decide on, it is important to proceed logically, with definite steps and ends in mind; any random approach is deadly. You also will want to organize your material with an eye to diversity. For example, it is refreshing for students if you follow a topic very heavy in mathematics with one that is more descriptive; a highly theoretical topic might be followed by one having direct application to daily life.

When you decide how to order the course, more specific planning should follow. Start by alloting blocks of time throughout the year for major topics. Subdivide these topics according to objectives and instructional activities related to each objective. Be sure to include time for lab work, films, guest speakers, field trips, review, and testing. This organization is essential for proper coordination of film orders, special speaker presentations and trips, all of which must be done well in advance. If you are not familiar with this process, many of the teacher's manuals listed in the references contain specific models.

LABORATORY WORK

To represent fully the "flavor" of physics, any course should include student laboratory work. Many of the scientific process objectives stipulated as observing, measuring, making and supporting conclusions, setting up an experiment, etc., require a lab setting. Lab work should be coordinated with class activities to reinforce, develop, or apply concepts. Experimental verification of a relationship is often preferred to a more tedious theoretical approach, which is less meaningful to some students.

A multitude of approaches to lab work is available to the teacher. Most text publishers offer a separate laboratory guide with their books, many of which are listed in the references at the end of this chapter. These make excellent sources of lab ideas.

Your choice in this area will be governed by equipment and space availability and student needs. Consider the amount of direction you wish to give your students. Should they be guided through a specific lab step by step and complete it in a minimum amount of time, or should they simply be given a problem or question and be allowed to try their own approach? Discovery method proponents place high value on a student finding out for himself. Critics of that method object to the time spent on "re-inventing the wheel" every lab period. Lab guidebooks which a student fills in as he proceeds enhance success and completion but are far removed from a true experimental experience.

Rather than choose one particular approach, consider your student's various abilities and offer several different lab activities all relating to the same topic. Besides offering some individualization of instruction, this option requires fewer pieces of the same equipment since not all students will be doing the same lab at any one time. It also offers the option of several lab experiences in one topic since students can rotate through the different labs. Class discussion will be more interesting when results of several experiments are applied. Most of the laboratory exercises in this book are intended to provide a general suggestion of activities and materials for labs. The teacher will determine specific material selection and themes.

Regardless of your choice, there are two elements of lab work that should be a part of the student's experience. The first is the idea of experimental error. Students, surprisingly, are often unaware that all physical measurements are approximations. They insist that if a result does not come out exactly right, a mistake has been made. The difference between a mistake and an experimental error (limitations to perfect accuracy) should be explained. You can develop the idea during the course by first identifying sources of error (divisions on measuring devices, techniques of measurement, variations between theory and actual experimental conditions, etc.) and then proceeding to estimations of the amount of various errors; include them in calculations. The degree of this development will again vary with the student.

The second element of all laboratory experience is some sort of lab report. It is essential that communication skills are included. Many different forms of lab write-ups are used, but most include a statement of purpose, some presentation of how the work was performed, data and observations, and a conclusion relating to the purpose. Students should understand that the influence of an experimental result in science is directly related to the ability of other scientists to understand and duplicate the experiment.

Use Reproduction Pages 3 and 4 to help orient students in writing reports. It may be helpful to use them simultaneously in that Reproduction Page 4 provides specific examples of the various parts of a lab write-up which are outlined in Reproduction Page 3. You may choose to do a "dry run" of the sample lab and have students submit a report similar to the sample with the exception that they will use their own measurements and calculations. This approach offers the advantage of guiding the student through a report without having to deal with additional problems related to specific subject matter. Since the exercise uses a familiar mathematical relationship of the circumference of a circle to its diameter, pupils can concentrate on the specifics of the report prior to encountering laboratory work dealing with physics related to their classroom instruction.

SOME SPECIFIC INSTRUCTION RECOMMENDATIONS

Class Atmosphere

A great deal of immediate student feedback is essential to be effective. An informed, open atmosphere is most conducive to feedback. Students should feel free to ask questions at any point in a presentation or to indicate that they are not following. This is easy to state but requires skill and technique to implement. Students tend to withhold questions or indications that "they do not get it", not wanting to appear "stupid" in front of their peers. Your classroom manner is influential in achieving the desired atmosphere.

First, you must be open to interruptions. You can indicate this verbally and by your body language. Mask some of your own frustration with patience and a direct answer or another example. Of course, if you perceive that an adequate response will require considerable time, or if for any other reason you will risk losing the rest of the class, you may have to speak to or provide help for a particular student outside the classroom.

Second, you will enhance your teaching effectiveness if you reinforce a student's willingness to participate in class discussion. If he answers a question correctly, evidence your pleasure with a smile, or through praise, or with a simple statement indicating that the student was correct (it is good practice to use his name on such occasions). If the response is incorrect, bring attention to some aspect of the student's answer that you can commend while correcting him. For example, a student may show through his vocabulary or application of pertinent ideas that he is following your presentation and still overlook something that produces a wrong answer. If students ask questions, you can precede your answer with "That's a good question," or "That's an unusual question," or "I'm glad you asked that." In the rare case where you cannot find anything in the student's behavior to reinforce, you can express your appreciation for the student's participation.

A Physical Object for Each Lesson

Since a physics class deals with the physical aspects of natural phenomena, each lesson should include at least one object to observe as an example of what is being discussed. In many cases this is no problem. In mechanics, for example, numerous weights, carts, springs, ropes, and other objects are involved owing to the nature of the subject. When direct observation is not possible, a model of the object will have to suffice. Radioactive decay can be represented by using a large number of dice; a chain reaction can be modeled by arranging matches or dominoes. If the entire phenomenon cannot be represented, some aspect of it usually can be. Gold foil can be brought in when Rutherford's Scattering Experiment is discussed; a cut-away portion of a T.V. picture tube will serve as an object when discussing electron beam control. In cases where no object is available, pictures, slides, or films make good substitutes.

Units

The fundamental notion that units are a part of every physical measurement is surprisingly foreign to many students, and it becomes even more difficult for them to grasp when more complex calculations are required. In order to prepare them adequately, devote some extra time and attention to this area. Appropriate units should be included in your presentation of concepts, and dimensional analysis should be discussed along with conceptual relations. The teacher serves as a model by including units in his blackboard solutions and presentations.

Regularly, demonstrate and emphasize that formula relationships predict units as well as magnitudes of the answer. The organization and unity of subject matter in a discipline such as physics is well demonstrated by the inter-relationships of the units included in all measurements.

In order to improve your student's background in this area, you might consider co-ordinating your efforts with teachers of other science courses, and especially with teachers of mathematics courses that are taken prior to the physics course. Simply discussing the need to include units in mathematical operations usually will not produce significant changes in this area since more pressing mathematics objectives seem to take precedence. You will be more effective if you ask the math teacher for some of his standard classroom problems or examples and recast them with an eye to creating similar options for him that deal with physical quantities as well as with numbers. For example, you can rewrite a standard calculation of the slope of a straight line using distance and time quantities rather than pure numbers. This results in a slope representing speed with appropriate units. A small amount of time and effort spent in this way makes a significant difference to those students going on to take physics.

Reproduction Page 5 is a summary of some physical quantities and their representation in the International System of Units (SI), a system advocated for universal use. This guidebook and most newer physcis texts employ SI units. You may want each student to have a copy for reference as new units are encountered during the course.

Computers and Calculators

A scientifically literate person is familiar with standard calculating tools used in his field. Pocket calculators have replaced the slide rule. Computer terminals are prevalent in almost all areas of endeavor. Your physics students should have experience with these devices. Relatively inexpensive hand calculators are available, and many pupils will already own one. Purchasing a calculator may be a financial burden on some students if required for the course and for this reason, you might consider having one or two desk calculators available to students in the physics room. These are also useful for quick teacher calculations during a class. Moreover, students may use them during labs and for homework calculations during their free time.

Many schools now have a computer terminal available for student use on a time-shared system. Ideally, a terminal is located in the physics lab. If this is not possible, any location allowing easy student access will do. Computor instruction should be carried out in stages. For example, when students are doing lab work that requires fairly tedious or lengthy calculations, you can inform them that an operating program is in the computer which will do these calculations. The program should be instructive, telling the pupil which buttons to push as well as generating the desired calculation. This does two things for the student: it allows him to manipulate the device successfully and it saves time. This experience motivates students to learn some programming.

Two class periods of instruction in BASIC language and general terminal operation are all that students need to begin writing useful programs and running them on the computer. You can conclude this portion of your instruction by requiring each student to write an original program which has some practical application. Each student writes his own program, runs it with some sample data, and turns in both the program and its results for evaluation. This guarantees that every student will gain experience in programming and some familiarity with the terminal. At this point, some students will be eager for more experience, whereas others will not be interested at all. You may encourage pupils to continue and refine their programming skills by accepting a computer program designed to do calculations for subsequent lab work as a substitute for the write-up for that lab. This offers an added advantage to other students who can use a particular program to save time on calculations. If the terminal is conveniently located, students can get quick, on-the-spot feedback on data gathered in the laboratory and return to their apparatus immediately if the results are not satisfactory.

Evaluation Ideas

Each of the following chapters contains specific activities and questions useful for student evaluation. The references at the end of the chapters include additional materials that you may use to construct your own tests and quizzes. They also list suppliers of additional ready-made forms. The evaluation process should be ongoing, requiring only the satisfactory completion of a project in some instances and various degrees of achievement in others.

The main instructional principle you should apply in any form of evaluation is immediate knowledge of results for the student—feedback. This serves to reinforce proper responses and to correct errors before they negatively influence subsequent learning. One of the simplest ways of doing this is to encourage an appropriate vocabulary during class discussions and to correct misused terms on the spot.

Short quizzes may be given once or twice a week as you exchange information with the class. When you give a quiz, you are saying, "Here is material I think you can handle." The class takes the quiz and corrects it immediately under your direction. When the scores are reported, the students are telling you, "Here is how well we understand the material at this point." If the scores are generally good, you can introduce new subject matter; if not, you should go back over the problem areas prior to taking on new material. Given in this context, quizzes should not affect a student's grade too heavily. A rule of thumb is that the average of all the quiz scores over a ten-week period is equal, in weight, to one unit test.

If your school has a test scoring machine, the immediate feedback principle is approximated for unit tests as well. Objective test questions can be scored quickly by machine, and the reinforcing and correcting processes should apply to the unit test on the following class day.

Preparing for a final examination by reviewing a whole year's work can become very dull for students. Here is a suggestion that provides motivation and an excellent review at the same time: Assign a specific topic for homework each night. Ask your students to review all the physics related to that topic and then to write a ten question, short answer quiz. The next day, collect each of the quizzes and choose ten of the best questions for a class quiz. This proves to be a very effective student review since the *asking* of a good question often requires more cognitive operations with the subject matter than answering it. Students are very pleased when one of their questions is chosen by the teacher and thus are encouraged to do a good job the night before. This results in good quiz grades, which are further reinforcement. But even this novel approach becomes routine after a number of times, and, as your students become more sophisticated, you might try a variation: Collect the student papers as before, but this time include in the class quiz the *answer* to a possible or likely question. In this variation, a student gets credit for writing any question related to the material currently under review that matches the answer given.

The emphasis of this chapter is on teacher strategies for organization of a physics course. It is appropriate to include a student's input as well. You may want to share Reproduction Page 6 with your students. It contains some tips from a successful pupil's point of view.

USING THIS GUIDEBOOK

The following chapters present a variety of student and teacher activities arranged by topics included in most physics courses. Some are fairly conventional; others are more innovative. Evaluation materials and suggestions are included for each topic. Additional resources are listed and discussed in the reference section at the end of each chapter, and a list of publishers and their addresses is included at the end. Special Reproduction Pages are correlated with the instructional activities. Remove and reproduce these for masters or overhead transparencies.

Whether you are a new teacher looking for good instructional ideas or an experienced teacher seeking to add to your repertory of proven classroom methods, this guidebook will be a valuable asset. It will help all your students relate physics to their own lives and, at the same time, provide a firm introduction for those students interested in continuing in the field.

Resources for Organizing a Physics Program

Below is a selected list of books and other materials useful in organizing a physics program. Addresses of publishers can be found in the alphabetical list at the end of this book.

The Project Physics Course Handbooks produced by Project Physics. Holt, Rinehart and Winston, 1981. A series of six volumes related to topics in the Project Physics Course. Each handbook includes textual material, activities, experiments, equipment notes, visual aides discussion, and resources used in a physics course. Volume 1 also includes a sample of course organization planning for the entire year.

P.S.S.C. Physics, 4th ed., by Haber-Schaim, Cross, Dodge and Walter. D. C. Heath, 1976. This is a textbook for P.S.S.C. physics. It includes student activities related to topics that can be done at home as well as in school. Questions and problems are at the end of each chapter.

Physics Handbook by the Bureau of Secondary Curriculum Development. The State Education Department of New York, 1970. A guidebook of demonstrations and experiments for high school physics. Notes on each demonstration are included.

The Physics Problem Solver edited by the Research and Education Association. Research and Education Association, 1976. Focuses on aiding the teacher in the preparation of lectures with demonstration problems. Problems of many descriptions are included for elementary as well as advanced students.

Goal Analysis by Robert F. Mager. Fearon Publishers, 1972. The sole purpose of this book is to help the teacher describe the meaning of the goals he hopes to achieve. It helps him to understand his own intents better and to be able to make better decisions toward their achievement.

Physics by D. Holliday and R. Resnick. One of the most quoted references in high school physics course materials, 1978.

Physics—Fundamentals and Frontiers by Robert Stollberg and Faith Hill (Teachers Manual).

Houghton Mifflin, 1975. Contains a suggested time schedule for topics in the textbook.

Science Objectives by the Committee on Assessing the Progress of Education. Committee on Assessing the Progress of Education, 1969. A brief description of a process employed in identifying objectives in science. Objectives are given for four age groups: 9, 13, 17, and young adults.

Physics for the Modern Mind by Walter R. Fuchs. Macmillan, 1967. An exploration of the theories behind the most advanced and sophisticated aspects of modern physics. Scientists who made specific contributions are discussed. Written for the general reader. A good teacher reference and selections are appropriate for students.

Mathematical Aspects of Physics: An Introduction by Francis Bitter. Doubleday, 1963. Discusses patterns in nature, data gathering, analysis, and experimentation. Discussions are appropriate for the layman or students.

Understanding Physics: Motion, Sound, and Heat by Isaac Asimov. The New American Library, 1969. A historical and philosophical treatment of topics in classical physics. Can be used as a teacher reference, or sections might be assigned to students.

Understanding Physics: The Electron, Proton, and Neutron by Isaac Asimov. New American Library, 1969. Complements Asimov's book on classical physics by treating topics in modern physics from a philosophical and historical point of view.

Understanding Physics: Light, Magnetism, and Electricity by Isaac Asimov. New American Library, 1969. Combined with the other two references by Asimov, this book completes the historical and philosophical treatments of most of the topics included in your course.

Biography of Physics by George Gamow. Harper and Row, 1961. This book presents both theories and biographical data of the great men in science. It gives the reader a feeling of what physics is, and what kind of people physicists are.

Physics and Man by Tor Ragnor Gerholm. The Bedminster Press, 1967. This work emphasizes the social, economic, political, esthetic, religious, and ethical implications of physical discoveries. It adds a great deal of depth to the teacher's knowledge and instruction.

Source Book in Physics by William Francis Magie. Harvard University Press, 1963. Presents extracts from important contributions made to the science

of physics from Galileo's time to 1900 A.D. Material is arranged according to a historical time sequence and the scientist involved.

Physics for Everybody by Germaine and Arthur Beiser. E. P. Dutton, 1956. An uncomplicated description of basic laws in physics, stressing their relationship to everyday experiences. An excellent reference for material relating instructional topics to the daily life activities of students.

Careers and Opportunities in Physics by Philip Pollack. E. P. Dutton, 1961. Provides information and advice on qualifications, educational requirements, and financial rewards for a wide range of special fields in physics.

Physics Demonstration Experiments, Volumes 1 and 2, by Harry F. Meiners. The Ronald Press Company, 1970. The result of an effort to bring together the best demonstration equipment and techniques of the past thirty years, these books describe demonstrations and the necessary equipment for lectures. Tests and sources of materials are included. Notes on a variety of instructional techniques are part of the works.

Great Experiments in Physics, Morris H. Shamos, editor. Holt, Rinehart, and Winston, 1959. The original accounts of twenty-five experiments that created modern physics. The initial nineteen experiments can be readily duplicated by first year physics students. The experiments lend an air of authenticity and a sense of history to the study of physics.

Physics Through Experiment by Dr. Richard Bamberger and others. Sterling Publishing Co., 1969. A book of fairly elementary experiments in physics, designed primarily as a guide for the beginning student of physics. Instructions on how to set up a laboratory notebook are included.

Experimental College Physics by Marsh White and Kenneth Manning. McGraw-Hill, 1954. Primarily a laboratory manual of experiments in physics. The manual emphasizes the objectives of lab work and the values to be obtained from experimenting. It also includes instructions concerning tabulation of data, graphical methods, and the techniques of analyzing and interpreting data. Special emphasis is given to student evaluation of errors involved in measurements.

Introduction to the Theory of Error by Yardley Beers. Addison-Wesley, 1957. A good teacher reference discussing the fundamental principles of the theory of error and those applications which are likely to be encountered by students.

Handbook of Physics and Chemistry, Robert C. Weast, editor. Chemical Rubber Publishing Company. A complete collection of tables, properties, and physical measurements. This reference should be available in the classroom. Students may need some initial guidance on how to find required information in this source.

Project Physics Readers produced by Project Physics. Holt, Rinehart and Winston, 1981. A series of six books. Each is a collection of articles related to areas of physics. Excellent enrichment material related to a wide variety of student interests.

Communicating with the Computer by Jacobs, French, Moulds, and Schuchman. Allyn and Bacon, 1975. An excellent student guide and text on basic programming if extensive work is done in this area. Useful for teacher instruction preparation and as a source of student exercises.

Preparing Instructional Objectives by Robert F. Mager. Fearon Publishers, 1962. Describes how to specify objectives. This work emphasizes the form of a usefully stated objective.

The Physics Teacher. A monthly journal primarily for high school teachers. American Association of Physics Teachers. Almost all aspects of information pertinent to teaching a physics course are included. A "must" for any physics teacher.

Scientific American. This periodical should be in your school library. In addition to major articles, this magazine contains brief notes about recent findings.

Science. This is the official journal of the American Association for the Advancement of Science. American Association for the Advancement of Science. A copy should be in the school library. Every issue contains one or more articles surveying recent research in a particular field.

American Scientist. Official publication of the Society of the Sigma Xi, an organization of scientists interested in research. Society of the Sigma Xi. Articles are similar to *Scientific American* in that they are written by research specialists for an educated, but not specialized audience.

The Science Teacher is the journal of the National Science Teachers Association. National Science Teachers Association. In addition to many articles concerned with improving science teaching, this journal carries review articles of recent research.

The New York Times. This newspaper prints current science news and has a staff of science-trained reporters to write its articles. In addition to science news of the day, these reporters give a great deal of background information, partly in the original news report, partly in special articles in the Sunday edition. Articles of special interest can be clipped and filed.

"Microcomputers! Applications to Physics Teaching" by R. Tinker and G. A. Strenger. *The Physics Teacher* (October 1978). This article (and several others in this issue) is designed to help you decide what computer system you can afford and use. Several instructional uses are suggested.

"Role Playing—An Effective Teaching Tool" by E. A. Peterson. *The Physics Teacher* (February 1980). Describes a technique of student investigation and subsequent interaction in a panel discussion where students view a phenomenon from the perspective of a famous scientist.

"Conceptual Physics. Turning Nonscience Students On to Their Everyday Environments" by P. G. Hewitt. *The Physics Teacher* (December 1972). Some good comments on physics instruction with many suggestions for relating the science to daily experiences. Although the non-science student is the focus, the suggestions are equally valid for science majors.

The Flying Circus of Physics With Answers by J. Walker. John Wiley and Sons, 1977. An entire book filled with those questions often asked of or by a physicist such as, Why does hot water placed in a freezer freeze before some colder water does? This book provides the questions, answers, and references for the answers.

Time. A weekly publication with a section devoted to science. Good general reading for students. Your school library should have this magazine.

Occupational Outlook Handbook. U. S. Dept. of Labor. U. S. Government Printing Office. This manual (published every two years) provides information on careers in science as well as other areas. The description includes nature of the work, places of employment, training, outlook, wages, and working conditions. A good resource for career education.

"The Evaluation of the Physicists Picture of Nature" by P. A. M. Dirac. *Scientific American* (May 1963). An excellent summary of physics from a historical and philosophical viewpoint.

Dear Faculty by J. A. Nordling. F. W. Faxon, 1976. This book is designed to involve students in using library resources. Following the guidelines suggested in this book, a similar learning program for physics can be developed.

Computer Mathematics by C. Conrad et al. Hayden, 1975. The authors employ mathematical structures to teach the workings of computers and the make-up of programming languages.

Skylab Experiments. NASA U. S. Government Printing Office, 1973. Information for teachers on the Skylab program and experiments, including suggestions on relevance to school curricula.

Physics Fun and Demonstrations by Julius S. Miller. Central Scientific Co., 1974. A demonstration book using toys to show basic physical concepts as well as standard demonstrations and experiments.

Teaching Science in Today's Secondary Schools by W. A. Thurber and A. T. Collette. Allyn and Bacon, 1968. A methods book.

Basic From the Gound Up by D. E. Simon. Hayden Book Co., 1978. An introduction to computer programming in the BASIC language. Assumes the reader knows nothing about computers; uses very little math.

Physics Project Cards by M. F. Fleming. The Center for Applied Research in Education. Twenty-five cards with instructions for self-contained investigations of an inquiry style. Can be used for independent study, make-up work, or rotating lab groups.

Thinking Physics by L. Epstein and P. G. Hewitt. Insight Press, 1979. Good examples and ideas with very little math. Relates physics to everyday experiences with illustrations. Conceptual questions and answers follow each section.

Physics and Man by T. R. Gerholm. Bedminster Press, 1967. The first section, "Physics and Society," contains some good general ideas on the importance and place of physics.

The Inspiration of Science by G. Thomson. Oxford University Press, 1961. Shows how a scientist thinks and works using examples from physics.

Science Books and Films. American Association for the Advancement of Science. Reviews of new science films and books providing information useful for selection. Published quarterly.

Resources for the History of Physics by S. G. Bush, editor. University Press of New England, 1972. For the teacher who likes to use historical anecdotes in his presentation, this work provides a listing of sources of references.

A Cinescope of Physics by J. Dowling, editor. American Association of Physics Teachers, 1979.

A compilation of physics films with analysis of each film according to physics quality, social relevance, photography, and other parameters.

"Contemporary Frontiers in Physics" by V. F. Weisskopf. *Science* (January 1979). A summary of where physics has been lately and where it is likely to go in the future.

"The Reading Levels of High School Physics Texts" by K. Kennedy. *The Physics Teacher* (March 1979). A good article to read prior to selecting a new textbook.

Resources for the History of Physics by Stephen G. Brush, editor. University Press of New England, 1972. Lists publications of interest to students and/or teachers who may wish to delve into the history of physics. A source of anecdotes for lectures or names and dates associated with a particular discovery.

"Physics Texts: An Evaluation Review" by Robert Lehrman. *The Physics Teacher* (November 1982). A good article to read prior to selecting a text. Many of the most used books are evaluated in this article.

For those interested in an Olympics-type physics competition, write to the Physics Olympics Subcommittee for a guide to setting up and conducting such events. An information booklet is also available from the Physics Department, Indiana University of Pennsylvania.

"Physics Olympics: Competitions for Secondary Physics Students" by David M. Riban. *The Physics Teacher* (November 1976). Good background reading if you are considering running competitions with your classes.

The American Science Film Association is a professional organization whose objectives are the promotion of film, T.V., and related communications media as instruments of science education and research. Membership includes a quarterly newsletter, science film and communication conferences, and referral services on films.

What's So Funny About Science? by Sidney Harris. William Kaufmann, 1977. This compilation of over 100 cartoons about science is a good source of humor for your classroom.

" 'Mission Improbable' Problems" by Doug Jenkins. *The Physics Teacher* (October 1981). Suggests a way to introduce humor and sharpen problem solving skills at the same time.

Exploratorium Cookbook I by R. Burman. *Exploratorium Cookbook II* by R. Hipschman. Exploratorium, 1981. Both books present a wide variety of projects that are useful demonstration ideas. Although some are fairly elaborate and costly, they make for good exhibits for open-house nights, etc.

The September, 1981 issue of *The Physics Teacher* has five articles which offer general ideas on demonstrating and specific demonstrations on several topics.

A Demonstration Handbook for Physics by G. D. Freier and F. J. Anderson. American Association of Physics Teachers, 1981. This work contains about 800 demonstrations well suited to every teacher of physics. The encyclopedia coverage of physics demonstrations has a wide range of sophistication. There is something for everyone from the beginning teacher to the veteran demonstrator.

SI: The International System of Units by Robert A. Nelson. American Association of Physics Teachers, 1981. A useful book for anyone concerned about SI and its relation to customary and metric units. Teachers can use this source to improve their understanding of SI and its relation to other systems. The book also presents much useful information on metric practice.

String and Stickey Tape Experiments by R. D. Edge. Department of Physics, University of South Carolina, 1981. A collection of experiments and activities using simple and inexpensive materials. Questions are posed in almost every experiment. The range is from middle school students to bright high school or college pupils.

"The Historical Approach to Science Teaching" by W. Bronwer and A. Singh. *The Physics Teacher* (April 1983). Discusses the advantages of a historical perspective in the teaching of physics.

"The Back of the Envelope," edited by Edward M. Purcell, is a monthly column in the *American Journal of Physics*. This article offers monthly order-of-magnitude problems with solutions following in the next month. A good source for teachers. In the January, 1983 issue, Purcell offers a one page "Round Number Handbook of Physics," which is his approximation for physical quantities.

How Fast Do Osyters Grow? by Norman F. Smith. Messner, 1982. This is an easy reading student guide for preparation of a science project. It will aid pupils in science investigations by helping with topic choice, planning equipment, recording data, drawing conclusions, etc. A book for beginning students.

How to Grow Science by Michael J. Moravcsik. University Books, 1980. This book deals with the sociology of the natural sciences. It may provide the interested instructor with several evenings of enjoyable reading plus a better understanding of the what, why, and hows of a scientist and the sciences.

"SI Notes" by the AAPT Metric Committee is a series of articles in *The Physics Teacher,* starting in February, 1983. This series is intended to assist teachers in using the SI system more completely and correctly.

A Biographical Dictionary of Scientists, 3rd edition, by Trevor I. Williams, editor. Wiley, 1982. Contains 1,100 biographical sketches. This reference book is suitable for both teachers and students. Each sketch is a few paragraphs in length accompanied by a brief list of further readings. The presentation is in non-technical language.

"Evaluation of the P.S.S.C. and Project Physics Handbooks" by V. Lunetta and P. Tamir. *School Science and Mathematics* (December 1981). The article describes how well each course's lab book does in providing student inquiry opportunity. Worth reading if the teacher is considering this approach.

University Physics by Sears, Zemansky and Young. Addison-Wesley, 1980. A standard college text which provides good discussion on most topics covered in a high school physics course. A good teacher reference.

Science Digest is a monthly publication good for the school library.

"Will the Real Science Please Stand Up" by Kendrick Frazier. *Sci Quest* (September 1981). This article distinguishes pseudoscience (UFO's, astrology, spoon bending, etc.) from science showing the misuse of logic and the distortion of data. Frazier discusses the effects of pseudoscience on science which lead to lower public esteem, loss of funds, opportunities and interest. Good teacher background.

Computer-Based Physics Lab by Richard A. Entelek. Ward-Whidden House, 1981. Offers fourteen computer programs in BASIC for many topics in a physics class. These programs are intended to help students in the analysis of lab work after data are collected. Notes for both student and teacher are included.

RESOURCES ON EVALUATION

Physics by Bonnie Maslin, editor. Park Lane Press. A paperback consisting of objective, multiple choice test questions in physics. Useful for making quizzes and tests.

Educational Criterion Measures by W. James Popham. Van Norstrand Reinhold Company, 1971. A method of obtaining information about the effectiveness of instruction. This method is more appropriate for evaluating the physics program than individual students, but can be generalized to apply to both.

Writing Behavioral Objectives and Criterion Tests by Richard G. Allen. Scott Graphics, 1972. A programmed text for educators who wish to learn how to write behavioral objectives and matching criterion test items.

Project Physics Course Tests by Project Physics. Distributed by Holt, Rinehart and Winston, 1981. A series of six test books arranged by topic. Several tests are included in each book. Objective questions are included.

Intentionality in Education by Mauritz Johnson. Center for Curriculum Research and Service, 1977. This book explicates the Johnson Model for Curriculum Development presented in this book. Detailed analysis of planning, implementation, and evaluation of a curriculum is presented. The relationship of the processes to general and local educational goals and constraints is thoroughly discussed.

"Physics Activities Examinations in Large Classes" by R. V. Eagleson. *The Physics Teacher* (October 1979). This article describes a method of using individual laboratory-activity examinations for evaluation in very large classes.

"What Are Your Students Really Doing in the Laboratory?" by John Penick. *School Science and Mathematics* (November 1981). This article presents a checklist using ten categories that teachers may employ to evaluate student behavior during a lab.

Physics Lab Experiments and Correlated Computer Aids by Herbert H. Gottlieb. Metrologic Publications, 1981. This book includes a lab manual covering usual topics in physics. The labs are "cookbook" type. Cassette or diskette computer programs are available. The programs are for verification and evaluation of lab work and are included in *Microcomputer Programs*.

Science Brain-Twisters, Paradoxes and Fallicies by Christopher P. Jargocki. Scribner's Sons, 1976. Contains 169 problem situations with answers. Most of the situations are appropriate for physics classes. They involve many novel and thought-provoking ideas.

The Ontario Assessment Instrument Pool, Physics, Senior Division. Science Teacher's Association of Ontario. This package contains over 400 multiple-choice questions for use in assessing the aims, goals, and objectives of a non-calculus based physics course. 1981.

The Classroom Test: A Manual for Teachers by J. M. Earls et al. Minnesota Mining and Manufacturing Company, 1970. Provides rules, illustrations, and procedures for the construction of three major types of objective test items.

2

Forces

INTRODUCTION

Force is a good concept to introduce early in your physics course because students already have good, intuitive notions about "pushes and pulls." This provides a solid starting base for a more sophisticated treatment of the topic using a wide variety of common experiences.

These experiences should enhance instruction and student involvement with the subject matter. Many teachers feel that a thorough understanding of the force concept is needed prior to incorporating it with other ideas to form more complex relationships such as those in dynamics or work and energy (Chapters 4 and 5).

A push or pull notion is an acceptable starting definition of a force, but you should expand the concept quite early in the study to incorporate a relationship to motion. Civilized man has been able to exert some degree of control over his physical environment by causing desired motions to happen and preventing undesired motions. We call this causative factor "force," and we study forces because of their effect on motion.

CONTENT OVERVIEW

The study of forces will require treatment of vector quantities and, in many cases, specific instruction in vector mathematics. A review of how to use a protractor to measure angles and the use of trigonometric functions and tables will help many of your pupils with this chapter. Allow time for such activities in your unit planning.

The experiences in this chapter treat composition of forces—finding the resultant of several forces acting concurrently—in a definite sequence of increasing complexity: First, calculate the resultant of two concurrent forces in the same direction; second, in opposite directions. The third step uses familiar mathematics to find the resultant of any two forces acting at right angles. Finally, the calculation of the resultant of any two forces acting at any angle is accomplished. If you desire, students can expand the preceding processes to find the net effect of several forces acting concurrently with very little additional instructional time.

Students seem to find the above sequence less abstract than the resolution process—replacing a single force with two components at right angles. The mathematics of resolution are essentially the same as for composition, so the main instructional thrust is at the concept and application of the process.

The main reason for interest in forces is their relationship to movement. To preserve this interest introduce equilibrium as a motion related concept. You may want to refer to portions of Chapter 4 for additional ideas. Students will quickly grasp the definition as it relates to objects at rest, but because of their limited analysis of experiences involving objects in equilibrium which are moving, you will have to spend more instructional time on this topic in order to show that the force relationship in both cases is the same. The resultant of all the forces acting on objects in equilibrium (either at rest or moving with constant motion) is zero. Include the notion of "equilibrant force" (note the spelling and pronunciation) as a problem solving concept at this point in instruction. When two or more forces act concurrently at a point, the equilibrant force is that single force applied at the same point that produces equilibrium.

It is likely that much of the discussion on forces will center around student experiences with mechanical forces, those exerted by muscles, machines, ropes, wires, and so on. It is appropriate to expand this experience so that the students' concept includes awareness of the five types of forces known to science. Three of these—gravitational, electrical, and magnetic—underlie most observable interactions. The other two—nuclear and weak interaction forces—should be mentioned, but examples that relate to pupils are rare because these forces exist only inside the nucleus.

This chapter concludes with an extended study of two forces which are among those most commonly experienced, friction and gravitation. Friction is a good choice because it exemplifies the idea that through our understanding of this natural phenomenon, we exert control over our environment. You may have to update information on the nature of frictional forces depending on the student text used. Many books describe friction as being caused by intermeshing of microscopically rough surfaces as well as molecular adhesion. Current thinking is more toward adhesion as the underlying factor even in the cases of surface roughness.

Student ideas of gravitation will probably relate mainly to astronomical notions—holding the planets and moons in orbit, for example. This makes a good starting point. Relating weight to a gravitational concept is also fairly straight forward since numerous experiences are available which you should use instructionally. Incorporate these notions as part of the larger, more powerful concept of universal gravitation, as described by Newton and measured by Cavendish. This will require classroom experiences to supplement everyday understandings. You may want to introduce some of Einstein's thoughts on gravitation and his general theory of relativity to fully describe the gravitational concept and its relation to the total organization of observations on natural phenomena, the field of physics.

OBJECTIVES

As a result of the learning experiences in this chapter, students should be able to:

1. Estimate the magnitude of several common forces in newtons.

2. Distinguish common vector and scalar quantities.

3. Represent a force graphically and interpret graphic representations of forces.

4. Determine the resultant of any two forces acting concurrently.

5. Resolve a single force into two appropriate components at right angles.

6. Distinguish objects in translational equilibrium from objects which are not.

7. Use the fact that for objects in translational equilibrium, the resultant force is zero, and solve equilibrium problems when one force is known and the directions of two others are implied.

8. Identify the direction of frictional forces in examples of moving or potentially moving objects.

9. Select which variable is being manipulated to either increase or decrease frictional force in several everyday examples.

10. Use $F_{fr} = \mu N$ to solve problems.

11. Calculate a coefficient of friction.

12. Predict the directions of gravitational forces between two masses.

13. Solve problems involving the use of the inverse square distance relationship in universal gravitation.

14. Solve problems using $F = G\dfrac{m_1 m_2}{s^2}$.

LEARNING EXPERIENCES

Topic I: Force—Definition, Measurement, Units

1. *Activity.* Ask your class for sentences using the word "force" or a derivative. As sentences are generated, record them or the main phrase on the blackboard or overhead. When a reasonably long and varied list exists, ask the class to try to extract common implications in the word—such things as strength, compulsion, constraint, and causation may result. Explain that the meaning of force in physics is essentially the same as in the examples. A second analysis of the examples dealing with those sentences which are closer to the physical use of the term will get at the "push" or "pull" notion. Be sure to point out that the reason for interest in this concept is its causative relationship to motion, which we are interested in controlling.

2. *Activity.* Ask your class to list several examples of things (objects) which are made to move in desired ways and several examples of objects which are made not to move. Identify the forces—pushes or pulls—involved in each of the examples. Emphasize the idea of control over motion during the identification. Feel free to make your own contributions to this activity either through initial examples or by providing additional diversity and scope during the class discussion

3. *Teacher Presentation*. Pass several masses of 100 grams around the classroom. Have each student "heft" the mass. Inform the pupils that the weight of these objects is approximately one newton, the unit of force in the SI system of measurement. Repeat the experience using weights of about 10 N and 100 N, identify the amount of force in each case. Explain that students should come to have a "feel" for the amount of force acting in everyday situations in newtons. Reproduction Page 7 shows several examples.

4. *Activity*. Newtonize the classroom! Tape large signs on a variety of objects showing the approximate force involved in newtons. The weights of several common objects will be the most obvious application, but don't overlook such things as the tension required to operate shades or drapes or to pull down the movie screen; the force required to open or close the door; or the force needed to push an object across a lab table. Use your imagination in this project. The teacher can prepare the room ahead of class time and simply let the students discover the "newtonization." Alternately, this may serve as a student project after measuring devices and techniques have been covered.

5. *Teacher Demonstration*. Arrange a series of springs of various stiffness. Hang several equal weights, one at a time, from the springs and note the changes in the length of the spring in each case. Reverse the procedure by removing the weights one at a time to show that the stretch depends directly on the total force applied to each spring. Next reproduce a particular distortion of one spring, indicating that the force involved is the same as when the previous amount of weight was applied. The spring distorts the same amount whenever a particular quantity of force is applied regardless of what is applying the force. Springs, because of this behavior, are used to measure force. Display several spring scales, graduated in newtons, to conclude your presentation.

6. *Student Laboratory*. The preceding teacher demonstration also can serve as a laboratory exercise. Arrange the laboratory as either a discovery or a verification lab depending on individual preferences or course theme. Be sure to prevent students from exceeding the elastic limit of their springs either through limiting the total distorting weight or through directions to the pupils. Any available distorting objects may be substituted for standard laboratory weights or masses, the only requirements being that all the objects should have approximately equal weight, and that they can be readily attached to the springs. Washers or nuts from a hardware store work nicely. At this point in the student's study, the total distorting force should be measured in "total number of objects" hung from the spring rather than in newtons.

7. *Student Laboratory*. A laboratory exercise dealing with Hooke's Law is appropriate at this point. It will reinforce the idea that the change in length of a spring is directly proportional to the force producing the distortion, the basic operating principle behind the spring scale. Several such experiments are cited in the references at the end of this chapter.

8. *Activity*. In order to reinforce the "feel" for various forces in newtons, have students in groups close their eyes and apply predetermined forces to spring scales. Feedback is provided by the other group members, initially by relating successive readings to the student operating the device. In later trials, students can note the actual final reading produced.

Topic II: Vector and Scalar Quantities; Representation of Force Vectors

1. *Teacher Presentation.* In order to point out the necessity of including direction in expressing vector quantities such as force, place a mass with a string attached to it on a demonstration table. Move the mass from its rest position to several different points on the table by pulling the string in different directions. Maintain the theme of control over motion by emphasizing that the desired motion is determined by the *direction* of the pull as well as the magnitude of the force. Quantities such as force which require direction for complete description are called vectors. Other quantities that require only magnitude for complete identification are called scalars. Several common examples of both vector and scalar quantities should reinforce these concepts.

2. *Activity.* Use Reproduction Page 8 as a homework assignment. It provides a basis for group discussion or evaluation of the distinction between vector and scalar quantities. Students should be able to support their categorization by discussing the specific direction involved in the vector examples or why a direction is not required in the case of scalar quantities.

3. *Teacher Presentation.* Draw an arrow on the board or overhead and label it as 5N, East.

Now, draw a second arrow, twice as long as the first and in the same direction. Label it as 10N, East

Request the class to identify a third arrow, half as long as the first and in the same direction. (Be sure to press for the direction as well as the magnitude in the expression.) Most students will catch on to the arrow representation of vectors quite rapidly. They should be able to identify yet another arrow equal in length to the original one, but in the opposite direction as representing 5N, West. Use as many examples of the representation as necessary to insure that the general rule is clear to all students: the length of the arrow represents the magnitude of the force; the direction in which it points corresponds to the direction of the force.

4. *Activity.* Use Reproduction Page 9 to instruct your students in direction conventions and graphic representation of force vectors. Note that all the examples show forces as "pulls." Point out that even if a force acts as a "push" it is represented as a pull by convention. Several quick examples will show that the motion of an object is the same regardless of whether a certain magnitude force pushes on it from the left, for example, or pulls toward the right. Some review of protractor use may be necessary at this time.

Since the length of a vector represents its magnitude, a scale relating the length of the arrow to the amount of force represented is required in each case. Sharp pencils and careful measurement of lengths are required for this Reproduction Page.

Topic III: Finding the Resultant of Concurrent Forces

1. *Teacher Presentation.* The resultant concept is a simplifying notion. It involves replacing several forces acting on an object with one force which produces the same motion effect. The concept is necessary since most motion is caused by many forces acting on a particular body concurrently. Analyze several common phenomena to reinforce this multiple force statement.

   Pull an object such as a brick across a demonstration table with a spring scale. Ask the class to note the motion while you note the scale reading. Repeat the pull a second time using two scales, each with the same reading as before. Ask the class to note the contrast in the motion. Repeat once more using one scale with the combined reading of the previous two. This should show the idea of a resultant force in a rather rough way since the motion with the single resultant force should be similar to the motion with the two forces. Several similar demonstrations will suffice to extract the rule: the resultant of any two forces acting in the same direction is simply their sum and the direction is the same.

2. *Activity.* Hand one end of a piece of rope to a student, mark the middle of the rope by tying a handkerchief or ribbon around it, and grasp the other end. Ask the student to pull on the rope and explain that you will pull in the opposite direction with an equal amount of force. Ask the class to note the motion of the marked portion of the rope. Now ask the student to pull harder as you also pull harder. Again note the motion of the marked section. Explain that the marker responds to the resultant of the two pulls. Now lay the rope on a table with no one pulling. Again ask the class to note the motion of the marked portion. In all cases, the marked portion will not move one way or the other. This shows that the resultant of two equal forces acting in opposite directions is zero.

3. *Activity.* Have pairs of students repeat the procedure outlined in the previous activity, except this time have them exert their equal and opposite forces on a ring or loop of wire using spring scales. Compare the readings in several instances.

4. *Demonstration.* In order to show that the resultant of two equal and opposite forces is zero, set up the apparatus which is sketched below.

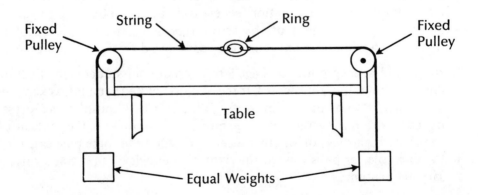

Several different pairs of weights may be used. In each case the resultant force on the ring is zero since it does not move. Represent the forces acting on the board or overhead. A modification of this arrangement is possible by disconnecting the strings attached to the ring and inserting two spring scales going from the ring to each string.

Discussion may ensue about the tension in the string. Students experience some difficulty understanding that the tension is the same as either force and not their sum. Ask what would happen to the scale readings if one of the weights was replaced by a fixed connection. Modify the apparatus to check on the predictions.

5. *Activity.* Use a desk chair on wheels and two lengths of rope to provide a series of instructive activities on resultant forces. Sit in the chair holding an end of one rope. Ask a student to pull you along. Now get twice as much pull by enlisting the aid of a second student using the other rope (some direction should precede this activity to prevent student over-enthusiasm in pulling). Note the effects of the combined forces on the motion of the chair. Repeat this exercise with the pulls in opposite directions and at right angles. Ask for a prediction on the *direction* of your motion prior to the right angle pulls. Previous experience with similar conditions will usually help students to state that the motion will be along a diagonal between the two ropes.

6. *Activity.* Reproduction Page 10 is a self-instructional sequence designed to illustrate the trigonometric solution of problems involving two forces acting at right angles. This procedure to find the resultant is appropriate for independent study, but you may supplement the instruction based on your judgment of student abilities.

7. *Activity.* Use Reproduction Page 11 to instruct students in a graphic solution to find the resultant of any two forces acting concurrently at a point. Emphasize the necessity of using sharp pencils and the need for careful measurement of angles and distances. Also, encourage students to use scale drawings which are large enough (about half a page in size) to minimize errors due to approximations of length.

8. *Demonstration.* Construct a device similar to the following prototype. Many alternate materials will work, so the directions are general. This apparatus will help you demonstrate the relationship between magnitude and direction of component forces and their resultant. This demonstration also provides a visual display of the dynamic interplay among the three force representations as they change.

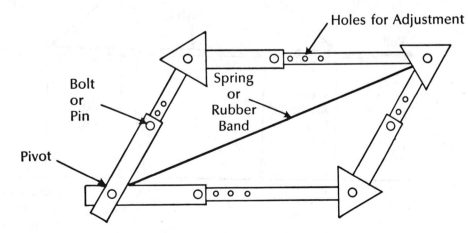

The sides of the parallelogram are constructed to be adjustable by using such materials as two sizes of metal tubing, slotted pieces of wood, or old curtain rods. If you wish, paint this arrangement using different colors to represent the component forces, the resultant, and the construction line portion of the parallelogram.

9. *Activity.* Use Reproduction Page 12 to provide practice in finding the resultant of two concurrent forces acting at angles other than 0° or 180°. You may specify either a trigonometric or graphic solution in each case or you may direct students to do both types of solution. One may also divide the class and have different groups do the problems with different approaches. Compare results.

Topic IV: Resolution of a Force

1. *Teacher Presentation.* Prior to engaging students in the resolution process, you should explain the need for such a procedure and the process. (If composition precedes this topic, the mathematics of resolution will not require a large portion of time.) Conceptually, resolution is similar to composition. In resolution we replace a single force with two forces acting at right angles (and in more convenient directions). Again, these two "components" will produce the same effect on the motion of the body as the original force did. Reproduction Page 13 provides several common examples of a single force to be resolved into two components. Use it as a supplement to your own presentation or as the basis for a class discussion.

2. *Activity.* Brain over Brawn. Have two of your more muscular pupils pull on opposite ends of a rope strung over two well anchored lab tables as shown in the diagram. (The rope must be fairly strong and not very stretchy for best results.) Mark the portions of the rope that coincide with the far edges of the tables as reference points. Explain that the problem is to pull one or both of these marked portions toward the center. Hopefully, the class will figure out how to do this. If not, have one of your smaller students push down on the middle of the rope between the tables and watch the reference marks. Very little downward force will cause the rope to pull inward. Discuss this with emphasis on the requirement that the rope sags (pulls in) in order to produce the balancing, upward component of force.

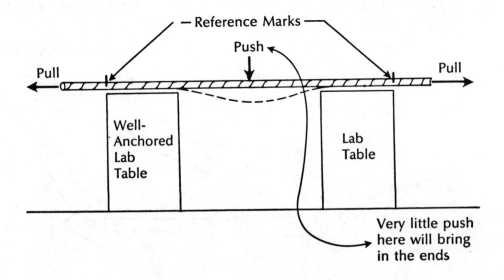

3. *Demonstration.* Show that a very small weight will raise a larger one by setting up the apparatus shown in the diagram below:

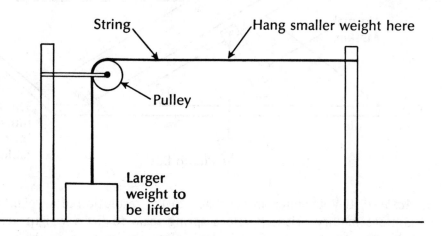

Discuss how the small force can be resolved into a fairly large tension in the string using force diagrams.

4. *Demonstration.* Show that the weight of an object on an inclined plane may be resolved into two components, one acting parallel to the incline and the other normal to the incline surface. The component parallel to the incline is easily demonstrated by releasing the object on the slope and noting that it slides down the incline. Consequently, a force must act parallel to the incline. The second component, the normal force, is not so obvious. If you use a flexible board for the incline, place a fairly heavy weight on it and note the sag in the board. Reproduce this sag by pushing or pulling normal to the surface.

5. *Activity.* Reproduction Page 14 is an example of the resolution of a weight on an incline into two components, one perpendicular and one parallel to the incline. An essential assumption in the solution is that the angle of the incline is equal to the angle between the normal component and the vertical direction of the actual weight. Although geometric proof of this relationship is possible, students get a better "feel" for it through the following demonstration: Fasten a ruler or dowel normal to a board and extending downward. Hang a plumb bob from the same point to represent the vertical direction of the weight. If the side of this incline arrangement is hung a bit over the edge of a demonstration table, you can adjust the angle of inclination from zero to 90° and note the corresponding angular relationship between the normal marker and plumb bob string.

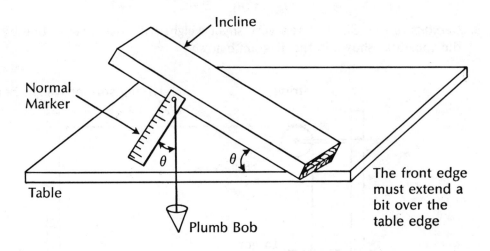

6. *Activity.* If you prefer an approach to the resolution of a weight on an incline that is more inquiry oriented, use a spring scale to lift a weight vertically up from a table top to the top of an incline. Note the reading on the scale. Next, pull the object up the inclined plane to the top and note the smaller scale reading. Begin your discussion with the question, "Why is less force required when the weight is pulled up the incline?"

Topic V: Equilibrium

1. *Teacher Presentation.* Define translational equilibrium as a motion concept. Any object in equilibrium will display constant motion—that is, it will be at rest and continue in that condition or, if it is moving, it will maintain the same speed and direction. Several examples should suffice to clarify the several aspects of the definition. Take care to insure that students do not include objects traveling in circular paths as part of this concept since the *direction* of the motion in this case is not constant but always changing.

   The force relationship for objects in equilibrium is relatively straightforward: If a body is in translational equilibrium, the net resultant force on it is zero. Several of the following activities are useful in supporting this relationship.

2. *Activity.* Re-investigate several of the resultant activities presented earlier in this chapter with special attention toward those which illustrate translational equilibrium and the zero resultant force.

3. *Activity.* Use commercially produced "force boards" as a student exercise to show that if a point is in equilibrium, the net force on it is zero. This activity also broadens the equilibrium concept by using three forces rather than the simple pairs used in the previous activity. Force boards allow the student to place a sheet of paper on a platform underneath three spring scales pulling on a center ring. The direction and magnitude of each of the scale forces is adjustable as shown in the sketch below:

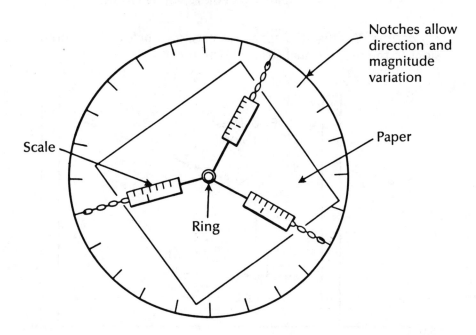

Students should record the direction of each force by tracing on the paper. The magnitudes are recorded from the scale readings. Of course, the center point is marked as well. With this data, the student can represent each of the forces to scale. Next, have the students pick any one of the three represented forces and label it as the "equilibrant." Graphic solution to find the resultant of the other two forces will show that this resultant is equal in magnitude but opposite in direction to the equilibrant force, thus producing the net force of zero on the ring. By comparison with others or by repeating the process with different directions and magnitudes, your students will quickly arrive at the following generalizations.

When several forces act on an object in equilibrium:

a. their net resultant is zero.

b. any one of them may be considered as the equilibrant.

c. the equilibrant is equal in magnitude and opposite in direction to the resultant of the other forces.

These relationships will be extremely useful for problem solving.

4. *Activity.* If commercial force boards are not available, do the preceding activity by using your own spring scales and mounting them on some plywood using nails or screws for the adjustment. Another option is to use three rubber bands instead of spring scales. In this case, the magnitude of each force is determined by the length of each stretched rubber band. (Uniform rubber bands are required.)

5. *Laboratory*. Arrange the apparatus as shown below. The purpose is to find the tensions in the two diagonal strings.

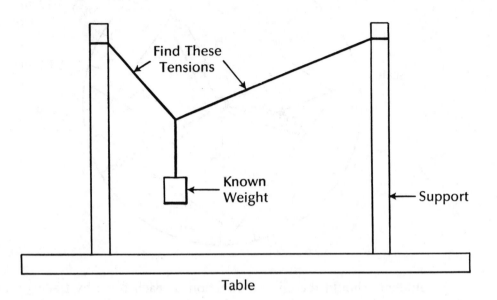

Table

Students should use the known weight as the equilibrant of the two unknown tensions. By representing the equilibrant force and the directions of the other two strings on a scale drawing, the student can draw in the resultant of the two unknowns by making it equal in length and opposite in direction to the equilibrant. Using this determined resultant as the diagonal of a parallelogram will allow the pupil to construct that parallelogram around the diagonal, thus determining the lengths of the two unknown sides. Relating these determined lengths to the scale for the drawing will produce the required tensions.

Students may check their results by attaching a spring scale to the point of intersection of the three strings and pulling in the direction of each string until the tension is released. The spring scale reading will approximate the actual tension.

6. *Activity*. Arrange several equilibrium problems similar to the previous lab activity for your students, except make the weights much heavier—more "life-sized." In this case, ropes replace the strings and sufficiently strong ceiling and wall supports are required. Objects such as cinder blocks or anvils provide the known weights. These objects may have to be weighed in pounds instead of newtons, depending on the type of heavy duty spring scales available for checking answers. Take special care in fastening the ropes in order to prevent accidents while students are gathering data. Some possible arrangements are sketched below.

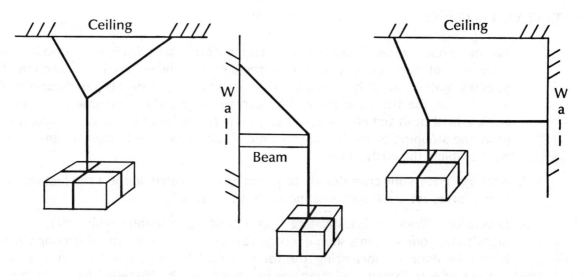

7. *Activity.* Students sometimes confuse the amount of force exerted by a length of rope or string with the actual length of the cord. Dispell this notion by having a student hold one end of a rope while you pull on the other end with a fixed amount of force. Pull initially with a short length (1 meter or so) and then with the full length of the rope (across the room). Show that the magnitude of the force does not depend directly on the length. Point out that what is determined by the dimension of the rope is the *direction* of the force.

8. *Activity.* Choose some common examples as the basis for problems similar to those in Activity 6. These should be solved by employing equilibrant concepts.

9. *Activity.* Place a cart on an incline as shown in the diagram below. Lock the wheels in some manner so it does not roll down the incline. Have the class resolve its weight into components parallel to and perpendicular to the plane. When the components are known, supply the equilibrant of each with strings passing over pulleys to appropriate weights. If the strings are attached to the cart properly (so that no unbalanced torques are produced), the plane may be removed without disturbing the cart.

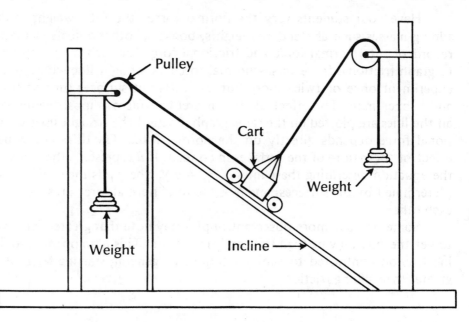

Topic VI: Friction

1. *Teacher Presentation.* Explain that frictional forces arise from attraction between molecules of two surfaces, and that these forces always act in a direction that opposes motion. Steadily push a book across a table. Ask the class to determine the direction of the frictional force. You can verify the class response by giving the book a hard push and noting that it stops due to the frictional force. A second hard push and stopping of the book, this time by allowing it to bump into an obstacle, will complete the verification.

2. *Activity.* Have your class discuss common examples that support the fact that frictional forces act in a direction opposite to the motion.

3. *Laboratory.* Prior to investigating friction and the variables which determine its magnitude, your students should recognize that the measurement of frictional forces is usually done by measuring the force needed to *overcome* friction and, using notions of equilibrium, deducing the magnitude of the frictional force. In this lab, which is outlined on Reproduction Page 15, pupils will drag an object such as a block of wood or a tray across a surface with steady speed. This is accomplished with either a spring scale or through the use of a pulley and weights as shown:

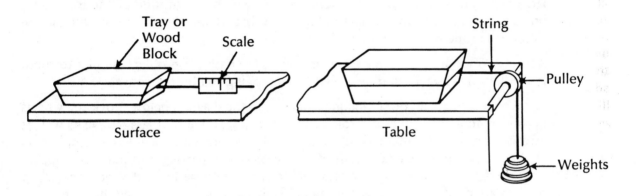

Have your students vary the normal force (the total weight in this case) by adding masses such as standard weights, books, or other objects to the tray. Keep a record of total normal force and frictional force for each of several trials—enough to graph frictional force versus normal force. A straight line will result. Repeat the experiment once or twice more but use different surfaces such as concrete, rugs, and rubber mats. The effect of the different surfaces is most readily observable if all the lines are plotted on the same graph. Each of the straight lines shows that frictional force depends directly on the normal force. The different slopes show the effect of the nature of the surfaces in contact. If μ represents the slope of each line, the equation describing these lines is $F_{fr} = \mu N$, where μ is the coefficient of friction (determined by the surfaces) and N is the total normal force pressing the surfaces to each other.

Some of your more observant pupils may note that greater force was required to get the tray moving than to keep it in motion. This is an opening to discuss starting friction contrasted to sliding friction. In general, starting frictional forces are greater than sliding friction.

4. *Demonstration.* A block of wood on an adjustable incline makes a simple demonstration of sliding versus starting friction. Place the block on the incline and slowly increase the angle until the wood starts to slide down. Once started, the block will accelerate, demonstrating that there is less frictional force while moving than when it was at rest (starting). Another variation is to adjust the angle so that the block just slides down when given a push. However, if the block is placed on the incline, it will remain until the slope is increased considerably.

5. *Activity.* Use Reproduction Page 16 as the basis for a discussion on how frictional forces are increased or decreased as desired by varying either the coefficient of friction or the normal force. Starting versus sliding frictional ideas are also included. Have students produce and explain several of their own examples.

6. *Activity.* Ask students to compose a short science fiction story entitled "The Day Friction Disappeared." Preliminary discussion can touch on the ideas that all knots, screws, nails, nuts and bolts, and the like depend on friction to stay in place.

Topic VII: Universal Gravitation

1. *Teacher Presentation.* The purpose of this presentation is to develop the general relationship describing universal gravitation, $F = G\dfrac{m_1 m_2}{s^2}$, by combining intuitions students already have regarding gravitational force. Each of the three variables, m_1, m_2, and s, the distance factor, are illustrated through thought experiments. First note that "weight" is the term usually applied to describe gravitational force. (Be sure to clear up any confusion with mass—the quantity of matter.) Place two masses on a table, a large one and a smaller one. Ask which weighs more. After the obvious answer is given, one can deduce that the amount of mass in an object determines the gravitational force on it. Next ask about the weight of the larger mass if it was transported to the moon. Relate the decrease in force to the effect of the second mass—the moon's mass—being less than the earth's. Finally, you can get at the inverse dependence with distance through questions concerning the weight of a mass as it is transported farther and farther away from the earth in a space craft. The inverse square relationship with distance will have to be accepted on faith by your students temporarily. Subsequent activities will support this hypothesis.

2. *Activity.* Newton's law of universal gravitation is the culmination of the work of many of his predecessors. If one arbitrarily chooses the Copernican theory as a starting point, then Galileo's consideration of the earth orbiting around the sun is a logical next step. Tycho Brahe's measurements of the positions of the planets followed by Kepler's laws regarding planetary motion also served as a basis for Newton's explanation of the motion through the law of universal gravitation. Newton's theory served as the basis for the work of Cavendish in measuring a value for G in a non-astronomical setting. Leverrier's extension of this theory led to the discovery of the planet Neptune. Similar perterbations of the planet Uranus led to the discovery of Pluto.

    Any of these works are appropriate as a research assignment for students. A total picture will result if different groups are assigned to each of the topics, and the resultant information is shared with the entire class. Some of the references listed at the end of this chapter are useful for this research.

3. *Activity*. Use Reproduction Page 17 as a worksheet to focus on the nature of the inverse square relationship in universal gravitation.

4. *Demonstration*. It is helpful to students to build a model of a torsion balance as used by Cavendish in order to understand and appreciate the extremely delicate measurement made in his famous experiment. The model will not work to make measurements but it does aid the student in understanding the operation of a torsion balance. Lead into this demonstration by asking, "If Newton is correct and all masses in the universe mutually attract, why then do two masses placed on the demonstration table not come together?" There are two plausable explanations: either there is no force of attraction or, if there is a force, it must be very small. Then set up a model of the torsion balance similar to the diagram below to aid in the explanation of its operation and to show how such a delicate measurement was made. Be sure to demonstrate that almost invisible twists of the string are "amplified" by the mirror and light and thus made measurable.

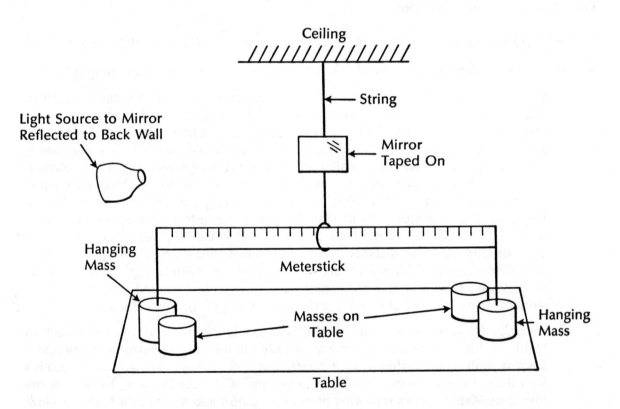

You may choose to follow this demonstration with a film loop from the references at the end of this chapter, which shows the Cavendish experiment with the speed of the light spot increased by time-lapse photography. Some of your students may choose to replicate this experiment. Commerically produced balances are available but the time required for the balance to reach equilibrium is longer than most lab periods. Replication also requires a building relatively free from disturbing vibrations.

5. *Activity.* Reproduction Page 18 is a problem in which students can calculate their weight using Newton's law of universal gravitation and appropriate conversion factors. It will serve to reinforce the idea that weights of objects are in fact described according to Newton's universal relationship, $F = G\dfrac{m_1 m_2}{s^2}$.

EVALUATION PROCEDURES

Short quizzes based on activities in this chapter should occur at several points in the instructional sequence. You may choose to grade the laboratory exercises as they are completed as well. Many of the Reproduction Pages and the discussions they generate will provide evaluation opportunity or serve as models for your own tests and quizzes. Reproduction Page 19 is a unit test on forces. It is in essay form. Give it in sections according to the numbered topics or as an entire unit test.

Resources for Teaching Forces

The following list of resources useful in teaching topics in this chapter is divided into two sections, audio-visual materials and print. Appropriate notations are included if the work is particularly well suited for either teachers or students. Publisher addresses appear at the end of the book.

Audio-Visual Materials

Vectors. Film. P.S.S.C. A lecture demonstration made to a high school class. Magnitude and direction in vector quantities are discussed as well as addition and subtraction of vectors.

Force of Gravity. Film. McGraw-Hill. Portrays historical development of gravity touching on the work of Copernicus, Kepler, and Galileo. Examines Newton's work in detail.

Forces: Composition and Resolution. Film. Coronet. Illustrates graphic methods of finding resultants and components using examples, models, and animation.

Friction (Advanced Science). Film. McGraw-Hill. Demonstrates that frictional force is independent of surface area, and that it is proportional to the normal force. Principles of surface lubrication are also demonstrated.

Issac Newton. Film. Coronet. Re-enacts Newton's contributions in mathematics, his theory of light, and his work on gravitation and laws of motion.

Gravity, Weight and Weightlessness. Film. B. F. Associates. In a lively style, this film relates weight to gravity. Weightlessness in free fall and satellites are also presented, as well as the studies of space scientists on gravity.

Forces. Film. P.S.S.C. Shows the Cavendish experiment. Compares gravitational force with electrical force.

Kepler's Laws. Filmloop. Ealing Corp. An explanation of Kepler's three laws. Planetary orbits in an inverse-square force field are programmed for display on a cathode ray tube.

Jupiter Satellite Orbit. Filmloop. Ealing Corp. Uses time-lapse photography to record the motion of Jupiter's satellite, Io. Explains the finding of Jupiter's mass from the period of revolution.

Determination of a Value for G—The Cavendish Experiment. Filmloop. Ealing Corp. Shows a laboratory apparatus being used to determine a value for the universal gravitational constant, G. Data is provided so that students can work out a value from the filmloop.

Principles of Lubrication. Film. International Film Bureau. Using models and demonstrations, this film illustrates frictional forces as dependent on normal force and coefficient of friction The second portion discusses lubrication in several forms. The latter section has an engineering slant; the first part closely relates to a typical physics introduction to friction.

Print

Gravity by G. Gamow. Doubleday Anchor, 1962. A brilliant discussion of one of the currently unsolved problems in physics.

"Newton" by I. Cohen. *Scientific American* (December 1955). A biography by one of the leading authorities on the subject.

The Planet-Girded Suns by S. L. Engdahl. Atheneum, 1974. This book is a history of the idea that inhabited solar systems exist in the universe. The first section relates the work of Bruno, Copernicus, Kepler, Galileo, Newton, and others.

Pioneer Astronomers by N. Sullivan. Atheneum, 1967. The first four chapters deal with Copernicus, Kepler, Galileo, and Newton.

Physics for the Inquiring Mind by E. M. Rogers. Princeton University Press, 1960. Chapter 2 has many sample problems in vector math.

Project Physics Text. Holt, Rinehart and Winston, 1975. A good deal of detail and additional references provided for selected topics in Unit 3, "Motion in the Heavens".

Physics—Its Methods and Meanings by A. Taffel. Allyn and Bacon, 1981. Chapters 3, 4, 8 provide references on weight, vectors, force, and gravitation.

P.S.S.C. Physics, 4th edition by Haber-Schain et al. D. C. Heath, 1976. Selected portions of Chapters 10–13 are references for topics in this chapter.

Physics Through Experiment by R. Bamberger et al. Sterling Publishing Co., 1969. Offers several simple experiments distinguishing mass and weight and variations in gravitational force on objects.

A Source Book in Physics by W. F. Magie. Harvard University Press, 1963. Pages 30 and 92 contain extracts from *Principia*, which demonstrates Newton's law of gravitation, and his *Third Book*, where Newton applied his mathematical theorems to prove the two elements of the law. Useful for some quotes.

Physics Teacher's Guide by D. Kutliroff. Parker Publishing Co., 1970. Chapter 5 suggests some demonstrations and activities with vector quantities, as well as a vector laboratory.

Knowledge and Wonder by V. F. Weisskopf. Doubleday Anchor, 1963. Chapter 3 of this book, written for the layman, deals with the law of gravitation. Relationships of several physical sciences are discussed.

The Watershed by A. Koestler. Doubleday Anchor, 1960. A biography of Kepler. Kepler, the man, emerges as a rich, if outlandish, character, deserving of immortality.

"Friction." American Institute of Physics, 1964. Selected reprints of a series of articles on friction. The material is fairly technical and not at all suited for most students.

The Rise of Modern Physics by H. Crew. Williams and Wilkins Co., 1935. Presents an account of the early work on combination of forces. Page 135 discusses mass versus weight.

"A Background to Newtonian Gravitation" by V. V. Ramon. *The Physics Teacher* (November 1972). This article provides some historical treatment of Newton's works. An excellent list of additional references accompanies the article.

"Use of a Puzzle to Teach Concepts of Circular Motion and Friction" by J. D. Logan. *The Physics Teacher* (November 1972). Part of the puzzle experiment presented requires the student to estimate a coefficient of friction.

"Normal and Frictional Forces: An Experiment" by H. K. Macomber. *The Physics Teacher* (December 1979). An analysis of frictional force on an inclined plane. A coefficient of static friction is determined from slopes of graphs.

Physics, The Pioneer Science by Lloyd W. Taylor. Dover Publications, 1959. Read Steven's treatment of the inclined plane in Chapter 6.

Historic Researchers by Thomas W. Chalmers. Scribner, 1952. Chapter 1 traces the development of our understanding of friction.

"Stick and Slip" by E. Rubinowicz. *Scientific American* (May 1956). Describes an interesting aspect of solid-friction phenomena.

Vectors—A Programmed Text for Introductory Physics. Appleton-Century-Crofts, 1962. An excellent book for the student who wants additional explanation and practice in vector additions and subtractions.

"Friction" by F. Palmer. *Scientific American* (February 1951). Some research on the still puzzling aspects of friction.

Vectors 1 and *Vectors 2*. Holt, Rinehart and Winston, 1971. The Project Physics Course Programmed Instruction Booklets for students. They deal with resolution and composition of vectors.

The Birth of a New Physics by I. B. Cohen. Anchor Doubleday, 1960. Chapters 6 and 7 explore the thinking and contributions of Kepler and Newton in a historical context.

3

Motion

INTRODUCTION

We live in a world of moving things. In order to understand why objects move—the causative and thus controlling factors—we must first accurately describe the movement. This chapter deals with such a description, kinematics, through the concepts of displacement, speed, velocity, and uniform acceleration. The scope is limited to motion in straight lines and uniform accelerations. Examples should be chosen, initially, from the wide range of common experiences shared by you and your students. Later, point out the dynamic nature of some less obvious phenomena such as molecular motion and temperature, the movements of bodies on an astronomical scale, and motion within atoms.

CONTENT OVERVIEW

The simplest concept and a good starting point is displacement. If a body moves, it is initially in one location, position A, and later in some new location, position B. Displacement is the representation of this position change. The directional nature of the change makes displacement a vector quantity since both magnitude and direction are involved. Students should grasp the vector idea readily if this chapter follows Chapter 2 in your course. If it does not, appropriate references to vector discussions in the previous chapter are a good idea.

Once motion from A to B is presented in terms of displacement, one might ask about time relationships for that motion. How long it takes to move involves the concept of speed or, if direction is taken into account, velocity. Students will have a good "feel" for these concepts from earlier courses, and this should serve as a basis for studying relationships with other descriptors such as acceleration.

Since a body may move at varying speeds at different points along its path from A to B (which is the most likely in real life movements), the idea of acceleration is necessary to complete the description of things moving. Pupils seem to grasp the notion of velocity as the rate of change of position with time but have considerable difficulty relating acceleration as the rate of change of velocity with time. Anticipate some confusion of velocity and acceleration definitions. Careful initial discussion and continued differentiation of these two concepts are needed in order to reduce fuzzy definitions to clearer perceptions through multiple instructional activities. Another problem area to watch for is the apparent paradox of "uniform acceleration". When students grasp the change notion, they sometimes have trouble with conceptualizing a constant (uniform) rate of change. Multiple examples will help to clear up the idea; also, avoid the phrase "constant acceleration" in your instruction, at least initially.

Kinematics in many textbooks is a chapter filled with numerous equations relating distance, time, velocity, and acceleration variables. This leads students to try to "find the right formula" in solving problems in this area. In order to avoid the formula approach, try to minimize problem solving formulas to two or, at most, three basic relationships: one for average velocity; the second being the definitional formula for uniform acceleration. (The third formula might be one that relates distance and time for accelerated motion.) A variety of problems stressing analysis of the physical situation will provide the required practice for successful use of kinematics relationships.

Space-time graphs complement verbal and mathematical descriptions of motion. Students will need to produce and interpret these graphic representations. It is helpful if the student can see the motion along with its graphic description in order to make the relationship between the two clear. Choose your laboratory activities and demonstrations with this in mind.

Basic measurements in the laboratory portion of this study involve displacement and time. Several options are available depending on equipment and type of motion to be described. Each option has advantages and shortcomings.

For slow moving objects, meterstick or tape measure and stopwatches offer direct measurement of distance and time as the motion happens. Students either mark off distances and record the time to cross each distance marker or mark the distance traveled after successive intervals of time.

Good stopwatches are costly, however, and this technique produces large measurement errors if the motion is rapid. For measurements on rapid movements, such as those displayed by objects falling under the acceleration due to gravity, spark timers or strobe photography produce more accurate results. Spark timers have the disadvantage of separating the measurements from the motion, since the distance record is made from a spark tape *after* the motion has occurred. A more direct measure might be more instructive to an introductory student.

Strobe photography offers a good compromise between directness and accuracy. One may use a strobe light in a darkened room or a light "chopping disc" mounted in front of the camera lens. Either technique can produce a record of the positions of a moving object during successive time intervals. This has the advantage of a record of the event in context—that is, the background shows. The spark timer only shows marks on a tape. Distance measurements can be taken directly from the strobe picture or, if real life size distances are required, the photo can be "blown up" using an opaque projector and a reference marker on the picture, or by using an overhead projector and the photo with pin holes marking the object in its various positions. The *Project Physics Course Teacher Resource Book* listed in the references at the end of this chapter has some excellent notes on strobe photography techniques for a physics class. Prior to choosing this option, you should consider the initial cost of the equipment and subsequent budgeting for film.

Photoelectric cells coupled to an electric timing device provide still another option for measuring time intervals. In this case, the moving object interrupts light to the cell, activating and stopping the timer as it passes over a distance interval.

Whichever option you choose, there should be no problem in finding plenty of examples of motion for the lab activities in this section. Such activities should make use of some of the variety of familiar motions in daily life: balls, cars, airplanes, bicycles, and so forth. Don't overlook people—racing, walking, jogging—as possible examples of the moving things to be described in this study.

OBJECTIVES

As a result of the learning experiences in this chapter, students should be able to:

1. Represent and interpret displacement and velocity as vector quantities.

2. Carry out the composition and resolution processes with displacement and velocity vectors.

3. Correctly use the terms speed, velocity, and acceleration in describing motion.

4. Solve problems using relationships among distance, time, velocity, and uniform acceleration.

5. Produce and interpret distance-time and velocity-time graphs of moving objects.

LEARNING EXPERIENCES

Topic I: Displacement as a Vector Quantity

1. *Activity.* Ask a student to stand in the middle of a cleared area of the room (a circle of about five meters diameter can be used). Now instruct the pupil to "walk two meters." At this point, one of two things will happen. The person may ask, "In what direction?" This will be a lead in to a discussion of displacement involving both a distance *and* a direction, and the necessity of both for effective communication regarding a change of position. Or the following may happen: The student may simply walk about two meters from where she was standing as per your instruction. Feign frustration, indicate that this is not what you wanted, and ask the person to go back and try it again. Several repeats and some acting on your part will soon convey the impression that there is a predetermined location where you wish the student to go, and that the *direction* of the motion is critical to communicating that command.

   Indicate that a change of position is called a displacement. Also indicate that because displacements involve both distance and direction, they are vector quantities. Discuss giving directions to motorists, airplane flight plans, and navigation in general as employing the idea of displacements.

2. *Activity.* A treasure hunt will reinforce the concept of displacement as a vector quantity. It also will provide students with a fun experience in representing and

interpreting displacement vectors graphically. The activity is in two parts. First, students produce a map (a series of graphically represented displacements) to a "treasure." Later maps are exchanged and each team follows a map made by another team. If successful, they will find the treasure. This is an out-of-doors activity—athletic fields and areas around the building provide good settings.

Distances are measured by pacing them off. Therefore, each student will need to know a correspondence between his pace and an equivalent distance in meters. Mark off a distance of 100 m (the sideline of a football field provides a good line), and have each student walk this course while counting his paces. This will provide information needed to convert paces to meters and vice versa. Some students will need instruction on how to determine directions with a compass. Remind pupils to walk in straight lines for each displacement by selecting some object in line with their desired direction and walking toward it. Advise teams to use simple directions such as 0°, 90°, 180°, etc. and to have each displacement terminate at some obvious marking point such as a tree, fence, or corner of a building. During the first phase of this activity, students choose some starting point and pace off several displacements, leaving a "treasure" at the end of the last one, and recording each displacement in order to produce a map. The map should be drawn to a scale in meters. The starting point and scale should be indicated and the displacements represented by the length of each vector. Their direction should be taken from a 0° indicator on the map. "Treasures" are at your discretion but a note with "words of wisdom" will suffice. Once the maps are completed, they are exchanged among the teams. Each team now has to interpret a map and follow it to find the treasure.

3. *Activity.* If your teams don't notice the obvious shortcut in Activity 2 (find the resultant of the several displacements graphically and locate the treasure in one displacement), ask about this after the exercise is completed. Note the process of finding the resultant displacement is similar to the process with forces (Chapter 2), with the exception that each successive displacement is measured from the termination point of the preceding one and the resultant is drawn from the original starting point to the end of the last displacement. Resolution is essentially the same as with forces.

4. *Activity.* Have a guest speaker from an engineering or surveying company talk to your class about how they measure displacements.

Topic II: Velocity as a Vector Quantity

1. *Teacher Presentation.* Have students time you as you walk across a pre-measured five-meter interval. Ask the class to calculate your average speed of walking. They will have no difficulty in dividing the five meter distance by the time required to make the trip. Summarize the relationship on the blackboard or overhead: speed $= \dfrac{\text{distance}}{\text{time}}$ or $v = \dfrac{s}{t}$. Now repeat the walk at about the same speed but in the reverse direction. Ask about the speed again, then ask what was different—the directional aspect should come out in the student's response. Point out that if we are concerned about

both speed and the *direction* of travel, velocity is the concept to use: velocity = $\dfrac{displacement}{time}$ or $\bar{v} = \dfrac{\bar{s}}{t}$ (Note the vector indicators over $\bar{v}$ and $\bar{s}$.)

2. *Activity.* Use Reproduction Page 20 to emphasize the distinction between speed and velocity.

3. *Activity.* Use the film loop *Vector Addition—Velocity of a Boat* as an exercise in resolution and composition of velocities. It is listed in the references at the end of this chapter. Students may use the loop individually by projecting it on some paper, or an entire group may use it by projecting it on a blackboard. In either case, the idea is to follow a chosen reference point on the boat as it moves and thus trace out the displacement while timing with a stopwatch. This technique requires synchronization of the start and end of the trace with the time. Synchronization is done best when directed by the person doing the timing, who says, "Ready . . . . start!" and "Ready . . . . stop!" Determine each velocity from these measurements.

In Scene 1, floating objects provide data for the determination of the velocity of a river. Scene 2 shows a boat heading upstream. Its velocity is the resultant of two components, the velocity of the river down and the velocity produced by the motor upwards. Since the resultant and one of the two components are already known, this scene provides for the calculation of the other component: the velocity provided by the motor which is maintained in the following scenes. In Scene 3, the boat will head downstream. Students can predict the resultant velocity (a combination of the river and motor in the same direction) and then project the scene to check the prediction. Scene 4 shows the boat heading across the river but its motor velocity is at right angles to the current resulting in a velocity along a diagonal. Again, predict the resultant (don't forget an angle for direction) and check the prediction with a measurement from the film loop. Scene 5 is intended to show a horizontal resultant when the boat points diagonally upward and travels across the river. A slight change in approach allows for a resolution process. For this scene, the velocity provided by the motor is resolved into two components; one upstream and equal in magnitude to the velocity of the river, and a second component which produces the observed horizontal movement. Measure the angle of the boat in this scene, and then use this angle and the known motor velocity to resolve it into upward and sideways components. The upward component should be equal to the current in magnitude. The horizontal component is compared to the observed velocity in the scene.

4. *Activity.* Guest speakers who teach flying or are involved in aviation or navigation can provide some interesting talks and practical applications of velocity vectors and their composition.

Topic III: Graphing Constant Velocity

1. *Laboratory.* Have students investigate distance-time relationships for objects moving with constant speed in a straight line. They should record distance traveled as a function of time and plot the data on a graph of distance versus time. The resulting straight line graphs show that for constant velocity, distance is proportional to time.

Some interpretation of this proportionality is helpful. From the graphs, students should be able to show that in twice the time, twice the distance was covered; three times the time covers three times the distance, and so on. An investigation of the slope of the line will show that it represents the speed of the moving object:

general equation for any straight line: $y = mx + b$

general equation for the distance-time graph: $s = vt + 0$

Have pupils calculate the speed of their objects from the slope of the graph.

In order to show that the relationships discussed are general for all constant velocities, you might have different groups work with different moving objects, and then compare similarities and differences in their results. The general relationships will be the same, the speeds (slopes) will be different.

Here are some suggested motions for this laboratory:

a. A toy, battery operated, car or bulldozer.
b. A cart or ball rolling down a long incline. (The incline must be just enough to overcome friction and produce the desired constant motion. Remember, grooves confine the object to a straight line.)
c. A glider given a push on an airtrack.
d. A puck on an air table or other low friction surface.
e. A person walking down a hallway.
f. A person jogging across a course.
g. A cart on a lab table with a string going to a pulley at the end. The weight is adjusted to

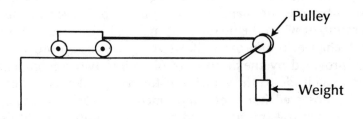

just overcome friction and keep the cart moving. (Your surface must be very regular for this one.)
h. A cart apparatus similar to the one above, except that an electric motor and gear system are used to wind up the string and keep the cart moving. (Be careful that the winding string does not build up on your take-up reel and thus increase the speed during the end of the trial.)
i. A car driving along a marked course in the school parking lot with steady speed.
j. A person on a bicycle going along a course at steady speed.

2. *Laboratory.* A second series of measurements, similar to the preceding lab, using the same physical situation will help emphasize that the slope of a distance-time graph represents the speed of the moving object. In this case, at least two repeats of the motion are used, one slow and one faster. Each trial will produce data for a straight line. If both lines are plotted on the same graph, the slope correspondence with speed is shown through a comparison of the two lines. Of course, your choice of

examples of the two constant velocities in this lab is restricted to set ups which will allow two different speeds.

Topic IV: Uniform Acceleration

1. *Teacher Presentation.* Most motion that we observe is not constant, it is changing. Objects speed up, slow down, and diverge from straight line paths. Acceleration is a concept that describes this change. Suppose two cars accelerate from rest and reach a speed of 50 km/hr. Did they both experience the same acceleration? The answer is, "It depends." It depends on how long it takes each car to undergo the change. If one car did it in 10 seconds and the other in 5 seconds, there is a difference in their accelerations. This concept, then, involves a time rate of change of velocity. In formula form:

$$\bar{a} = \frac{\Delta \bar{v}}{\Delta t} \quad \text{where } \bar{a} \text{ is the acceleration,}$$

$\Delta \bar{v}$ is the change in velocity and Δt is the time required for that change. Note that acceleration is a vector quantity in that a direction of change is implicit in this concept. The mathematical relationship is often expressed as:

$$\bar{a} = \frac{\bar{v}_f - \bar{v}_i}{t} \quad \text{In this case, } \Delta \bar{v}$$

is written out as the difference between a final velocity, v_f, and an initial velocity, v_i. The time required for the change to occur is t.

Present several examples of velocity changes and reasonable times for those changes to occur. Be sure to include at least one example of an object slowing down in order to discuss negative acceleration (or deceleration) as an example of the general relationship. Some attention should be given to the units for acceleration in your examples. In the SI system, they will be $\frac{m}{s^2}$, since acceleration is a rate of change of a rate of change of position.

2. *Activity.* Have students refer to Reproduction Page 21 in order to arrive at a relationship among acceleration, velocity, time, and distance.

The resulting formula, $\bar{s} = \bar{v}_i t + \frac{1}{2} \bar{a} t^2$, combined with the definitional equation for acceleration, are sufficient to solve a wide variety of problems characterized by uniform acceleration. Several problems are offered in Reproduction Page 22.

3. *Activity.* Problem solving in this area often perplexes students. They often tend to read a problem and search for a formula that will produce the correct answer. If one is not at hand, they encounter a brick wall and cannot proceed. Practice in doing a wide variety of problems will eventually produce competence in analysis skills, which should be stressed over rote formula application. Reproduction Page 23 presents a series of steps that help a student proceed with analysis of a problem. Use of this approach to problems in physics is not restricted to ideas in this chapter. It is useful throughout the course. This is a good point for introducing

the steps because their function of allowing analysis, even if the approach is not immediately obvious to the pupil, will be especially valuable in initial problem solving in accelerated motion. You should emulate this approach in examples worked out for the class.

4. *Demonstration.* Objects falling freely under the influence of gravity provide many examples of uniformly accelerated motion. Show that all freely falling objects near the surface of the earth accelerate at the same rate by dropping several masses of different weights. If released simultaneously, all objects will hit the floor at the same time, showing that their accelerations due to gravity must be the same.

5. *Demonstration.* Air friction and terminal velocity. Follow the preceding demonstration with a second in which you drop a piece of paper and a metal weight or rock. In this case, the heavier object will hit before the paper. Your class will probably attribute the difference to air friction but you should verify this hypothesis. First, wad the paper into a tight ball and repeat the drop (the paper will now fall more rapidly than before but still somewhat slower than the heavier weight). Next, do the following demonstration.

6. *Demonstration.* Use a "guinea and feather" tube to show that, in fact, any differences in the acceleration due to gravity in the previous cases were due to air friction. This tube contains a coin and a feather. When the tube is full of air, quickly invert it. The coin will fall with a clunk while the feather flutters down. However, when most of the air is removed from the tube, the feather and coin drop together.

7. *Activity.* Show the film loop, "Acceleration Due to Lunar Gravity," listed in the references. It provides an interesting version of the previous demonstration, but this one is done by astronauts on the moon.

8. *Activity.* Assign three students to research the conversation concerning falling objects of different weights in a translation of Galileo's *Two New Sciences*. Following the research, these pupils might act out the classic argument between Aristotlian logic and Galilean experiment for the rest of the class.

9. *Activity.* Do the dollar bill trick. Hold a dollar bill with one hand. Release the bill and catch it with the fingers of your other hand, which have been around the paper but not touching it.

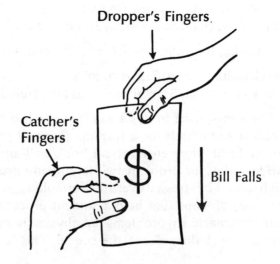

Dropper's Fingers

Catcher's Fingers

Bill Falls

Offer the dollar bill to anyone in the class who can catch it. They may place their fingers anywhere around the bill (but not touching it) prior to the drop. In order to prevent financial loss, follow this procedure in releasing the bill: Do not look at the catcher; release the bill while you are in the middle of a sentence addressed to the class; let the bill fall from your fingers by a slight release of pressure—don't open your fingers quickly. The reason for these steps is to avoid tipping off the catcher as to when the drop will happen. The reaction time for most people is too long to catch the money. Following several trials, do an analysis of the trick (or have your students figure out how long the bill is "catchable"). The physics is that one can only catch the bill during the time period involved in falling its own length. Air friction is negligible during this portion of flight so the bill is a freely falling object. Using the known value of the acceleration due to gravity, $g = \dfrac{9.8m}{s^2}$, the measured length of the dollar in meters and $\bar{s} = \dfrac{1}{2}\bar{a}t^2$, one can calculate the maximum time allowed to catch it. This is shorter than most reaction times for such an exercise.

Ask the class to speculate on why you *could* catch your own drop, while others could not get the dollar.

10. *Activity.* Use the acceleration due to gravity to measure reaction time by having pairs of students take turns releasing a meter stick while their partner catches it. The catcher first grasps the meter stick at the bottom in order to align the bottom of his hand with the end of the stick. Maintaining this orientation, he next loosens his grip until his hand no longer makes contact with it. The dropper, who was holding the stick, now releases it in a manner similar to the previous activity. Some of the stick will fall through the catcher's hand before the object is "caught."

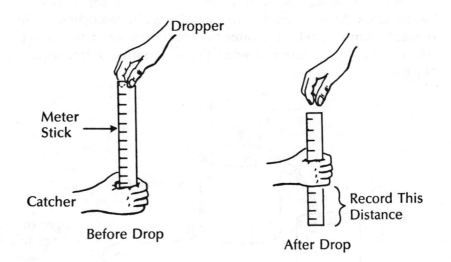

Dropper

Meter Stick →

Catcher

Before Drop

Record This Distance

After Drop

Record this distance. The average of several trials is used to calculate reaction time, just as in Activity 9. Students may compare times for left versus right hands, males versus females, or note the effect of "practice" on reaction time with appropriate record keeping. Compare class results to the dollar bill activity in order to predict who might catch the dollar.

Topic V: Graphing Accelerated Motion

1. *Activity.* Almost all student texts refer in some way to Galileo's descriptions of uniform acceleration resulting from his measurements on bodies moving down inclined planes. Student research into this aspect of his work is a good way to lead into the laboratory work which follows. Several references at the end of this chapter are appropriate for such an assignment.

2. *Demonstration or Laboratory.* A replication of Galileo's experiment. Galileo had to "dilute" the acceleration due to gravity with an incline because he lacked sufficiently fine time-measuring devices. Replicate his experiment by using a long track such as a board or V-shaped metal stock. A long wire, anchored with turnbuckles and supporting a trolley device, stretched across the room at an incline also will work well for this exercise. This is available from supply houses but you can easily make your own using some pulley wheels.

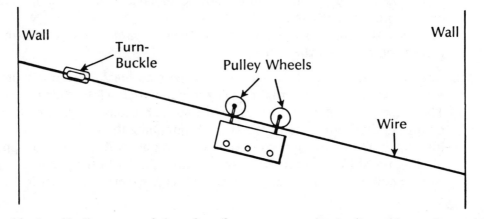

Mark off distances of 1m, 2m, 3m, etc., on the incline. Keep time with a "water clock." Such a device consists of a graduated cylinder which collects water released from a vessel. The water flow is started when the object on the incline is released; the flow is stopped when the accelerating object reaches a particular distance marker.

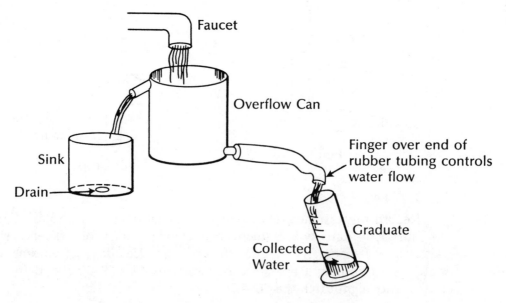

In this experiment, distance is in meters and time is in milliliters of water collected. Students should plot points on a distance-time graph as they are obtained. Several repeats at each distance will produce a cluster of points.

This is a good opportunity to discuss experimental error. Besides producing the parabolic distance-time graph, this experiment provides data for the calculation of instantaneous velocities at each distance marker by using v ave. $= \frac{s}{t} = \frac{v_i + v_f}{2}$.

v_i is zero in each case, and v_f can be determined. Have students plot these values against the corresponding time. The slope of this straight line graph equals $\frac{\Delta v}{\Delta t}$ and is the acceleration. Compare that value with subsequent values arrived at when repeating the experiment with steeper inclines. What would the value be if the incline was vertical $\left(9.8 \frac{m}{s^2}\right)$?

3. *Laboratory.* Repeat the preceding activity with modern equipment. Use stopwatches, a spark-tape, or strobe photography for timing. An inclined air track or table can replace the wire or board. Again, data of distance and time provide the base for calculation of velocities at various points. Distance-time and velocity-time graphs should be done by students. Acceleration values are obtained from the slope of the v versus t plot. Compare measurement errors with the previous version where the water clock was used.

4. *Laboratory.* The acceleration due to gravity. Use a spark-timer or strobe photography to obtain distance versus time data for a freely falling object. As in the previous experiments, students should plot and analyze distance-time and velocity-time graphs. The slope of the latter will give a value comparable to $9.8 \frac{m}{s^2}$. In this lab, you might use an alternate approach in determining velocities at various points in the flight: Calculate the average velocity during each successive time interval by dividing the distance traveled during that interval by the time interval. Plot these velocities against the *mid-time* of each interval for the velocity-time graph.

Although spark-timers and strobe photography provide convenient timing for freely falling objects, other arrangements will produce acceptable measures. Mechanical devices are available which synchronize the drop of a ball with the start of a watch. The ball drops onto a lever which stops the clock, thus measuring the time of fall. The mechanism is adjustable for a variety of heights. Another device initiates the drop with a peg mounted on the side of a rotating phonograph turntable. The object falls onto the turntable, marking its location on some paper with carbon paper underneath. The angle between the peg and the mark, combined with the known angular velocity of the turntable, allow for a computation of the time of fall.

5. *Laboratory.* One of the simplest ways to obtain a value for the acceleration due to gravity is through the use of a pendulum. Its period, T, length, l, and acceleration, g, are related by $T = 2\pi \sqrt{\frac{l}{g}}$. In this approach, the length is measured and the period is determined from the frequency obtained by timing the pendulum swings over many oscillations. Reduce errors by keeping the swing arc small.

6. *Laboratory.* Another approach for the determination of g involves the use of a timing device such as photo-relays or an oscilloscope to measure an average velocity of

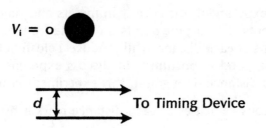

$$v_i = 0$$

$$d \qquad \text{To Timing Device}$$

a falling object over a small distance interval, *d*, near the end of the fall. The average velocity at this point approximates v_f. If the time of fall, *t*, is measured and the object is dropped from rest ($v_i = 0$), then *g* is calculated from $g = \dfrac{(v_f - v_i)}{t}$.

7. *Laboratory.* Distance-time and velocity-time graphs should be produced for other accelerations. Calculations are similar to the previous inclined plane and free fall exercises. Here are some possibilities:
   a. Cart accelerated by means of a hanging weight.

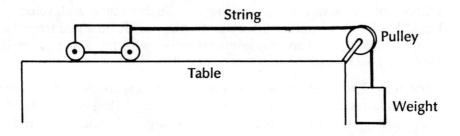

   b. Study decelerated motion by letting a cart or ball travel down an incline which terminates on a horizontal surface. Some track may be required to maintain a straight line path while slowing to a stop.
   c. A large pulley supports two slightly different masses at opposite ends of a string. By adjusting the mass difference, the resultant acceleration can be very small.

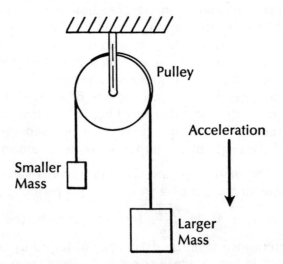

   d. Very slow linear accelerations result from a yo-yo with a thin axis and large body.

With these arrangements, a metronome, pendulum, or stopwatch is used for time measurements. Mark off successive distance intervals.

ASSESSING ACHIEVEMENT OF OBJECTIVES

Ongoing Evaluation

The extent to which students have mastered concepts covered under the five topics in this chapter may be measured by any of the activities assigned to class members as individuals, particularly the laboratory activities. Responses to the problems on Reproduction Page 22 may also be used for evaluation.

Final Evaluation

For an overall assessment of the student's grasp of the concepts in this chapter, construct a test directly from the list of objectives presented at the beginning. The unit test may be in essay form or short answer-objective type, depending on local preferences. Such an examination might include questions on:

1. Interpreting displacements and/or velocities from vector representations and producing representations, given the quantities.

2. Finding the resultants of two or more displacements and velocity components.

3. Resolving a velocity and/or displacement into components.

4. Discrimination of the terms speed, velocity and acceleration.

5. Recognizing appropriate units for quantities studied in this chapter.

6. Solving distance, time, velocity, acceleration problems such as those on Reproduction Page 22.

7. Producing and interpreting graphs related to various motions.

8. Interpreting laboratory data as related to descriptions of moving objects.

Reproduction Page 24 contains some examples of graph relationships. Use it as a source of test questions or for student review prior to the unit test. Use Reproduction Page 25 as a quiz, part of a final test, or as a source of ideas for additional kinds of questions.

Resources for Teaching Kinematics

Below is a selected and annotated list of resources useful for teaching the topics in this chapter. It is divided into audio-visual materials and print materials. Notations are added if the material is specifically for either teacher or student reference. Addresses of publishers or distributors can be found in Appendix A.

Audio-Visual Materials

Galileo's Laws of Falling Bodies. Film. Encyclopedia Britannica. Uses slow motion and freeze-frame photography to show experiments with the inclined plane and free falling bodies, both in the atmosphere and in a vacuum.

Galileo: The Challenge of Reason. Film. Learning Corporation of America. A dramatic account of the conflict between Galileo's scientific thinking and the Church's authority. Although Galileo recants, it is his view which dominates the West in succeeding centuries. Several experiments are shown but the thrust of this film is on the man and his conflicts.

Straight-Line Kinematics. Film. P.S.S.C. Distance, speed, and acceleration are discussed. Graphs of all three versus time are generated using a car. Relationships via slopes and areas from graphs are shown.

Galileo's Experiment: On the Moon and on the Earth. Filmloop. Spring Green Multimedia. Shows a hammer and a feather being dropped simultaneously on the moon and on the earth. The moon sequence offers a dramatic effect to this experiment.

Inertia. Film. P.S.S.C. Uses low friction dry ice pucks and flash photography in contrasting constant and accelerated motion. Distance-time graphs are produced and analyzed. Discusses the principle of inertia.

Mechanics Lesson 7: Falling Bodies. Film. Encyclopedia Britannica. Deals with the kinematics of falling bodies and demonstrates falling bodies in a vacuum and in air.

Velocity and Acceleration. Film. Coronet. Defines motion and explains and demonstrates velocity and acceleration. Animation is used to illustrate both positive and negative acceleration due to gravity.

Vectors. Film. Modern Learning Aides. Uses models to show vector displacements in two and three dimensions. Introduces vector addition.

Vector Kinematics. Film. Modern Learning Aides. Introduces velocity and acceleration vectors and shows them simultaneously for various motions. Circular and simple harmonic motion are also included.

Vector Addition: Velocity of a Boat. Filmloop. Ealing Corp. A boat travels in a river. Scenes are photographed from above. This loop provides for the combination of velocity components, one due to the motor and the other due to the current in the river. Various combinations are shown. The student can measure the velocities and calculate the various combinations before checking his answer with the loop picture. This loop offers the advantage of showing the motion associated with the vectors that describe it.

Acceleration Due to Gravity: Method I. Filmloop. Ealing Corp. A heavy ball falls freely past a measured background. Two intervals are marked and students time the fall during slow motion photography. The rate of fall is measured over the intervals. Using the given slow motion factor, the student computes the acceleration due to gravity.

Acceleration Due to Gravity: Method 2. Filmloop. Ealing Corp. A ball falls freely during slow motion photography through four 20 cm intervals. If the student uses the average speeds at each interval as approximations to instantaneous velocities, he can compute the acceleration of the ball.

Galilean Relativity: Part 2—Object Dropped from Aircraft. Filmloop. Ealing Corp. Side and head-on views of a flare dropped from a moving airplane in slow motion and freeze frame. The student can time the motion and compute the displacement, velocity, and acceleration of the flare for the horizontal and vertical viewpoints.

The Velocity Vector. Filmloop. Ealing Corp. A spot moves on the oscilloscope screen of a computer. The computer measures the speed and direction of the spot and displays this information on the screen in the form of an arrow—the velocity vector of the spot.

The Acceleration Vector. Filmloop. Ealing Corp. Starts out the same way as the previous filmloop; then the change in the velocity (the acceleration vector) is displayed.

Velocity and Acceleration in Free Fall. Filmloop. Ealing Corp. A dot on a cathode ray tube moves representing an object thrown upwards. Vector arrows showing the magnitudes and directions of the velocity and acceleration during the flight are displayed.

Analysis of a Hurdle Race—I. Filmloop. Ealing Corp. Slow motion in this filmloop allows the measurement of average speeds during successive one—meter intervals. Data of speed versus displacement may be graphed. The racer's acceleration may also be calculated.

Analysis of a Hurdle Race—II. Filmloop. Ealing Corp. A continuation of the previous loop. This loop shows two more scenes of the hurdle race photographed at a slow motion factor of 80. Again, data taken from the projection allow graphing of the motion.

Distance, Time, and Speed. Filmloop. Ealing Corp. The purpose of this loop is to provide a set of seven different problems dealing with relationships among distance, time, and speed. Solving the problems will give added facility in dealing with situations where one or another of these parameters is unknown. One advantage of this approach is that students see the motion related to the problem they are to solve.

Print

"The Role of Music in Galileo's Experiments" by S. Drake. *Scientific American* (June 1975). Describes how Galileo handled the problem of time measurement without having a reliable clock.

P.S.S.C. Physics by Haber-Schaim, et al. D. C. Heath, 1976. Chapter 9, "Motion Along a Straight-Line Path," has some good presentations on graphic representation and analysis of motion.

The Birth of a New Physics by I. B. Cohen. Doubleday Anchor, 1960. Aristotelean concepts of motion are contrasted with the inertial and accelerated motions of modern physics in Chapters 2 and 5.

Biography of Physics by G. Gamow. Harper and Row, 1961. The last part of Chapter 2 presents some of Galileo's experiments and quotes from the *Dialogues*. Gamow tries to chart a midway course between the man and the basic laws of mechanics which he discovered.

Great Experiments in Physics by M. H. Shamos, editor. Holt, Rinehart, and Winston, 1959. Chapter 2 presents a portion of a translation of Galileo's works with notes accompanying the translation. The notes relate what Galileo said to more conventional expressions.

The Science of Movement by L. Basford. Sampson Low, Marston and Co., 1966. This book tackles the job of making physical laws exciting and understandable through the use of ingenious illustrations. Pages 36–40 would be good reading for a student having difficulty with equations.

Physics Demonstration Experiments by H. F. Meiners. Ronald Press, 1970. Chapter 7, "Kinematics," presents numerous demonstrations appropriate

for this unit. Although several require specially made devices and a corresponding large amount of time to reproduce, others might be very useful for your course. This is a teacher reference.

Physics and Man by Tor Ragnar Gerholm. Bedminster Press, 1967. Chapter 19, "From Galileo's Inclined Plane to Einstein's Red Shift," sets the stage for an introduction to relativity.

Understanding Physics: Motion, Sound and Heat by I. Asimov. New American Library, 1966. Chapter 2 on Falling Bodies. This work is a good supplement to the student's formal textbook. Galileo's inclined planes and timing problems, acceleration, and free fall are discussed.

Source Book in Physics by W. F. Magie. Harvard University Press, 1969. Chapter 1 gives a brief biography of Galileo and then continues with translations of some of his work. Good teacher background but most students would not profit from this material.

"The Measurement of g in an Elevator" by H. Kruglak. *The Physics Teacher* (November 1972). Describes an experimental approach to obtain a value for g from data used for an average velocity-time graph from elevator motions.

"The Physics of Sport Activities" by W. C. Connolly. *The Physics Teacher* (September 1978). This article describes strobe photographic analysis techniques for various sporting activities. High interest is generated among students when they study their own motion.

"Measuring g with a Phonographic Turntable" by T. A. Scott. *The Physics Teacher* (December 1978). An elaboration of one of the experimental techniques listed in this chapter.

"Graphic Solutions for Velocity and Acceleration Problems" by L. Wilhite. *The Physics Teacher* (March 1979). Presents a novel approach to the analysis of motion problems which are moderately complicated through the use of graphs.

"An Accurate Direct Reading Accelerometer" by P. W. Hewson et al. *The Physics Teacher* (January 1979). Provides details on the construction of an accelerometer to measure accelerations directly rather than through distance-time relationships.

"Do the Leaning Tower Experiment with One Hand" by P. Latimer. *The Physics Teacher* (May 1979). Describes a technique for simultaneous release of two objects for free fall.

"Air Track to Demonstrate Sailing into the Wind" by R. E. Benenson, et al. *The Physics Teacher*

(October 1978). This short article is useful in showing vector components and how they apply to a sailboat.

"An Aid for Kinematics" by D. V. Sathe. *The Physics Teacher* (November 1979). Suggests a technique to show that the area under a velocity-time graph represents the distance traveled.

"Physics of Basketball" by Peter Brancazio. *American Journal of Physics* (April 1981). This article can provide the teacher with interesting material for analysis of motion studies. Some students might read the comparison of theory and practice.

4

Dynamics

INTRODUCTION

The preceding chapters acquainted students with the ways that physicists describe motion and forces. This chapter puts both concepts together. Dynamics deals with the relationships between forces and the motion they control. Sir Isaac Newton (1642-1727) investigated most of these relationships, which we now know as Newton's laws of motion. These laws, which have been tested for over two hundred years, make excellent examples of good physics: simple, concise, thoroughly reliable descriptions applicable to a wide variety of natural phenomena.

One measure of the degree of civilization attained by any society is its ability to control the environment. Through our knowledge of dynamics we have reached a relatively advanced position in this area. Think of all the things that represent our degree of civilization and ask how many of them are the result of our knowing how to control motion by bringing appropriate forces into play. Because our students have grown up in this highly developed society they already "know" a great deal about dynamics—they just don't know it as "physics." Your job is to systematize this experience and to show its relevance in areas that are not yet a part of the student's background.

CONTENT OVERVIEW

Newton's first law, a description of the property of inertia, describes motion when a resultant force of zero acts on any object. When a net force other than zero acts, acceleration results, and Newton described this phenomenon in his second law. (Acceleration in a circle is also considered here.) Most students know the third law of motion as "action and reaction." What they do not know is that Newton was describing *forces* in this law. Here you will have to explain how acceleration can occur if all forces come in equal but oppositely directed pairs, a seeming paradox.

The concept of linear momentum is a logical combination of the idea of inertia, the

51

tendency of all masses to maintain constant motion, and the idea of velocity, the quantity of motion that the object has. Linear momentum can be thought of as the "quality" of motion. Keeping the dynamics theme, you can relate impulse to momentum by using Newton's second law and a little elementary algebra, as indicated in Reproduction Page 26.

Finally, conservation concepts can be introduced and stressed, first as a relationship in dynamics and then as a major tool used by physicists in more recent research. Much of our knowledge about atomic and subatomic particles relies on our understanding of conservation, as we shall see again in subsequent chapters.

Concepts in dynamics are basic to all student texts in physics and should be considered core material. After completing the core material, more advanced students could consider interactions among several masses in more than one dimension, or angular momentum and frames of reference linked to Newtonian relativity.

If the following presentations and activities produce their intended results, students will have enriched perceptions of the world they live in. They will have observed that this abstract "stuff" called physics is really quite simple; it is also apparent in common daily life activities. Specifically, this study will provide insights into forces and the motions they control.

Students may understand, possibly for the first time, the basis for using seat belts as life saving devices. The physics behind driving at a reduced speed can help students understand how energy is saved. Perhaps, this knowledge will encourage their participation in energy conservation as it pertains to driving.

OBJECTIVES

As a result of the learning experiences in this chapter, students should be able to:

1. Use the word "inertia" with scientific precision.

2. Give practical examples of Newton's first law.

3. Identify phenomena involving inertial behavior.

4. Describe the forces involved in constant motion.

5. Use Newton's second law to predict quantitative and qualitative results in linear and circular motion.

6. Cite examples of Newton's third law of motion, describing forces in the pair and their effects.

7. Use the words impulse and momentum in a scientifically correct manner.

8. Identify various moving bodies according to the amount of momentum they possess.

9. Describe situations where an object undergoes a change in momentum in terms of $\bar{F}\Delta t = \Delta m\bar{v}$.

10. Solve problems where a change in momentum is equated to impulse.

11. Cite examples showing conservation of momentum.

12. Solve problems for both elastic and inelastic collisions in one dimension by using conservation of momentum principles.

LEARNING EXPERIENCES

Topic I: Newton's First Law: Inertia

1. *Teacher Presentation.* Review the ideas studied in the chapters on forces and motion. Explain that the class is now beginning the study of dynamics, which relates forces to the motion they control. Explain also that Sir Isaac Newton first investigated this area. He summarized his findings in what are now known as Newton's laws of motion. Ask the class if anyone remembers Newton's first law, or anything about inertia. (Usually several students will recapitulate ideas they learned in previous science courses. If they don't, you will have to get the ball rolling.) As the discussion progresses, itemize correct statements on the board or overhead. After some discussion, the list, roughly shaped, might look like this:

    Newton's First Law: Inertia

    - an object at rest will stay at rest
    - an object in motion tends to stay in motion
    - at the same speed in the same straight line
    - a shorter way to say it: all objects tend to maintain constant motion . . . if no unbalanced force acts
    - a property of matter

    Ask the class to consider some examples of objects at rest in the room. (Jokingly watch one for a minute to "be sure it *does* stay at rest.") Ask for a description of the forces acting on the object. A couple of repeats of this will convince the class that, in such cases, the resultant force must be zero.

    Now ask for examples of objects moving with almost constant velocity. Draw some diagrams representing the forces acting on them. It should become clear after several examples (and non-examples) that objects maintain constant velocity only if there is a zero resultant force acting upon them.

2. *Activity.* Divide the class into small working groups. Have each group develop several additional examples of objects that describe constant velocity. Show that the resultant force is zero in each case. Have each group select one of their examples to share with the entire class.

3. *Activity.* Ask the class why a reduction of speed limits to 55 m.p.h. results in a saving of gasoline. Ask them to relate their discussion to Newton's first law. Raising the appropriate questions, focus the discussion on the forces acting on an automobile moving at constant velocity on a flat road. Reproduction Page 27 will facilitate the discussion.

    It may be necessary, at this point, to talk about the increase of the air frictional force proportional to the speed of the car. Most students have felt this force. Ask what air frictional force they would feel if they stuck their hand out the window while sitting in a car that was not moving. They would feel none, of course. If the car was moving, they would feel the retarding force—a very great force if they stuck out their arm at a very high speed. In short, air friction increases with speed. The driving force, produced by burning gasoline in the engine, balances the retarding frictional forces. All four forces must be balanced if the car has constant velocity. It can be deduced that driving one mile at higher speeds will require more driving force (and gasoline) than driving that same distance at 55 m.p.h.

4. *Activity.* Some of your more artistic students may want to produce a display of the preceding activity for your bulletin board or school display case. This could be coordinated with driver education or consumer education class work.

Topic II: Newton's Second Law

1. *Teacher Presentation.* If objects are to describe constant velocity, the resultant force on them must be zero. What happens if it is not zero? Give several quick examples: drop an object; have a cart accelerate, using a pulley attached to a falling weight; mention accelerating a car. Ask what factors affect the amount of acceleration an object experiences. The class should discern that the acceleration depends directly on the magnitude of the resultant force and inversely on the mass of the object. Ask for examples to support these relationships. From the mathematical expression $\bar{a} = \dfrac{\bar{F}}{m}$, we can solve for $\bar{F}$, getting $\bar{F} = m\bar{a}$, a common mathematical form of Newton's second law. You should discuss units at this point, since the unit of force, "the newton," can be defined as the amount of force required to produce an acceleration of $1\,\frac{m}{s^2}$ on a 1 kg mass. Mathematically: $1\,N = (1\,kg)\left(1\,\frac{m}{s^2}\right)$, or a newton $= kg\,\frac{m}{s^2}$.

2. *Activity.* Using a small cart and a hanging weight to accelerate the cart via a system of pulleys, proceed to demonstrate, qualitatively, that the cart's acceleration depends directly on the magnitude of the unbalanced force and inversely on the mass of the cart. Set the cart on the floor or on a long demonstration table. In order to produce acceleration over a sufficiently long time interval, fix the pulley at cart level and run the string to another pulley fixed at the ceiling. Let the weight fall from ceiling height. If additional time is desired, a combination of pulleys from the ceiling can be used. Show the effects of varying forces and then those of varying masses loaded on the cart. Have the class predict the comparative acceleration. Be prepared to discuss the question of whether or not the entire weight acts on the cart while it is accelerating.

3. *Activity.* Students have already observed that, when air friction is not a large factor, all falling objects accelerate at $9.8\,\frac{m}{s^2}$ near the earth's surface. Lead a class discussion describing this phenomenon in terms of Newton's second law. You may want to weigh several measured masses to show that the weight to mass ratio is always $9.8\,\frac{m}{s^2}$. The discussion should be generalized to show a special case of the second law in which $\bar{F} = m\bar{a}$ is expressed as $\bar{wt.} = m\bar{g}$, where $\bar{g} = 9.8\,\frac{m}{s^2}$.

4. *Activity.* Many of the examples set forth in texts to illustrate inertia are more appropriately applied as examples of both inertia and acceleration. An unbalanced

force acts on a portion of a body and the portion accelerates (2nd law). Another part of that same body experiences very little unbalanced force and describes constant motion (1st law). Examples are given in Reproduction Page 28.

Ask your students to redescribe the examples in terms of Newton's laws. They should be able to describe what produces the accelerating unbalanced force; also to explain why, in terms of zero resultant force, the constant motion continues. Diagrams would be helpful. You might want to assign examples to individuals or small groups and have them demonstrate and explain them to the rest of the class. The teacher should do at least one as a model of how the assignment is to be done.

5. *Activity.* Have the students generate their own list, one similar to Reproduction Page 28.

6. *Activity.* Discuss the function of automotive seat belts and/or air bags in terms of Newton's laws. The discussion should include the following ideas:
a. A driver moves at the same speed as his car.
b. His body has inertia and will continue to move at this speed until decelerated by an unbalanced force.
c. If no significant force acts on his body, it will continue moving even though his car stops as a result of a collision.
d. If his body is to be decelerated quickly, large forces are required.
e. What can exert these forces and what are their effects on a human body?
Students should be able to cite examples during the discussion. Some activities to indicate the magnitude of the forces involved or calculations of these forces might be included. Selected students may work up a bulletin board presentation or do a project on this topic.

7. *Activity.* Tie a string to a rubber stopper and swing the stopper in a horizontal circle at a steady speed. Ask the class why this is an example of accelerated motion. Students should perceive that an unbalanced force is required to maintain the motion, and that, even though the speed is constant, the velocity is always changing because the *direction* of the velocity differs at different times. Then ask the class to predict what would happen if the string broke at various points in the circle. Show them that the stopper would move in a straight line tangent to the circle by releasing the string at those various points.

8. *Activity.* Explain that the inward force in Activity 7 is called the centripetal force, and that it accelerates the mass out of a straight line into the circular path. Ask the class what variables in the motion relate to the amount of centripetal force required to keep the object moving in a circle. Usually the class will deduce that the mass of the object and its speed will produce direct effects. These effects can be made visible by running the end of the string through a piece of fire polished glass tubing and allowing various hanging weights to provide a variety of centripetal forces corresponding to different speeds and masses in circular orbit.

9. *Activity.* The effects of the radius of the circle on the required centripetal force are not as obvious as the mass and speed variables. The following exercise draws upon student experience to determine the effects of the radius.

Draw a large arc on the board to represent a curve in a road. Ask the class to imagine driving a car on this road at some fairly high speed. Now draw a smaller arc—a second, sharper turn. Ask the class which turn would be easier to negotiate in the same car at the same speed. Relate "easier" to the amount of force required on the car to make the turns. When it is agreed that the smaller one would require the larger force, complete each arc, making two circles, and point out the inverse effect of the radius of each on the required centripetal force.

10. *Teacher Presentation.* Put the equation for Newton's second law ($F = ma$) on the board. Below this general expression, put the equation for centripetal force $\left(F_c = \dfrac{mv^2}{r}\right)$. (The effect of the squaring of the speed variable should be shown experimentally at some point.)

$$F = ma$$

$$F_c = \frac{mv^2}{r}$$

Upon inspection, students will observe that a in the second law corresponds to the $\dfrac{v^2}{r}$ term in the centripetal force expression. We call this term the centripetal acceleration: $a_c = \dfrac{v^2}{r}$.

11. *Activity.* Have students use Reproduction Page 29 and relate variables in $F_c = \dfrac{mv^2}{r}$ to the examples described.

Topic III: Newton's Third Law

1. *Teacher Presentation.* Have your students strike their desk tops with one hand. Ask what forces acted, the direction of the forces, and what each acted on. Explain that in his third law, "action and reaction," Newton stated that forces always come in pairs, equal in magnitude but opposite in direction. Now instruct the students to hit their desks again, but very hard this time. What indications are there that the forces are equal? The apparent possibility of a zero resultant force should be dispelled at this time by remarking that the two forces acted on *different* objects, one downward on the desk, and the other upward on the hand. Each produced its respective effect. Be sure that your students are able to identify what exerts each force in the pair, what each force acts on, the respective effects of each force, the difference in direction, and the equality of the magnitudes.

2. *Activity.* Using a fan cart or a similar device, discuss the application of the third law to the device. Show that the blades push the air backward. Some smoke mixed with the air will make this visible. The reaction force will drive the cart in the opposite direction. If you wish to challenge your students, you can complicate the demonstration by attaching a piece of cardboard to the cart directly behind the propeller. The cart will not move now, even though the blades turn. This can be explained by a multiple application of the third law. Finally, ask if the cart would operate in a vacuum.

3. *Activity.* Discuss tables and benches—things that support objects—in a third-law context. Students are very sure that an object placed on a table top pushes down on

the table, and that the table must push back up on the object in order to support it, but they wonder how the table "knows" how much upward force is required.

Using an elevated meterstick supported at both ends, demonstrate that a weight placed in the middle distorts the stick, and that the stick's tendency to resume its original shape produces the upward force. The more weight used, the more distortion and the greater the upward force. Explain that more substantial surfaces do the same thing, but the distortion is not obvious to the naked eye. Ask how this relates to a trampoline.

4. *Activity.* Get a basketball and throw it to a student. Ask someone to describe this action according to Newton's third law. Point out that the effect of the reaction force on the thrower is not obvious. Then stand on a platform mounted on small ball bearing wheels and throw the ball again. You will move backward slightly. If you can borrow a large number of basketballs from the athletic department, you can propel yourself across the room on the platform by throwing basketballs handed to you by a student.

5. *Activity.* Some students may wish to investigate jet and rocket engines.

6. *Activity.* Building and demonstrating a rocket-propelled device makes an interesting project, at least for some students. Several variations are possible, including mounted CO_2 capsules, model rocket and jet engines, and a wagon with a CO_2 fire extinguisher mounted on the rear. Balloon driven model cars might also be included.

7. *Activity.* Have your students analyze each example in Reproduction Page 30 with Newton's third law in mind. Their analyses should state clearly what exerts each force, what each force acts on, the direction of the forces, and the effects of each force in the pair.

Topic IV: Momentum, Impulse, and Conservation

1. *Teacher Presentation.* One way of describing the property of inertia is to say that an object tends to maintain the state of motion it is in. The more mass the object has, the more inertia it shows. (Relate several examples to support this.) The concept of inertia would provide a more complete description if it included the amount of mass and the motion of the object. Momentum, the product of an object's mass and velocity, does just this. It is usually represented by the symbol p, and it's mathematical relationship is $\bar{p} = m\bar{v}$. Notice that momentum is a vector quantity due to its relationship to velocity. Objects may have relatively large amounts of momentum by having a large mass, such as an ocean liner; or by having high velocities, such as a rifle bullet; or by having medium amounts of both mass and velocity, such as a person on a motorcycle. In each case, the momentum is calculated by taking the product of the mass times the velocity.

2. *Activity.* Ask a student to catch a mass of one or two kilograms with his hand when you drop it from a height of about one-half meter. Have him catch it once again. Now ask the student to catch it again, but not to move his hand downward as he catches it. And, in order to be sure he doesn't, tell the student he must put the back of his catching hand against a table top. Get set as if you are about to repeat the drop, but *do not actually drop the mass*! Your student and most of his

classmates will immediately articulate the potential consequences—broken fingers, bruised knuckles, etc.—had you dropped the mass. Thank your volunteer and re-mark that they must already know about this aspect of physics. Discuss why the force would be greater in this case, even though the change in the momentum of the mass would be the same. The time factor for the momentum change should be discussed as having an effect on the required force. Reproduction Page 26 can now be used to formalize notions of impulse and change in momentum.

3. *Activity.* Tell about the following event, which actually occurred on the New Jersey Turnpike.

A gentleman was having trouble starting his car and needed to get it moving at 30 m.p.h. before the engine would turn over. Since there was no hill around, he asked a fellow motorist for a push. The motorist gently eased his car up behind our stalled friend's vehicle, accelerated gradually and attained the desired speed. The gentleman's car started and he took off under his own power. Some time later he stalled again and this time explained his problem—the need to move at 30 m.p.h. —to another motorist, who agreed to help. Unfortunately for our friend, this motorist hadn't taken physics. The motorist backed up some yards, floored it, and was going about 30 m.p.h. when he crashed into the back of our friend's car. The car started, of course—but damages were estimated at $3,000.

Discuss this event in terms of impulse and change in momentum.

4. *Activity.* Prepare students to discuss the phenomena on Reproduction Page 31 in terms of impulse and change in momentum variables.

5. *Teacher Presentation.* To introduce the concept of conservation of momentum, suspend a flask with a small amount of water in it from the ceiling. Use long strings attached to a wire cage designed to hold the flask in a horizontal orientation. Gently insert a moistened rubber stopper into the mouth of the flask. Explain that this is an "isolated" system, meaning that there are no net external forces acting on it. Point out that the momentum of the stopper is zero, the momentum of the flask is zero, and the momentum of the entire system, therefore, is zero. Explain that conservation of momentum means that this system will always have the same amount of momentum (zero in this case), although the states of motion may change. Indicate that conservation concepts are a physicist's major tool. They are readily demonstrable in many instances, but not in all. Yet we believe in them, and apply them in uncertain areas to obtain new knowledge, as in atomic physics.

Ask the class to predict what will happen if the flask is heated. (They should be able to see that the stopper will pop out in one direction and the flask recoil in the opposite direction.) Ask how momentum can be conserved when it seems to have changed—originally it was zero and now two parts of our system are moving. It should be recalled that momentum is a vector quantity and that the net momen-tum could be zero if the momentum of the stopper in one direction is cancelled by the momentum of the flask in the opposite direction. This would require the small massed stopper to move with a relatively high velocity compared to the larger massed flask.

Now to verify the prediction, heat the flask and water with a burner. Special cautions must be taken: paths along which the stopper and flask (and some hot water) will travel must be cleared; initially, the flask must be slowly and evenly heated; the water must be brought to a boil by placing the burner on a support below the flask; the teacher as well as students must stand a good distance away from the system; everyone should wear safety glasses in case the flask breaks due to a flaw or uneven heating. Although less spectacular than the flask system, a suspended platform with a cocked sling-shot device to propel a ball may be substituted.

6. *Teacher Presentation.* Repeat Activity 5 but produce higher velocities by inserting the stopper more firmly into the mouth of the flask. Note that even though the velocities are different, the conservation of momentum concepts still hold true.

7. *Activity.* Show that momentum is conserved in situations where the initial condition is not zero. Use two platforms, large enough to stand on, and *mounted* on small ball bearing wheels. With a little practice, you should be able to get a running start, jump upon a platform with both feet, and coast across the room. Now you can set up some collisions. (You may want to precede this activity by discussing elastic and inelastic collisions, so that students can recognize both.) Of necessity, measurements of mass and velocity will be rough at this time. Use notions such as twice the mass, half the velocity, and the like.

    Elastic collision: Choose a volunteer who has about the same mass as you. Have him stand on a motionless cart in the center of the room. Explain that you will collide with him—that you will come together and simultaneously push away from each other, using your hands as bumpers. Discuss the momentum of the system before the collision and the conservation of that amount, and ask for a prediction of what will happen after the collision. Produce the collision and analyze it from a conservation of momentum aspect.

8. *Activity.* Repeat the previous two activities in a variety of ways:
    a. Elastic collision with both riders approaching each other at about the same speed.
    b. Both riders initially at rest pushing off from each other.
    c. Elastic collision with a stationary cart having twice as much mass as you do (two student riders).
    d. Inelastic collision with two stationary riders.

    After trying as many variations as the class wishes, you might complete this activity with an inelastic collision between two riders of equal mass approaching each other at equal speeds. The zero momentum after the collision (both parties standing still) greatly impresses students.

9. *Activity.* More precise measurements using a variety of masses and velocities should generalize the concept of conservation of momentum. Strobe photography or electronic timing of a variety of collisions of dynamics carts, gliders on air tracks, frictionless pucks, etc., would be appropriate here. If you do not have such equipment, or the facilities in which to use it, several audio visual substitutes may be used. These are listed in the references.

10. *Activity.* Animated cartoons often consist of exaggerations, delays, or omissions of dynamics notions which produce their humorous effects. Picking out these effects and analyzing them makes an excellent review or evaluation technique and is fun for the class. Several options are possible. Obtain several films for class view-

ing and analyze them as a group; have individual students view some at home on T.V. or at a movie and report their observations to the rest of the class; ask others to relate dynamics to cartoon art.

EVALUATION PROCEDURES

Short quizzes based on activities in this chapter should be given at appropriate points in the instructional sequence. Items in Reproduction Pages 28–31 also may be used. Reproduction Page 32 is a unit test on dynamics. It can be given at the end of this chapter or broken up according to the numbered topics and subsections in this unit.

Resources for Teaching Dynamics

Below is a list of resources useful in teaching topics in dynamics. It is divided into audio-visual materials and printed material. If a particular source is especially appropriate for students or teachers, this is noted in the reference. Addresses of publishers appear alphabetically at the end of the book.

Audio-Visual Materials

Force and Motion. Film. Coronet. Investigation of force, mass, acceleration, and their relationships. Inertia, momentum, and reaction are introduced.

The A.B.C. of Jet Propulsion. Film. General Motors Corporation. Explains basic principles of jet propulsion. Newton's third law is discussed in cartoon form.

Inertia. Film. P.S.S.C. Demonstrates inertia using low friction dry ice pucks and flash photography. Shows acceleration is proportional to force when mass is constant.

Inertial Mass. Film. P.S.S.C. Develops the relationship that acceleration is inversely proportional to mass, with constant force. Compares inertial and gravitational masses.

A Million and One. Film. P.S.S.C. A short, unusual film of a flea pulling a massive dry ice puck showing that even very small forces, if unbalanced, produce acceleration.

Frames of Reference. Film. Encyclopedia Britannica. Shows effects of moving frames of reference in producing fictional forces in them.

Elastic Collisions and Stored Energy. Film. Ealing Corp. Demonstrates various collisions between dry ice pucks. Points out that energy is conserved in an elastic collision.

A Matter of Relative Motion. Filmloop. Ealing Corp. Collisions of two carts are viewed from several different frames of reference.

One-Dimensional Collisions I. Filmloop. Ealing Corp. Slow-motion photography of elastic one-dimensional collisions. Measurements are possible by group or individual student. Student questions included.

One-Dimensional Collisions II. Filmloop. Ealing Corp. A continuation of the preceding filmloop.

Inelastic One-Dimensional Collisions. Filmloop. Ealing Corp. Measurements are possible individually or as a group. Student questions included.

Two-Dimensional Collisions I. Filmloop. Ealing Corp. Slow-motion photography of elastic collisions in which components of momentum along each axis can be measured.

Two-Dimensional Collisions II. Filmloop. Ealing Corp. A continuation of the preceding loop.

Inelastic Two-Dimensional Collisions. Filmloop. Ealing Corp. Measurements are possible; student questions included.

Scattering of a Cluster of Objects. Filmloop. Ealing Corp. Shows conservation of momentum when a moving ball collides with six stationary balls in slow motion. Individual or class measurements are possible. Student questions included.

Recoil. Filmloop. Ealing Corp. A bullet is fired from a model gun. The sequence is filmed in slow motion. Conservation of momentum is demonstrated by taking measurements of the gun and bullet velocities. Questions included.

Colliding Freight Cars. Filmloop. Ealing Corp. Railroad cars collide. Slow-motion photography allows measurements which show conservation of momentum. Questions included.

Dynamics of a Billiard Ball. Filmloop. Ealing Corp. Slow motion-photography of a moving billiard ball striking a stationary one. Measurements are possible to show conservation of both linear and angular momentum.

Explosion of a Cluster of Objects. Filmloop. Ealing Corp. A powder charge is exploded at the center of a cluster of balls of various masses. One ball is temporarily hidden. The position and velocity can be predicted using conservation of momentum.

Print

Physics as a Liberal Art by J. Trefil. Pergamon, 1978. Chapter 7, "The Newtonian World," provides some insights not available in most student texts.

Of a Fire on the Moon by N. Mailer. Signet, 1971. The second portion of this book (describing the Apollo moon landing) contains a good discussion of Newton's laws.

A History of the Sciences by S. F. Mason. Collier Books, 1962. Includes a good history of Newton's period and a description of his role in founding the Royal Society.

Biography of Physics by G. Gamow. Harper and Row, 1961. Chapter 3 presents Newton's contributions, including his laws of motion.

Understanding Physics: Motion, Sound and Heat by I. Asimov. The New American Library, 1969. See Chapter 3, "The Laws of Motion," and Chapter 6, "Momentum."

"The Physics of Somersaulting and Twisting" by C. Frohlich. *Scientific American* (March 1980). An interesting application of Newtonian mechanics. Conservation of angular momentum is shown.

Physics and Automobile Safety Belts. U. S. Government Printing Office. Each section contains classroom demonstrations, examples and problems, lab work, and programmed instruction. Use as a supplement and source of test questions.

The Birth of a New Physics by I. Cohen. Doubleday Anchor, 1960. An excellent history of the development of the dynamics of motion.

A Source Book in Physics by W. F. Magie. Harvard University Press, 1935. See the section on Newton.

"What Is Centrifugal Force?" by R. P. Bauman. *The Physics Teacher* (October 1980). This article is good reading for the teacher. It discusses various definitions and applications of centrifugal forces.

"On the Derivation of the Centripetal Acceleration Formula" by E. Zebrowski, Jr. *The Physics Teacher* (December 1972). Presents a derivation of the centripetal acceleration formula which the author has found to be successful.

"Physics and the Bionic Man" by A. O. Stinner. *The Physics Teacher* (May 1980). Some T.V. feats are analyzed from a dynamics and conservation point of view.

Air Track Physics: A First Semester Laboratory Manual by Harold J. Metcalf. Kendall/Hunt, 1980. Provides several experiments on air tracks related to topics in dynamics.

"Explaining the 'At Rest' Condition of an Object" by J. Minstrell. *The Physics Teacher* (January 1982). This is a research summary of student concept development related to balanced forces. Worthwhile teacher reading prior to instruction on statics.

5

Energy

INTRODUCTION

This chapter introduces the concept of energy. The introduction is in the context of mechanics, but you should broaden the student's perspective with many references to the use of energy forms other than mechanical (for example, heat, electromagnetic, nuclear, chemical, and electrical).

The greatest idea underlying all sciences is the energy concept. If one was to choose a substitute word for physics, energy would be the logical choice. It is the most "powerful" concept in our study; that is, the single concept of energy has applications over an extremely wide range of physical phenomena, and far greater application than most other ideas encountered in the study of physics. This concept is also an excellent example of good science in that it is a relatively simple description of numerous physical behaviors.

Although energy is a very powerful concept, it also is very abstract when compared to other concepts such as matter, for example. We cannot identify energy per se with our senses as we can with mass. Energy is more intangible. It takes many forms, several of which are included in this study. If energy is so basic to our scientific organization, but at the same time so abstract, how can we study it? The answer is that we can observe the *effects of transfers* of energy and use the main concept in understanding the observed exchange. We can detect directly—with our senses—certain parameters that are related to energy: mass, temperature, velocity, shape, phase, position, chemical make-up, charge position, but none of these is energy. We determine energy by forming combinations of these parameters according to sets of algebraic expressions (formulas). Each formula, when applied to its appropriate system, leads to a value. This energy value will have the same dimensions as work—a concept *related to energy exchanges* but not synonymous with energy. Energy expressions, when coupled with the fact that energy is conserved (the total energy at the end of any process is the same as when the process started), form an extremely useful approach to many physical phenomena. Energy conservation is a natural law. Algebraic relationships describe the workings of that law.

Capitalize on the high interest in energy-related phenomena arising from our current "energy crisis." Point out that this crisis is not due to a shortage of energy but rather to problems associated with many of our conventional transfer mechanisms. The depletion of fossil fuels and the energy stored in them is at the heart of most of our current energy problems. This does not mean that we are running out of energy; it means that the solution will involve conservation, plus tapping some of the other sources available to us. Our problem is to find transfers other than the ones we have been using for some time. Understanding the transfer concept is imperative to understanding our problems and evaluating proposed solutions.

A second way to heighten student interest in this topic is to emphasize the reverse of the "energy crisis." We now have available the means to control large amounts of energy in the nuclear area. This control makes for a large range of possibilities. Nuclear energy may be a means to world destruction or the way to a peaceful, prosperous future. The science underlying atomic energy and its transfers is simply a good description of natural behavior. But the nature of the control—for prosperity or destruction—will be determined by our social and political behaviors.

Since energy is the prime mover, and people can decide on the direction of the motion, it is important that we understand more about energy and its transfer.

CONTENT OVERVIEW

Many textbooks define energy as the ability (or capacity) to do work. This definition is easy for students to memorize but it distorts the nature of the concept. Several other texts refrain from offering any definition at all. It seems that an accurate definition of energy is something that must develop—a concise, thorough statement eludes us. We will have to start at a familiar, concrete point and work toward understanding the greater abstraction. View this chapter as a formal *beginning* to energy. The rest of your course should expand the concept far beyond the initial experiences provided here.

Approach the study of energy through a more concrete idea, work. This uses notions of force and distance already familiar to your students. Numerous mechanical energy ideas will evolve through the mechanism of work.

A related concept, power, is a useful descriptor of the dynamic aspect of transfers of energy. Some special care is required to differentiate power (the rate of energy transfer) from the energy itself since students have probably used the two terms synonymously in previous experiences. A number of activities and questions in this chapter will help to make the distinction.

Use the broad categorizations of kinetic and potential energy for analysis of several mechanical energy transfers; also as a way to study and then implement the law of energy conservation. This relationship demonstrates the simplifying effect of the energy concept. Point this out by referring back to some of the problems studied through dynamics and kinematics constructs but contrast the complexity of earlier solutions with a conservation of energy approach to the same problem. Falling objects and inclined plane problems provide good examples.

This study of mechanical energy is a starting point for the study of other forms and transfers. This intangible "stuff" (energy) can manifest itself in motion or position. Additional studies of electricity, heat, light and other radiations, chemical energy at the atomic and molecular level, and nuclear energy will expand the energy concept. These various forms, and the scientific and social questions related to them, will make this study extremely important and exceptionally timely for you and your students.

OBJECTIVES

If all the topics in this chapter are chosen by the teacher, the student should be able to:

1. Define work and compute work done using $W = \bar{F} \cdot \bar{s}$.

2. Determine the work done from a force versus displacement graph.

3. Define and compute power through $P = \dfrac{W \text{ or } E}{t}$

4. Classify forms of energy into two groups: potential and kinetic.

5. Solve problems involving the calculation of gravitational potential energy and kinetic energy.

6. Use energy relationships and conservation of energy in the analysis and solution of problems.

LEARNING EXPERIENCES

Topic I: Work

1. *Teacher Presentation.* Define work as the product of a force times the distance that force moves something, $W = \bar{F} \cdot \bar{s}$. Note that work is a scalar quantity even though it is the product of two vectors, force and displacement. From this equation, you should also show that the units for work are N • m. This combination of units is the joule, a unit for work. One joule of work is done when a force of one newton moves something through a displacement of one meter. Demonstrate this by pulling a block or similar object across a table with a spring scale through a measured one meter interval. Choose the object so that the initial value of the force is about one newton. Vary this approach using different objects and forces and different distances. Ask the class to calculate the work in each case from the scale reading and measured displacement. Additional variations are possible by lifting objects with the scale and pulling them up inclined planes. Ask your class to describe the effects of doing the work in several cases (the lifted objects are up higher; so is the object on the incline; objects dragged over a horizontal surface will be slightly warmer due to friction).

2. *Teacher Presentation.* Relate the following story to your class: Suppose a person got a job that was to pay $50/hr. The job was to hold a heavy object weighing 75 lbs. in his arms for a long time. (You might demonstrate this for a short time.

Exaggerate the effort required to support such an object.) At the end of the first day, the worker was very tired and his muscles were quite sore, but he had held the object for six hours. When he went to collect his pay, the boss, who was a physicist, informed the fatigued worker that his earnings for the day were zero since he had not done any work! Ask for an explanation of this travesty from the class. (No work, in the physical sense, was accomplished since the force exerted did not move the object through a displacement.) If the same boss advertised another job—pushing as hard as you can against a wall all day for $100/hr.—would you take it?

3. *Demonstration.* Formal study of simple machines used to be included in most physics courses. Devices such as a pulley system, levers, and inclined planes make good instructional tools when teaching about work and relating that concept to the daily experiences of students.

   Arrange three such devices to show that a small force, $F_{(E)}$, can lift a larger force, $F_{(R)}$.

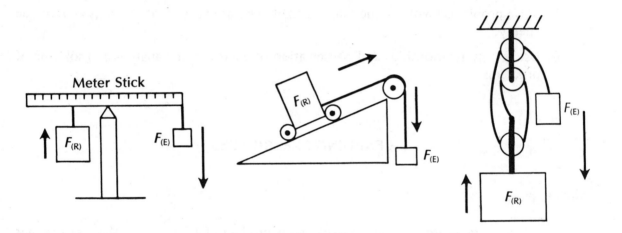

Ask "How can this be?" Students will very quickly ascertain that although a smaller force does lift a larger weight in each case, the smaller force must act through a much greater distance. Most pupils will intuitively guess that the work done is just about the same for the $F_{(E)}$ and $F_{(R)}$. If not, verify this approximation by taking measurements of each weight and the corresponding distances moved, and then calculate the work comparison. Summarize by noting that machines such as these often "make work easier"—not by reducing the *amount* of work needed but by changing the form. In physics, just as in many other endeavors, you don't get something for nothing. In these demonstrations the increased force out of the machine is "paid for" by greater distances required for $F_{(E)}$, although the work involved is just about the same. (This is a good way to lead into conservation of energy ideas to be presented later in this chapter.)

4. *Activity.* Use Reproduction Page 33 to further develop the work concept through simple machines. The points to emphasize are that these devices change the form of the work done but not the amount. In some cases larger forces are produced; in other cases, a smaller force but greater distance (and thus velocity) results.

Students must first recognize the machine involved and then analyze the work transformation which each uses. This may be done by individual pupils, small groups, or the entire class.

5. *Laboratory.* Students set up several simple machines (levers, inclined planes, and pulley systems) and take measurements to calculate the work input and work output. If you wish, students also can calculate the efficiency of each machine: the ratio of the work output to the input, usually expressed as a percent. (This calculation may lead to discussions of more complex machines and "wasted" work. Some insight into energy problems may result from knowing that many automobiles, for example, have efficiencies in the 20 percent range.)

Several variations in the construction of these devices will indicate the measurement techniques needed for forces. If the effort force is upward, spring scales are satisfactory. Downward forces are measured by hanging enough weights on the system *to just operate it.* Distance measurements should be as large as possible, and the distance the resistance moves should be used in conjunction with the corresponding distance through which the effort force moves. Reproduction Page 34 offers several alternate arrangement ideas for these devices.

Some notes about construction and measurement follow:

Lever. In order to avoid having the weight of the meterstick affect results, balance the stick on the pivot point before adding the weights; include the weight of the hangers with the respective force measurements.

Inclined Plane. The distance of $F_{(E)}$ is the length of the incline; the distance the $F_{(R)}$ moves is the height. If a board is used, be sure to consider its thickness in making these distance measurements.

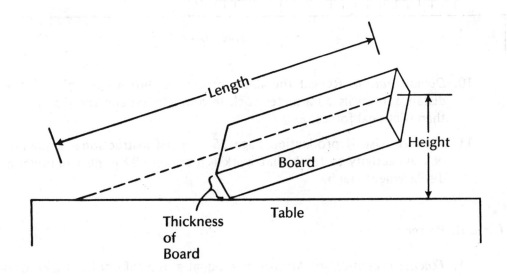

Pulley. The weight of the movable pulley(s) is not considered part of $F_{(R)}$.

6. *Activity.* Groups of students may enjoy designing, building, and measuring a "Rube Goldberg" device with simple machines. Essentially, this is a combination of several simple machines in which the $F_{(R)}$ of one is the $F_{(E)}$ for the next. In this measure-

ment, only the initial and final work is measured. Intermediate exchanges (not measured) will cause efficiencies to be much lower than the previous lab.

7. *Activity.* Groups of students can make models of various devices that use the work transformation principles of these machines. The model should show the practical device and relate its operation to the machine principle used. Diagrams and pictures are good for this relationship. The muscular-skeletal system of the human body is a high interest project of this type.

8. *Demonstration.* Slowly drag a wooden block across a lab table with a spring scale over a one meter course marked off in 10 cm intervals. As each interval is crossed, call out the scale reading (it should be constant). Have students record this displacement and force data and then graph $\overline{F}$ versus $\overline{s}$. An analysis of the resulting graph and a comparison of the calculated work with the area under the curve will show the correspondence between the two measures.

9. *Demonstration.* Arrange a series of different horizontal surface materials and inclined planes at several angles and repeat the previous activity. Again, have the class record displacement and force data for a graph and calculate the total work done by using the sum of the areas under the curve. Be sure the distance intervals are marked off along the inclines and not in a continuous horizontal line. It's a good idea to have intervals terminate at each boundary to simplify graphing.

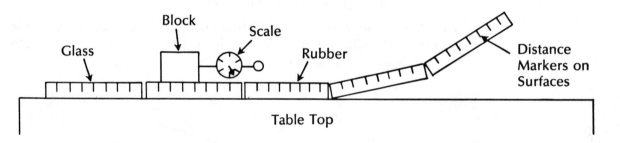

10. *Demonstration.* Repeat the above procedures but lift the block vertically against distance intervals on a meter stick in order to expand the graph concept to other than frictional forces.

11. *Activity.* Use Reproduction Page 35 as a self-instructional sequence, homework, or class activity to teach that work is represented by the area under a force versus displacement graph.

Topic II: Power

1. *Teacher Presentation.* Arrange two equal groups of books, bricks, or other objects on the floor next to a demonstration table. Slowly lift each of the objects in the first pile onto the table above. Ask how the total work might be calculated. Repeat this for the second group of objects but do the job much more rapidly. Ask for a way to measure the total work and a comparison with the work in the first case (the work in each case will be the same). Now ask for the obvious differences in

the two exercises. This will lead into the concept of power as the time rate of doing work. Formalize the results of the discussion and represent power through the equation, $P = \dfrac{W}{t}$. Note the units for power will be $\dfrac{J}{s}$. Introduce the watt as the equivalent power unit.

2. *Activity.* Have selected students do some research on "horsepower." Various pupils could look into such areas as the history of how the unit of power came into use, its relationship to ft · lbs/sec and watts. Investigate horsepower ratings of several common devices. Automobile engines are a good starting point.

3. *Laboratory.* People often compare their power outputs with animals. Alligator wrestling and novelty races that match a person against a horse are some examples that your students might be aware of. In this lab, each student will have the opportunity to measure his power output in doing an exercise. Comparison with a horse is via the horsepower concept. Have students discuss some of their findings from the previous activity as a lead-in to the lab. Note that in this case, forces are measured in pounds, distances in feet, and time is in seconds. Bring out the relationships equating 1 H.P. to 550 ft · lbs/sec and to 746 watts. The students will need this information to convert their measured power output into horsepower and watts. Here are some suggested activities for this laboratory. In each case work is calculated and combined with the time required for the power calculation:

- Climbing ropes in the gym. Distance is measured from hands when standing on the floor to highest point touched on the top of the rope.

- Running up a flight of stairs. You need stairs with a stairwell that enables measuring the vertical distance from bottom to top; or measure the vertical height of one stair and multiply by the total number.

- Lifting weights. Measure the distance covered in one lift and multiply this by the number of repetitions; only upward displacements are counted. Be sure to add the weight of the bar to the weights on it for the force calculation.

- Chin ups. Similar to lifting weights on the distance calculation.

- Push ups. To estimate the force, have the student do one very slowly with his hands on a bathroom scale. Put some books under the toes to the level of the scale. Use this scale reading for the force measure. Distances are measured from the floor to the chest for full arm extension. Total distance is the upward displacement times the number of push ups done in the measured time period.

Results of these measurements, when converted into horsepower, will usually be less than 1 H.P. Occasionally, a fairly good sized and speedy student will develop more than 1 H.P. when doing an activity using the large muscles of the legs.

Take advantage of competition, if it develops, by having pupils design their own experiment with analysis of the variables used to provide maximum power. Reproduction Page 36 is a general guide to this exercise. Use it as it is or modify it to fit your particular experimental theme.

Topic III: Potential Energy, Kinetic Energy, and Conservation

1. *Teacher Presentation.* Slowly raise a mass from the demonstration table to some height above the table. Ask what effect is produced by the work you have done. The mass is in a new position above the table. Doing more work raises the object even higher. As a consequence of being in this position, the *mass* can now do work. If released, the object falls and could crush some peanuts or turn a wheel or pound a nail, if appropriate connections are supplied. Explain that the mass has energy in this position, and that the amount of energy stored is equal to the work done to store it. Show this relationship by raising several different objects to various heights and then dropping them onto some clay or play dough. (The deformation of the clay or dough is used as a crude measure of the work done.)

   Work and energy, then, are related and work units are appropriate for expressing amounts of energy. Derive the formula for gravitational potential energy, $PE_g = mgh$, by converting the work to raise the object, $W = \bar{F} \cdot \bar{s}$, into the appropriate energy expression.

2. *Activity.* Ask the class for examples of other forms of potential energy besides gravitational. Focus the discussion on the position relationship to the energy. You may want to illustrate some of the examples by "launching" paper wads or some similar object with rubber bands, springs, bent meter sticks, and the like. In this discussion, mention chemical potential energy and relate it to electron positions.

3. *Activity.* It should be clear to students from earlier presentations that gravitational potential energy is not converted directly into work when the object falls. Rather, an intermediate step exists between the potential energy and the doing of the work. The potential energy is changed into energy of motion, kinetic energy, and this form eventually does the work. Use Reproduction Page 37 as an aid in arriving at an expression for kinetic energy. Note that it is not critical what form the potential energy takes initially; the changing of that energy into movement provides for the kinetic energy expression, $KE = \frac{1}{2} mv^2$. Be sure to emphasize the analysis of units to show that this energy expression works out to joules. The conservation of energy is implied in this approach, but additional activities will highlight this most basic relationship.

4. *Laboratory.* Gravitational potential energy. Use an arrangement as shown in the sketch below to show the relationships between gravitational potential energy, mass, and height. The potential energy is measured by how far a nail is driven into a piece of soft wood by various masses after falling from different heights. This is accomplished by starting the nail with a hammer and then directing various metal cylinders onto the nail head through the use of a large diameter cardboard tube such as a mailing tube. Varying the height of drop will produce data that shows that the potential energy (as measured by how far the nail is driven in when hit) is directly proportional to *h*. Data may be displayed on a graph. The use of various masses from a fixed height will show the dependence on *m*. Good results in this lab depend on the fit and centering of the mass, its even drop through the tube, friction, and uniformity of the soft wood. If some of these factors are problematic, you may choose to do this procedure as a qualitative investigation rather than the

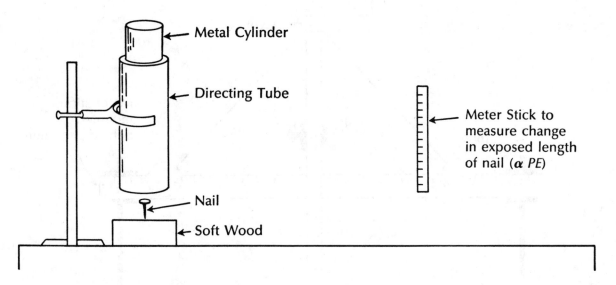

quantitative one suggested. If you do not want to duplicate this procedure in lab, several of the film loops listed in the references show a version of this approach which allows measurements of similar data.

5. *Activity*. Stand on a chair against a wall and extend a heavy pendulum bob so that it just touches your nose. Release the bob and let it swing out, then back to your nose. Comment on your confidence in physical laws, especially the law of conservation of energy. Point out that, in this pendulum, energy is continually converted from potential to kinetic and back during the swing. Ask why the bob would not come back and break your nose. Some students who are not yet convinced of energy conservation may want to try this activity. If so, be sure they don't flinch and that the bob is not inadvertently pushed during the release.

6. *Activity*. The previous activity is even more impressive when arranged in a room with very high ceilings such as a gym. Use a bowling ball in a mesh sack and wire for the pendulum string. The longer period of swing leaves more time for a student to think about conservation of energy while the bob swings back, especially if the student is the one standing with his back against the wall!

7. *Demonstration*. Do a more careful analysis of the pendulum with the apparatus shown below.

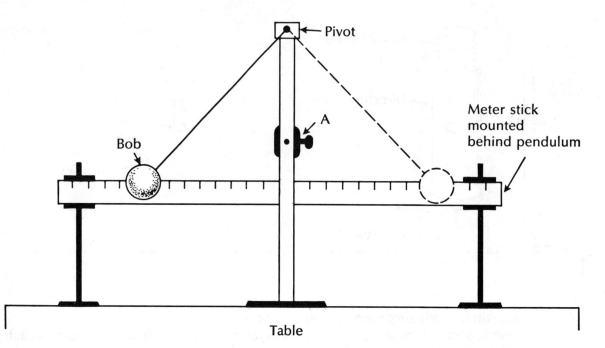

Table

Show that if the pendulum is started level with the meterstick at one side, it will swing as high on the other side (discounting frictional losses at the pivot point and to the air). Point out the near equivalence in the exchanges from potential to kinetic energy. Use this equivalence to calculate the velocity of the bob at its point of lowest swing.

   With the pendulum at equilibrium, show how the force necessary to pull it to the side is very small compared with pulling it straight up. Note that the product of the force and the distance—the work—is the same for equal elevations.

   Check to see if your class really grasps and can apply energy conservation with the following modification of the apparatus: Clamp a horizontal rod (A in the diagram) so that the string hits the rod as it swings past and thus goes in a smaller radius arc. Ask if it will still come back to the same position and why. Next ask your pupils to predict the location of the horizontal rod that will just cause the pendulum to loop around. Demonstrate the prediction(s) and request the rationale used to make the prediction.

8. *Activity.* Divide the class into small groups. Each group is to investigate one (or all) of the following phenomena and prepare an analysis in terms of energy transfers and conservation:

   a. A version of a child's toy consisting of a large diameter cardboard cylinder is produced by stretching a rubber band between its ends and along a central axis. A weight is attached from the center of the rubber band. When this system is rolled, the weight winds up the rubber band until the kinetic energy is converted to potential in the form of the wound rubber band; then the band unwinds making the cylinder roll back. If started down a slight incline, this device will eventually stop and reverse itself.

   b. A yo-yo illustrates conversion of potential to kinetic at the bottom and then back to potential as it rewinds. If you use a yo-yo that will "sleep" at the bottom, ask why it must be started with a flip of the wrist if it is to return all the way up.

c. A mass bobbing up and down on the end of a coiled spring, or a glider on an air track oscillating due to springs on both sides, are used as energy transformation devices.

d. Spin a hard boiled egg on a smooth surface and compare it to a fresh egg. If the fresh egg is stopped momentarily, and then released, it will resume spinning; the hard boiled egg will not. Why? Because all of the motion of the hard boiled egg is stopped, while the fluid inside the fresh egg continues moving for a short time.

e. Use a double incline as shown with very slight slopes. Tracks with a cart or pieces of glass and a cylinder will show energy transfers slowly enough to permit identification of the various energy states.

f. Have students discuss a roller coaster in terms of energy conservation and transfer. A model arranged as shown would be even better. Will the cart make it over the hill? Why?

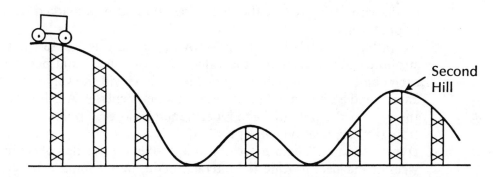

g. Buy a commercial model of a hydraulic ram or construct one from some bottles and tubing as shown. Water is driven up into the reservoir by pinching the rubber tubing several times interrupting the flow.

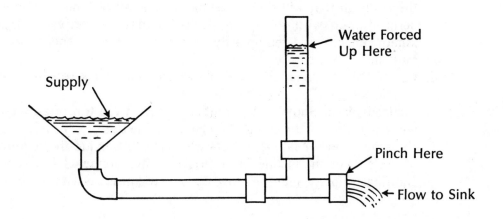

9. *Activity.* Show that mechanical systems "lose" energy due to friction, although the energy is not really lost in the sense of disappearing—it is converted into heat. Have students bend a piece of wire back and forth rapidly and feel the rise in temperature; have them hold a rubber band lightly against their lips and stretch it noting the temperature rise; have a student touch a piece of lead that has been pounded with a hammer; rub the palms of the hands together; rub two sticks together and note the temperature increase, and so forth.

10. *Activity.* Use Reproduction Page 38 as a source of problems to be solved using conservation of energy relationships and energy expressions presented thus far. Note that several of the problems are similar to those encountered in the kinematics section but the solutions will be much simpler using energy relationships.

11. *Laboratory.* Energy measurements and the conservation concept may be introduced through lab work, or the laboratory can serve as an instructional and reinforcing medium. Based on your instructional preferences, arrange several or all of the following laboratory ideas. The specific form is determined somewhat by the equipment you have available.

   a. Falling objects. Take data to measure the potential energy before a mass is dropped and its kinetic energy just before the object hits a reference surface. The mass and distance measures are straightforward but the timing necessary for the velocity will require automatic measure using a spark tape, strobe photo, oscilloscope triggered at the beginning and end of a marked distance interval, or photocells.

   b. An instructive variation on the above procedure is to use the spark timer or strobe to obtain data for the calculation of kinetic and potential energies at each point during the fall. Graphing the results will show a decrease in potential energy and a corresponding increase in kinetic energy. A third graph, displaying the sum of the potential and kinetic energies at each point in the fall, will illustrate the conservation concept.

   c. Dynamics carts. These devices will approximate elastic collisions if spring devices or magnets provide the interaction during the impact. In several collisions of one cart moving into a second, initially at rest, data are taken to show that the kinetic energy of the system before impact is equal to the sum of the kinetic energies of each cart after impact, thus illustrating conservation. Use various masses. Strobe photography is especially convenient for such measurements. A very high speed strobe rate and high velocities may even produce data *during* the collision that will show a temporary "loss" of kinetic energy. Further experimentation with the spring device or magnets can verify that this "lost" kinetic energy was temporarily stored as potential energy in the bumping mechanism.

   d. Use collisions similar to those above on an air track to show conservation of kinetic energy.

   e. Inclined plane. Show that potential energy at the top of an inclined air track will equal the kinetic energy of a glider at the bottom. Measurements similar to those outlined for falling objects will serve to provide the required data. Vary the heights of the incline for a variety of measurements. For very slight angles, the final velocity may be slow enough to measure with a stopwatch over an appropriate distance interval, or v_f can be calculated using the average velocity for the entire run. Then use $v_{ave.} = \dfrac{(v_f + v_i)}{2}$ to find v_f.

f. To show the transfer of elastic potential energy to kinetic energy on an air track, have students experiment with a spring or rubber band as the launching device for a glider. They should take data for a force versus distance graph. The area under this curve will give the potential energy for any measured distortion. Replicate this distortion on the air track, release the spring or rubber band, and then measure the kinetic energy of the glider.

If time or equipment does not allow the student to try these laboratory suggestions, you may use some of the film loops in the references that show similar arrangements and allow some student measurement. In any event, the film loops provide good introductory or supplemental activities for these labs.

12. *Activity.* Individual student research and reports based on references from this chapter may be appropriate for your class. Here are a few topics. You can add many more to this list.
   a. Perpetual motion machines.
   b. Conservation of energy in satellite and planetary orbits.
   c. Meandering rivers from an energy point of view (good for earth science students).
   d. The industrial revolution from a work-energy viewpoint.
   e. The development of simple machines and effects on cultures.
   f. Steam engines—Watt and Newcomen.
   g. Count Rumford.
   h. Leonardo da Vinci and energy conservation in the 15th century.
   i. Simon Stevin and his laws of statics in 1905.
   j. Galileo's energy argument in analysis of a frictionless inclined plane.
   k. Energy in biological systems.
   l. A report on the efficiencies of various mechanical devices such as cars, motors, furnaces, etc.
   m. A look at sports from an energy viewpoint.

ASSESSING ACHIEVEMENT OF OBJECTIVES

Ongoing Evaluation

The extent to which students have mastered the six objectives in this chapter can be measured by several of the activities included, especially the laboratory work and write-ups. Reproduction Pages 33, 35, and 38 may be evaluated or used as models for quiz questions.

Final Evaluation

For an overall evaluation of a student's grasp of the concepts in this chapter, construct a test directly from the objectives. Otherwise use Reproduction Page 39, which is an objective examination dealing with the topics in this chapter. The questions may be changed into essay type by a few word changes, eliminating the options, and directing pupils to show all work and reasoning used to arrive at their answers.

Resources for Teaching Energy

Below is a selected list of resources useful for teaching energy concepts. The list is divided into audiovisual materials and print. If a source is especially useful for teachers only or students only, this is noted with the citation. Addresses of publishers can be found in the alphabetical list at the end of this book.

Audio-Visual Materials

Kinetic Energy. Filmloop. Ealing Corp. Uses slow-motion photography to show the direct measurement of speed and the dependence of kinetic energy on speed and on mass.

Conservation of Energy. Film. P.S.S.C. Traces energy from coal to electrical energy in a power plant. Quantitative data is taken in the plant.

Energy and Work. Film. P.S.S.C. Shows that work is a useful measure of energy transfer. Uses experiments to show that work is the area under a force-distance curve.

Energy: Harnessing the Sun. Film. Sterling Educational Films. Presents an overview of alternate energy sources.

Alternate Energy. Sound Filmstrip. C. Clark Co. An outline of the many modern approaches to alternate energy sources.

Energy: Understanding and Managing a Critical Resource. Filmstrip/cassette. Prentice-Hall Media. A five-part presentation designed to introduce the law of conservation of energy. The accompanying teacher's guide provides questions and activities. Besides introducing the energy concept, many energy issues are discussed.

Finding the Speed of a Rifle Bullet, Method 1. Filmloop. Ealing Corp. A bullet is fired into a block suspended by strings. The speed of the block is measured directly by timing its motion in slow-motion photography.

Finding the Speed of a Rifle Bullet, Method 2. Filmloop. Ealing Corp. Similar to the first filmloop, but the speed is found by measuring the vertical rise of the block and using conservation of energy.

Conservation of Energy: Aircraft Takeoff. Filmloop. Ealing Corp. Flying with constant power, an aircraft moves horizontally at ground level, rises and levels off. Kinetic and potential energy can be measured at three levels.

Conservation of Energy: Pole Vault. Filmloop. Ealing Corp. Demonstrates that the total energy of a pole vaulter can be measured at three points: just before takeoff, the energy is kinetic; during rise, the energy is partly kinetic, partly potential, and partly elastic potential energy of the pole; at the top it is all potential energy.

Gravitational Potential Energy. Filmloop. Ealing Corp. Shows that potential energy depends on weight and height through data which can be graphed.

A Method of Measuring Energy—Nails Driven into Wood. Filmloop. Ealing Corp. Shows that a nail, driven into a piece of wood, penetrates proportionally to the number of repeated blows.

Conservation of Energy. Filmloop. Ealing Corp. Presents a series of three experiments in which energy in some form is converted into kinetic energy on an air track.

Coupled Oscillators. Filmloop. Ealing Corp. Two long, simple pendulums which are coupled, exchange energy.

Print

"The Conservation of Energy" translated by J. R. Mayer. In *A Source Book in Physics* by W. F. Magie. Harvard University Press, 1963.

"Newton" by I. Cohen. *Scientific American* (December 1955). A biography.

Sir Issac Newton by Edward Andrade. Doubleday Anchor, 1965. A biography.

Physics, The Pioneer Science by L. W. Taylor. Dover Publications, 1959. Read Chapter 17.

Power by M. Ruhemann. Sigma Books, 1946. Read Chapters 1–4.

The Two Cultures and a Second Look by C. P. Snow. Cambridge University Press, 1964. The scientist as a "black box."

"Demonstration: A Nail Driven into Wood" by D. P. Zicko. *The Physics Teacher* (January 1980). A good follow up demonstration using ideas developed in the filmloop on the same subject. Nails are driven into a board by hand.

"Energy and the Automobile" by G. Waring. *The Physics Teacher* (October 1980). Provides many examples and figures (numerical values) which apply to cars. These can make good homework assignments.

"Student Power" by J. H. Nelson. *The Physics Teacher* (December 1972). This short article discusses an experiment where students calculate the horsepower they develop. This leads into a discussion of power.

"Demonstration of the Conservation of Mechanical Energy" by L. Chinn. *The Physics Teacher* (September 1979). Describes an energy conservation experiment using a pendulum.

Energy and Fuels by W. Kaplan and M. Lebowitz. H. Milgrom, editor. Rosen Press, 1976. A part of the Student Science series, this work is a review of the energy problems and possible solutions facing us. The writing is appropriate for the average high school student.

"Are Stairs 'Inclined Planes'?" by Mario Iona. *The Physics Teacher* (October 1980). Teachers should read this short article before using stairs as examples of inclined planes.

"Energy Is Not the Ability to Do Work" by Robert L. Lehrman. *The Physics Teacher* (January 1973). Good teacher reading on energy definition from a historic perspective.

"Energy Experiments for Non-Science Majors" by David R. Sokoloff. *The Physics Teacher* (February 1978). Describes four simple energy experiments that are relatively inexpensive. These experiments can be offered during this unit or in other sections (e.g., heat, light, electricity).

Energy by Stephen Lowell. J. Weston Walch, 1978. Explores the energy crisis and its possible solutions. It presents students with problems and policies to think about and discuss.

6

Heat

INTRODUCTION

The previous chapter discussed energy in general terms. This chapter is devoted entirely to phenomena related to heat. This form of energy accompanies almost all transfers either as a side effect or as an intermediary between potential energy and work. Heat energy is a most important and common form. Because of this, your students share an especially large number of experiences with heating effects. Instruction based on these experiences will develop understandings about the behavior and effects of heat energy that go well beyond the initial common sense notions. Unification of heat concepts under the broader construct of energy will strengthen general understandings as well.

Your students are well aware that heat cooks their foods and warms their houses during cold weather—two fairly important functions—but they may not have thought about heat in relationship to making the family car run or its use in the production of electricity, two other common and important ways in which heat energy and its control affect our culture. Almost all modes of transportation—from jet planes to elevators—utilize heat in the series of transfers that produce the final form of the work involved. Even more basic to human existence are the effects of heat on climate and on maintainance of body temperature, two effects that affect life itself as well as life-style. Clearly, it is important to understand an energy form as basic to our lives as heat.

The current energy crisis and concurrent increasing costs of producing heat make knowledge of the nature and transfer of this energy form critical consumer information. Student interest in factors affecting heat transfer may increase when pupils realize that the only reason a heating system is needed in homes or other buildings is to continually replace heat which is lost to the environment. A similar point can be applied to the human body and the principles underlying down jackets and thermal underwear in winter, or the cooling effects of perspiration during hot weather.

Utilize these ideas and others that you can think of as a way to heighten student interest in this topic. Explore each phenomenon in more detail in the context of the activities presented in the following pages.

CONTENT OVERVIEW

Energy itself is an abstract concept. Heat, or thermal energy, is that portion of the internal energy of a substance that produces certain effects when transferred. These heating effects are fairly obvious in many cases but their explanations become a little more abstract due to the molecular constructs which make up the theoretical base used in analysis. It is a good idea to review the assumptions of the kinetic molecular theory:

- Matter is composed of large numbers of tiny particles called molecules.

- These molecules are in constant motion.

- In collisions between molecules (if no chemical reaction happens), momentum and kinetic energy are conserved.

The molecular concept is abstract in the sense that one cannot observe molecules directly (except for a few of the very largest ones). Most of the evidence supporting this construct is indirect and the molecular behavior must be inferred from such evidence. You may want to illustrate this with several short demonstrations such as Brownian motion, diffusion of gases, or evaporation if your students' backgrounds lack such experiences.

A note on safety: Several of the activities in this chapter utilize mercury. Inform your students of the hazardous effects of such heavy metals on the human body, and that mercury can enter the body through skin contact or be inhaled as a vapor. Appropriate measures for inadvertent spills involve thorough cleaning of any mercury. A less obvious problem is due to mercury in thermometers. When a thermometer breaks (and several will each year), the mercury released accumulates in cracks in tables and floor covering materials. It is easily overlooked and often not removed through normal room cleaning. This accumulation, coupled with poor ventilation (many schools reduce fresh air ventilation in the winter to save energy), can produce mercury levels in the air of laboratories which are above acceptable levels.

Eating food in the laboratory is generally not a good idea. It should be prohibited during these activities and several others (such as those involving radioactive materials) as a safety precaution.

One final note on measurement and units: SI units are used throughout this book. In this chapter, however, you may want to use C.G.S. units of grams and calories, especially in lab work, since the kilocalorie and kilogram may be somewhat large for the heat calculations and masses used. If you feel that introducing the smaller system will present more confusion than convenience, the SI units are fine but values will be decimals less than one in many calculations.

OBJECTIVES

If all of the topics are chosen by the teacher, at the end of this chapter the student should be able to:

1. Use the terms temperature and heat correctly in discussions.

2. Use the Celcius and Kelvin temperature scales for reporting temperatures, in problem solving, and in discussions of temperature measurement.

3. Define, measure, and use the concept of specific heat in laboratory and problem solving.

4. Use the kilocalorie and/or calorie correctly in discussion, laboratory, and problem solving.

5. Calculate the amount of heat involved in particular exchanges from information of effects (temperature and/or phase changes).

6. Apply the first law of thermodynamics—the law of heat exchange—in laboratory and problem solving.

7. Predict the effects of variables on heat transfer in everyday phenomena.

8. Interpret graphic displays of heat versus temperature for a sample.

9. Explain and predict various expansion and contraction effects through molecular and heat concepts.

LEARNING EXPERIENCES

Topic I: Distinguishing Temperature and Heat

1. *Demonstration.* Use student intuition to formalize the fact that temperature and heat, although related, are not the same. Place two beakers with equal masses of warm water on a demonstration table. Have your students note the equal temperatures and then ask which can give out more heat. Now pour off about half of the water from one beaker. Again question about the heat comparison. You may have to get at the "heat" notion by asking which beaker of water could melt more ice. Repeat the comparison and questioning using equal masses of water but at different temperatures. Finally, use a larger mass of cool water compared to a smaller amount of warm water. The last question cannot be answered from simple class observations but it sets the stage for further discussion. This demonstration should instill the idea that temperature and heat are *not* the same.

2. *Teacher Presentation.* Follow the above demonstration with a formal presentation. Explain that temperature is a measure of the average kinetic energy of the molecules of a substance. Heat energy, by contrast, is only measurable through the effects it produces (temperature or phase change) when transferred from one substance to another. Heat, then, is a portion of the total potential and kinetic energy of the molecules of a substance (its internal energy), while temperature is related to only the average kinetic energy of the molecules.

3. *Activity.* To emphasize the average kinetic energy idea in contrast to total energy, try the following height analog: Return to the two beakers of warm water, one with much more water (and thus heat) than the other. Again show that the temperatures are the same. Now state that height will be analogous to kinetic energy. Have students make a record of the height of every person in the class. Calculate both the "total class height" and the "average height." Record these values for the next day. As part of a homework assignment, each student polls five other pupils in the school recording each height, calculating the "total height" and "average height." Combine

student polls the next day arriving at the "total sampled height" and the "average sampled height." Your results will show a much greater total height when compared with the class figure but the average for both groups will be nearly the same. Relate this analog to the two beakers of water once again.

This activity focuses on the average notion in temperature and allows you to point out that not every member of the sample is of the average value, some are taller, some shorter. This will be useful in later studies of heat and temperature.

Topic II: Temperature Scales and Measurement

1. *Activity.* Show that the human body can sense relative temperatures by asking your students to first touch a textbook. It will give the sensation of cool. Next ask pupils to touch a metal object or a floor tile. This sensation will be cooler than the text. Point out that both objects have been in the same room for some time and are probably at the *same* temperature. The human body senses temperature by the direction and rate of heat transfer that occurs. Heat leaving the body results in various degrees of "cold" sensation. That is why the metal felt cooler than the paper text. Heat was conducted away from the warmer body at a greater rate since metal or tile is a better conductor. When heat flows from warmer objects into our bodies, we feel varying degrees of warmness depending again on the rate of transfer, which is often (but not always) dependent on the temperature difference.

2. *Activity.* A student report on "wind chill factor" in weather reporting would be interesting at this point, and it would focus on rate of heat loss in the human body.

3. *Activity.* Have two student volunteers place one of their hands in two large beakers of water. One student gets a beaker of ice water; the other, a beaker of very warm (but not burning) water. Both students report their sensations to the class. Verify the sensations with thermometer readings from each beaker. Now both students place the same hand in a single common beaker of lukewarm water. One will report the sensation of cool while the other will report a warm sensation, even though they are sampling the same actual temperature. Discuss the explanation in terms of heat transfer from warmer to cooler. Point out the need for more objective measures of temperature.

4. *Activity.* Use Reproduction Page 40 as a basis for class discussion, small group analysis, or homework on body sensation of relative temperature.

5. *Teacher Presentation.* Use Reproduction Page 41 while discussing the operation, scale basis, and relative advantages of the Farenheit, Celcius, and Kelvin (or absolute) temperature scales:

Farenheit. This scale is still used in the United States in weather forecasting and cook books but is being replaced by Celcius readings during metrification of our measurement system. Farenheit used the coldest temperature ($0°F$) he could get in a laboratory with a mixture of salt, ice, and water for his zero point. He used body temperature (around $100°F$) as his second fixed point.

Celcius. This is the thermometer used in most lab work. Fixed points are the ice point, $0°C$, and the boiling point of water, $100°C$. The scale has a disadvantage shared with Farenheit in that the numbers are arbitrary; at $0°$, for example, there *is* some average kinetic energy; 4° is *not* twice as much average molecular kinetic energy as 2°, etc.

Kelvin. This scale uses the same size divisions as Celcius but starts with a zero point (absolute zero) which corresponds to a condition where molecules have a minimum amount of kinetic energy. Kelvin thermometers have the advantage that 200°K, for example, *is* twice as hot as 100°K. (The average kinetic energy at 200°K *is* twice the amount at 100°K.)

6. *Laboratory*. Uncalibrated thermometers, available from most scientific supply houses, are used to reinforce the calibration principle of a thermometer. Roughen the glass with emery paper enough to take pencil marks without blocking visibility of the mercury column. Students can find the freezing and boiling points of water, mark off these fixed points, and divide the space between these points into ten equal spaces to locate 10 degree Celcius intervals. Once calibrated, these thermometers can be checked against commercially calibrated ones and used to measure air temperature (inside and out of doors). Students can compare their readings.

7. *Demonstration*. Principle of a thermometer. Insert a one hole rubber stopper with a 40 cm length of glass tubing in a large flask filled with water. Make the water more visible by adding food coloring or, better yet, some flourescent dye and use an ultra violet light source. Press the stopper into the flask. Water will rise in the tubing. Mark the initial position of the water and heat the flask with a bunsen burner. Students may note that the water level drops initially; then it rises as the liquid expands up the tube. This drop is due to the glass expanding first when heated. The greater amount of water soon dominates the demonstration. The thinner the glass tubing, the more the response is amplified.

8. *Activity*. Galileo's Air Thermometer. Have students research and construct an air thermometer. It consists of an arrangement similar to the one sketched below.

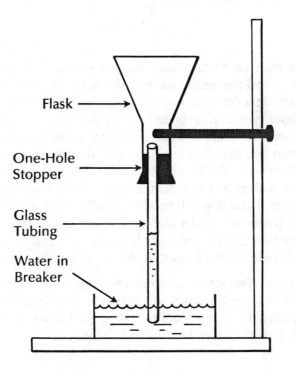

Flask

One-Hole Stopper

Glass Tubing

Water in Breaker

Support the thermometer from above as shown with the end of the tube under water. Heat the bulb so that air bubbles out. When the bulb cools, water is drawn up into the middle of the tube. Students can mark this level and calibrate the thermometer using another temperature and a commercial thermometer as a reference. This is a very sensitive device that will respond to changes in air pressure as well as temperature.

9. *Demonstration.* Make a thermocouple and connect the wires to a sensitive galvanometer. The galvanometer should be either a large lecture type or a projection type used with an overhead. See the reference section of this chapter for a source of directions for construction.

10. *Laboratory.* Determination of absolute zero by extrapolation. Use a commercially available apparatus which consists of a metal bulb in which some gas exerts pressure. This gas pressure registers on a gauge connected to the bulb.

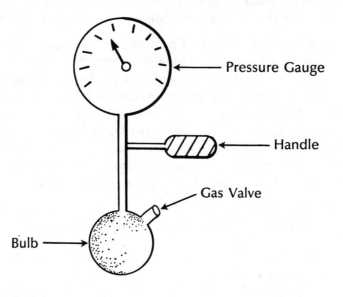

Be sure students relate the gas pressure to collisions between the moving molecules and the inside walls of the bulb. Slowing down the molecules produces fewer and less forceful collisions, thus reducing the pressure reading. Of course, the temperature is also related to this motion. Several readings of bulb temperature in degrees Celcius and the corresponding pressure determine a straight line relationship when graphed. For such a graph, the temperature axis should go from around −300°C up to +100°C, and the pressure from zero up to the highest reading produced. Readings at room temperature, in ice water, and in boiling water should be used. Careful plotting will produce straight lines which, when extrapolated to a zero pressure (minimum molecular motion), intercept the temperature axis near −273°C. By using different amounts of air in the bulb and even different gases, the resultant data will yield several lines that all converge near absolute zero when extrapolated.

11. *Laboratory.* Absolute zero from the volume of a gas. Data of volume versus temperature of a confined gas will also provide a theoretical value for absolute zero, if extrapolated to a zero volume value. Such data are obtained using apparatus for Charles' Law discussed later in this chapter.

12. *Activity.* Several topics from this section are appropriate for student research and reports. Here are a few suggestions (several of the references at the end of the chapter provide good starting points): Celcius temperature; the Farenheit scale; absolute zero; cryogenics; triple point temperature; wind chill factor; pyrometers; thermistors; and temperature sensitive paints. You and your students may suggest other topics during discussions.

Topic III: Heat Energy and Effects of Transfers

1. *Demonstration.* Show that mechanical work is often transformed directly into heat by repeating some of the activities in Topic III (#9) from the chapter on energy. Supplement this demonstration by taking the temperature of a bottle of mercury, closing the container, and shaking it vigorously for a couple of minutes. Insulated gloves will prevent transfer of heat from your hand. After the shaking, several degrees of temperature rise are noted.

    Hold a rounded point nail with the head removed in a drill chuck. Press this nail against a piece of hardwood and operate the drill. Smoke will soon be seen. A similar arrangement with the drill and a hollow metal tube (with a closed end) in the chuck will boil some water inside the tube. A small hole near the top of the tube but below the chuck will allow steam to escape and provide evidence of boiling for your class.

2. *Laboratory.* Students can verify that the work done by some lead shot falling from a measured height produces a temperature change in the lead. About 1 to 2 kg of shot in a cardboard tube, stoppered at both ends, will do. One of the stoppers is one-holed to allow the insertion of a thermometer to record initial and final shot temperatures. Once the initial temperature is recorded, the thermometer is removed, the hole plugged, and the tube is inverted so the shot falls the length of the tube. The number of inversions (50–100) and tube length (and thus the total height for falling) are two independent variables that are manipulated to show differential temperature changes in the shot.

3. *Activity.* Student research into "caloric" and the work of Count Rumford and James Prescott Joule would add some historic perspectives on heat as an energy form and its relationship to work. References at the end of this chapter provide good starting points for this assignment.

4. *Teacher Presentation.* Explain that heat energy is measured only when it is transferred and then only indirectly through the "effects" which result. The effects are either a temperature change or a phase change. It is the temperature change produced in water that is used as a standard for heat measurement. Since heat was not always considered a form of energy, units for such quantities are not joules (although heat units are often converted into an equivalent expression in joules), but kilocalories or calories. Formalize the kilocalorie as the amount of heat required to raise one kilogram of water one Celcius degree. You may also relate a similar definition of the calorie and perhaps the B.T.U.

    It is helpful for students to get a "feel" for how much heat one kilocalorie represents by applying a bunsen flame to a beaker containing one kilogram of water long enough to produce a one degree temperature change in the water.

Compare this crude demonstration to a similar one in which .5 kg of water are raised two degrees, and relate these effects back to the definition.

5. *Laboratory*. Students already know that the amount of heat that can be transferred depends on the mass of the object involved and the temperature change it experiences. Have students perform some of the following experiments, which show that a third variable, determined by the type of matter involved, also affects the quantity of heat exchanged. This variable is called specific heat of the substance. Follow this series of experiments with a summary. Include the units for expressing specific heat and an equation expressing the amount of heat involved in producing a temperature change in any material: $Q = m\,c\,\Delta T$, where Q is the amount of heat energy, m is the mass of the substance, c is its specific heat, and ΔT is the temperature change.

a. Balance styrofoam cups containing equal masses of cold water at the same temperature on a platform balance. Place equal masses of two different metals in a boiling water bath and then place each in one of the cups. Note the difference in the temperature increases.

b. Use a set-up similar to that above but use equal masses of two different liquids in the cups. In this case, equal masses of the same metal go from a boiling water bath into the two liquids.

c. Use two similar bunsen flames to heat a suspended metal mass and an equal mass of water in a beaker for the same amount of time. The metal will become much hotter than the water. Splash water on the metal and it will sizzle while the water in the beaker is still cool enough to touch.

d. Another version of procedure "a" is to place a metal mass in one of the cups after the metal has been in a boiling water bath. Then add boiling water to the second cup of cold water until the balance is re-established. Again, the cup that got the equal mass of boiling water added to it will show a greater temperature rise.

e. Use several different metal cylinders, each having the same mass and equal cross sectional areas. (These are available from most scientific supply houses.) Heat all of the samples in a boiling water or steam bath and then use tongs to carefully place and hold each sample on the surface of a block of paraffin wax or ice. The different amounts of ice or wax melted, as measured by the depth of the holes formed in them, will demonstrate the differential amounts of heat transferred.

6. *Laboratory or Demonstration*. Place a mixture of ice and water in a beaker. Apply a bunsen flame to add heat at a constant rate. Take temperature readings of the water at set time intervals. Plot temperature versus time (which is proportional to the heat added) as data is taken. Observations of what is happening in the beaker should also be noted. Continue heating and recording temperatures through the melting stage until the water is boiling for a time. The resulting graphic display will "flatten out" during the melting stage, then rise as the water is warmed, and then flatten again as boiling occurs. The question to raise is, "What happened to the added heat when the graph was flat?" Discussion will lead to a determination of phase changes (fusion and vaporization) that require heat in order to happen. Note that during these changes of phase, the temperature did not change. Introduce the concepts of latent heat of fusion and latent heat of vaporization. Relate

this behavior to molecular energy by noting that, in such phase changes, the average kinetic energy of the molecules (temperature) did not change. The added heat produced a change in the positions of the molecules, thus manifesting a change in the molecular *potential* energy.

7. *Teacher Presentation.* Use Reproduction Page 42 to formalize latent heats of fusion and vaporization of water. Point out that other substances behave similarly but the amounts of heat and temperatures for phase changes vary with the material. You might direct students to Reproduction Page 43, which shows heat values for several substances, and illustrate the point in that manner.

    Note that the processes are reversible, so *removal* of the appropriate amounts of heat will produce solidification and condensation.

    Finally, show that the amount of heat involved is dependent on the mass and the appropriate latent heat. $Q = m\, l_f$ and $Q = m\, l_v$.

8. *Laboratory.* Students can demonstrate that substances lose heat with no temperature change by plotting a temperature versus time curve while some water freezes. A mixture of crushed ice and alcohol in a beaker provides a temperature of about $-15°C$. If some water is placed in a small test tube fitted with a one-hole stopper and a thermometer, the curve will again flatten as the water in the test tube approaches zero degrees Celcius and solidifies. Shake the tube before reading the thermometer to prevent supercooling.

9. *Demonstration or Laboratory.* Balance two styrofoam cups with cold water in them on a platform balance. After showing that steam and boiling water are at the same temperature, bubble some steam through one of the cups, then add an equal mass of boiling water to the other cup to restore the balance. The greater temperature increase in the cup that got the steam shows that more heat is supplied by steam (through condensation) than by boiling water at the same temperature.

10. *Activity.* Give students some practice in calculating the amount of heat required to produce various effects, and the use of reference tables, prior to combining such calculations in the next section. Use Reproduction Page 44 as a source of problems in conjunction with the tables from Reproduction Page 43.

Topic IV: Conservation of Heat Energy

1. *Demonstration.* Use three beakers, two smaller ones and a larger. Place hot water in one small beaker, noting the temperature; use cold water in the other small container, again noting the temperature. Now pour both into the larger beaker. Ask your class for a prediction of the resulting temperature and an explanation. The following points should be drawn from the discussion that follows: Heat was exchanged in the mixing, going from the higher temperature water to the lower; this exchange continues until both reach the same temperature, equilibrium; energy is conserved, so the heat lost by one water sample was gained by the other. This is the first law of thermodynamics, which is essentially a conservation of energy statement applied to heat, Q Lost = Q Gained.

2. *Demonstration.* Show the conservation principle applies to heat related to phase changes, specifically, cooling by evaporation. Have students measure the tempera-

ture of some liquid alcohol. Then remove the thermometer from the bottle and note the quick decrease in the reading. The vaporizing alcohol acquired its heat of vaporization from the thermometer, thus causing the temperature to drop. Similarly, alcohol swabbed on students hands will cause cooling of the skin.

Make or use a hydrometer. Show the lower temperature resulting from swabing one bulb with alcohol, or some other violatile liquid, when compared with a dry bulb.

Discuss the cooling effect of perspiration on the human body.

3. *Demonstration.* Show through calculations on the board that the vaporization of two grams of water removes enough heat to cool and freeze about ten grams of water starting at room temperature. Follow this calculation by freezing some water by boiling it. The boiling, in this case, is produced by lowering the pressure rather than adding heat. (You may want to discuss vapor pressure and boiling points and demonstrate these effects before continuing.) Place about 10 ml of water from a tap on a watch glass in a vacuum chamber as shown below. Suspend the water over a dish of concentrated sulfuric acid that is used as a dehydrating agent.

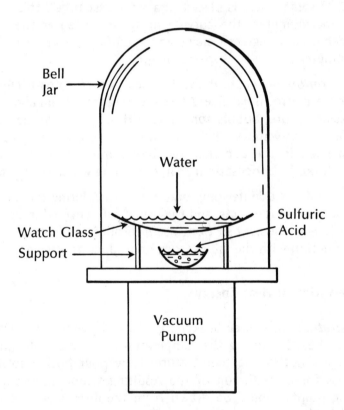

If your pump is good and the system well sealed, the water will boil quickly at first and then slow down as the temperature lowers. Even if boiling stops, continue for a couple of minutes, since vaporization through evaporation is still removing heat from the water. If you are successful, remove the ice formed (being careful of the acid below), and pass it around for students to feel. They often don't believe that the ice formed is, in fact, "regular ice" that is cold.

4. *Activity*. Reinforce the conservation of energy idea by assigning problems in heat exchange which are more complex than earlier calculations. (Most textbooks contain many of these.) Reproduction Page 45 is a student guide to setting up solutions to such problems. Use it before the assignment and subsequent lab work which involve similar calculations. It will allow students to proceed into a problem even when confused by the initial complexity.

5. *Laboratory*. Have your students replicate an exchange of heat measurement similar to your initial demonstration, except that they should carry out a calculation to predict the final temperature of a mixture of two water samples in a calorimeter. One sample of hot water is added to a calorimeter containing the cooler sample. Values for the masses, specific heats, and initial temperatures are needed. When the experiment is complete and the final temperature determined, students can calculate the final temperature and compare values. Remember, the calorimeter cup will be part of this calculation.

6. *Laboratory*. Most text books or accompanying lab manuals describe methods to experimentally determine specific heats, heats of fusion of ice, and the heat of vaporization of water by the method of mixtures. These experiments should follow at this point since they employ conservation of energy as their base and provide for experimental verification of values used in earlier calculations. Here are some brief notes on these experiments:
   a. Specific heat. The student heats a metal sample and places it in a calorimeter with water in it. Appropriate measures of masses, initial and final temperatures, and specific heats are used to calculate the specific heat of the metal.

      Minimize heat exchanges with the environment by starting with the water slightly below room temperature and ending slightly above. Choose metal to water mass ratios that will produce temperature changes of several degrees. Too much water will result in large errors due to very small temperature changes. Be sure the water in the calorimeter is sufficient to cover the metal. Results of this experiment are not always satisfactory when compared to accepted specific heat values but repeats with different metals will show correspondence.
   b. Latent heat of fusion. The student adds ice to water in a calorimeter and takes data for the calculation of the latent heat of fusion. Use crushed ice rather than shavings. Let the ice stand in the room for awhile to be sure it is up to zero degrees Celcius. Be sure students dry off the ice just before adding it to the calorimeter. The mass of the ice is measured by the increase in the water in the calorimeter at the end of the experiment.
   c. Latent heat of vaporization. Steam from a boiler is bubbled through water in a calorimeter. Use a trap to prevent entry of hot water along with the steam. Because of the high amount of heat added to the calorimeter by steam, warn students that the final temperature will be measured more quickly in this experiment than in earlier ones. Too high a final temperature produces large errors due to heat exchanges with the environment.

7. *Activity*. Use Reproduction Page 46 as a summary of effects presented thus far. It consists of several everyday phenomena related to the physics of heat and temperature. In each case the student should explain the described event in terms of concepts discussed in class. This Reproduction Page can be the basis of class or small group discussions, homework, or evaluation.

Topic V: Thermal Expansion

1. *Teacher Presentation.* Explain that, with few exceptions, substances expand when heated and contract when cooled. Relate this behavior to molecular motion. Solids expand due to an increase in the amplitude of vibration of the molecules, causing them to move farther apart because of the increase in thermal energy. Liquids behave similarly. Gases, too, expand due to increased kinetic energy of the molecules. Emphasize this molecular analysis during the next series of demonstrations.

2. *Demonstration.* Choose several of the following to show thermal expansion and discuss effects and uses of such behavior.
   a. Refer back to Galileo's air thermometer, Topic II, #8, focusing on the expansion of the air with increasing temperature.
   b. Ball and ring. Show expansion in solids with a metal ball that will just pass through a ring at room temperature. Heat the ball and it will not pass through until the ring is also heated. Note that heating the ring *increases* the internal diameter of the ring and does not force it to close. Discuss applications in fitting mechanical parts and why rivets are heated prior to installation.
   c. Refer back to Topic II, #7, and relate the principle of a thermometer to expansion of a liquid.
   d. Hang a small weight from some high resistance wire as shown below. It will move up and down in response to contraction and expansion of the wire as current is turned off and on.

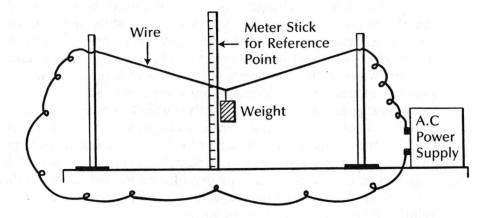

   Ask about the amount of sag in power lines in summer compared to winter.
   e. A variation on "d" is to arrange a pendulum which just clears a table top and then apply the current. The expansion will cause the hanging weight to hit the table as it swings. Measurements of the period of such a pendulum arrangement when hot compared to cold can lead into a discussion of errors in timing devices due to expansion.
   f. Show differential expansion of two metals using a compound bar (bi-metallic strip). This device will bend when heat is applied. Commercially produced bars are available or you can make one by riveting together thin strips of copper and iron or steel.

g. Use your compound bar to demonstrate its use in a thermostat control device shown below. The light bulb is analogous to a furnace. As the bar heats, it bends and breaks the connection powering the bulb. The resultant cooling causes the bar to straighten and once again make the contact to turn the bulb back on. The required temperature change for operation is determined by the spacing between the contact point and the bar.

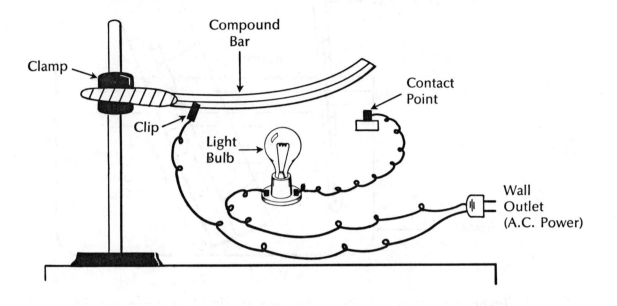

h. Bring in a commercial thermostat, an automobile cooling system thermostat, and an automotic choke from a car. Have students inspect the controls and observe their operation as temperature is changed. Discuss other applications of similar devices.

i. Show the effects of differential expansion and contraction on brittle substances by using some glass tubing. First, trap some water in the top end of the tube, holding it there with your finger and air pressure. Next, heat the other end in a flame. Release the water. The cool water will cause the internal portion of the glass to contract while the outside is still hot, and the tubing will crack. Use appropriate safety measures to protect from flying glass and be sure to keep your fingers away from the top end, since steam will rush out when the water contacts the hot glass at the other end.

3. *Laboratory.* Have students perform a calculation of the coefficient of linear expansion using standard laboratory apparatus. At least two different metals should be measured to show that the coefficient is dependent on the type of material.

4. *Laboratory.* Verify that the volume of an ideal gas is directly proportional to temperature (Charles' Law) by subjecting a volume of confined gas to different temperatures. Plot volume versus temperature to show the linear relationship. Here are two ways to obtain the data:

a. Use some capillary tubes with one end closed. Heat the tube with a match and then quickly place the opened end in some mercury. Hold it there as the tube cools and draws in some mercury (this uses Charles' Law). The mercury has now trapped the air in the tube. Attach this arrangement to a metric ruler and immerse the tube in various temperature water baths. The volume is proportional to the height of the air column.

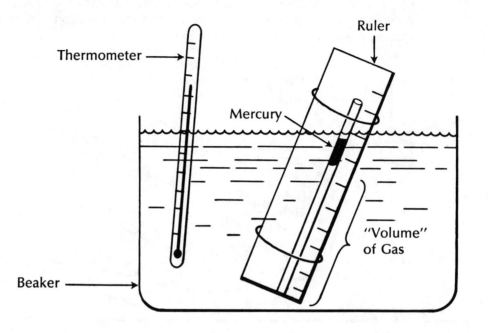

b. Immerse a syringe with its needle end sealed in a beaker of water. Read off the volumes of the confined gas directly from the syringe in cubic centimeters. The temperature corresponds to the water temperature. Twist the piston a little before each volume reading to free up any sticking.

5. *Demonstrations.* Show the relationship between the temperature of a gas and work through the following activities:
   a. Pop a cork out of a flask by heating the air in it. Wet the stopper before placing it in the flask to form an air tight seal. Don't force the stopper in since very high pressures will be needed to pop it out. Discuss the pressure increase due to increased molecular motion.
   b. Release a carbon dioxide fire extinguisher. Note that the expanding gas did work, and that the energy used to do this work came from the gas, thus cooling the carbon dioxide enough to freeze it. (You may also get into sublimation as your class sees the dry ice disappear back into the gaseous state without going through a liquid phase.)
   c. A fire syringe consists of a closed tube with a tight fitting piston. A piece of tinder is placed in the bottom of the tube, the piston is pushed down quickly, and the increased temperature of the air causes the tinder to ignite. Relate this to compression ignition in diesel engines.

   In each of these demonstrations, emphasize the relationship between heat, work, and temperature of the gas. When a gas does work, its temperature decreases; when work is done on the gas, its temperature increases.

6. *Activity.* Many industrial arts departments will have "see through" models of automobile engines. Obtain one, if you can, and investigate the operation of such a "heat engine."

7. *Activity.* If you have a working model of a steam engine, this would be a good point to analyze its operation using the concepts of heat, temperature, expansion, and pressure through molecular motion.

8. *Activity.* Have students research Hero's engine, build a working model, and explain the operation to the class. Another group may use a pulse jet from a model airplane to explain and demonstrate jet engines as "heat engines."

9. *Activity.* Students can make a model of a steam turbine by directing a steam jet from water boiling in a flask toward a series of propellors or pinwheels mounted on a shaft. Again, the sequence of heat to internal energy of a gas to work should be stressed.

10. *Activity.* Students can research and report on refrigeration systems and their operation as an application of the ideas discussed in this section. Reports on various types of heat engines will substitute for the model making when time or equipment is not available.

Topic VI: Heat Transfer

1. *Teacher Presentation.* Introduce this topic with the following joke: Three physics students are assigned the task of deciding what is the most amazing invention of all time. As they discuss their assignment, one girl suggests the jet plane, saying that through this invention, she could travel half way around the world in a matter of hours. The second student agrees that the jet is quite remarkable but proposes that the telephone is even more amazing, since she could talk with someone on the other side of the world in just a matter of minutes with this invention. The third girl listens to the first two suggestions but offers her own: the Thermos bottle. She argues that with a thermos, you can put something hot in it and it stays hot, *or* you can put something cold in it and it stays cold. The other two students agree with those statements but ask, "What is so amazing about that?" The third girl answers, "What is so amazing is . . . how does it know?"

   The Thermos or vacuum bottle is a good example of the prevention of heat transfer. Its design minimizes transfer through radiation, convection, and conduction. You may want to describe each of these processes and then show how the construction of the bottle reduces each process.

2. *Activity.* Divide the class into three groups, making each group responsible for investigating one of the three heat transfer methods. Their eventual task is to present their findings to the other groups through explanation, demonstrations, and applications. Each group may be graded on this project by giving the group whatever average grade is attained by others in the class on a quiz on the assigned heat transfer method. The teacher serves as a consultant to the groups providing suggestions and equipment as needed.

3. *Activity.* Home insulation against heat transfer is an important part of our nation's energy conservation efforts. Use Reproduction Page 47 in the following manner. Distribute the list to the class and ask what all the items have in common. The first answer will probably be "heat insulators." Then ask what mechanism is used by each item. The notion of trapped or "dead" air is common to each device. You may want to assign more detailed reports on each item to your students. These reports could deal with advantages, disadvantages, and uses of each item. Perhaps your class can add to the list.

ASSESSING ACHIEVEMENT OF OBJECTIVES

Ongoing Evaluation

The extent to which students have mastered the concepts covered under each topic can be measured by many of the activities suggested in each section. Periodic quizzes also provide evaluation information. Laboratory reports and participation in discussions, as well as individual reports on assigned topics, provide for additional assessment.

Final Evaluation

For an overall view of the student's understanding of the concepts in this chapter, you can construct a unit test directly from the objectives. Questions may also be chosen from Reproduction Pages 40, 44, 46, and 48. Reproduction Page 48 consists of several common phenomena related to Topics V and VI. Students are to explain each in terms of appropriate concepts in this chapter.

Resources for Teaching Heat Concepts

Below is a selected list of resources useful for teaching heat concepts. The list is divided into audio-visual materials and print. If a source is especially useful for teachers only or students only, this is noted with the citation. Addresses of publishers can be found in the alphabetical list at the end of this book.

Audio-Visual Materials

Behavior of Gases. Film. P.S.S.C. Shows Brownian motion and other evidence for molecules. Boyle's law and a gas pressure model are presented.

Carnot Cycle. Film. McGraw-Hill. The Carnot cycle is explained. Shows how heat is absorbed and rejected during cycle and defines the Kelvin temperature scale.

Demonstrating the Gas Laws. Film. Coronet. Discusses Boyle's and Charles' laws and then goes on to describe the Combined Gas Law.

Kinetic-Molecular Theory. Film. McGraw-Hill. An introduction. Deals with molecular motion, kinetic energy, and preparation for further study of the gas laws.

Mechanical Energy and Thermal Energy. Film. P.S.S.C. Illustrates bulk and random molecular motion. Thermal conduction and the absolute temperature scale are presented.

Temperature and Matter. Film. McGraw-Hill. Deals with changes in phase and the unusual properties of matter at extremely low temperatures.

Properties of a Gas. Filmloop. Ealing Corp. Makes measurement runs by counting pucks hitting one wall during a short time interval; also investigates the relations represented by the universal gas law. Shows the effect of isothermal and adiabatic compression of a single puck.

Finding Absolute Zero. Filmloop. Ealing Corp. Examines absolute zero through a pressure-temperature relationship of gas in a metal sphere which is subjected to various temperatures.

Boyle's Law. Filmloop. Ealing Corp. Shows an experiment where the volume of air in a syringe decreases as more weights are added to the plunger.

Thermal Expansion of a Gas. Filmloop. Ealing Corp. Uses a Galilean air thermometer to show that gases expand when heated.

The States of Matter. 16mm film or video-cassette. CRM/McGraw-Hill Films. A good introduction to kinetic theory and the states of matter as related to temperature. Various models are used to illustrate properties. The presentations are not highly technical.

Finding Absolute Zero. Filmloop. B.F.A. Educational Media. Use as an alternative to the experimental procedure suggested in this chapter, as a supplement, or for student self-study.

Print

"The Conduction of Heat in Solids" by R. L. Sproull. *Scientific American* (December 1962). Provides further insight into the solid state. Discusses heat and electrical conduction.

Count Rumford by S. C. Brown. Doubleday Anchor, 1962. A biography.

Cryogenics by M. McClintock. Reinhold Books, 1964. A descriptive account of extreme low temperature research and some applications.

The Early Development of the Concepts of Temperature and Heat: The Rise of the Caloric Theory by D. Roller. Harvard University Press, 1950. Rumford's experiments on heat produced by friction and Davy's experiments.

Heat Engines by F. Sandfort. Doubleday Anchor, 1963. The theory and practice of thermodynamics in Chapters 3, 4, 5, and 6.

Scientific American (May 1956). "Amateur Scientist" section has two rubber band heat engines.

"Alternative Automobile Engines" by D. G. Wilson. *Scientific American* (July 1978). Discusses the advantages and limitations of engines other than the gasoline type.

"Entropy" by G. Gamow. In *The World of Physics* by A. Beiser, editor. McGraw-Hill, 1960. A clear and simple description of the concept.

"Farenheit and Celcius, A History" by E. R. Jones, Jr. *The Physics Teacher* (November 1980). A brief account of how these two people designed and calibrated thermometers.

"Cooling a Cup of Coffee" by R. D. Edge, editor. *The Physics Teacher* (October 1979). Describes a technique to produce a cooling curve to show that rate of heat loss is proportional to temperature difference.

"Insulation and Rate of Heat Transfer" by V. D. Pynadath. *The Physics Teacher* (September 1978). A simple experiment which clarifies some of the basic physics involved in heat transfer.

One, Two, Three . . . Infinity by G. Gamow. Mentor Books, 1957. Read Chapter 8.

The Quest for Absolute Zero: The Meaning of Low Temperature Physics by K. Mendelssohn. Halsted, 1978. Describes some of the phenomena that arise at low temperatures and the people involved in research in this area.

A Source Book in Physics by W. F. Magie. Harvard University Press, 1963. See the selections on Newton, Amontons, Farenheit, Taylor, Black, Rumford, Davy, Gay-Lussac.

Water: The Mirror of Science by Kenneth Davis and John Day. Doubleday and Anchor, 1961. Chapters 1 and 5 discuss the internal energy of water.

Robert Boyle's Experiments in Pneumatics by J. B. Conant. Harvard University Press, 1950. Some good material on Boyle and Boyle's Law.

"What Is Heat" by F. J. Dyson. *Scientific American* (September 1954). Development of the concepts of heat, temperature and thermal energy.

"Negative Absolute Temperatures" by W. G. Proctor. *Scientific American* (August 1978). Temperatures not colder than zero but hotter than infinity.

"Heat of Vaporization of Water" by P. O. Berge and J. E. Huebler. *The Physics Teacher* (October 1978). The authors describe a simple and inexpensive method for measuring the latent heat of vaporization of water.

Knowledge and Wonder by V. Weisskopf. Doubleday Anchor, 1963. See Chapter 4.

Solar Energy Experiments by Thomas W. Norton. Rodale Press, 1977. Presents a range of solar experiments from the very simple to quite complex. The book would be a good self-study source for teachers.

Geigy Scientific Tables by C. Lentner, editor. Medical Education Division, Ciba-Geigy Corporation, 1981. This work has some interesting tables (starting on page 228), which provide information on energy expenditure by people while they do various activities.

"The Role of the Second Law of Thermodynamics in Energy Education" by Uri Haber-Schaim. *The Physics Teacher* (January 1983). Good teacher reading on the topic of energy and its definition. The remarks suggest ways to refine student energy ideas using heat concepts.

"Launching a Career in Solar" by Terry Brennan. *Solar Age* (August 1982). Provides a list of books, slides, films, helpful organizations, materials, and supplies if a teacher wishes to develop a unit (or a course) on solar energy.

"Freezing-by-Boiling Apparatus That Does Not Require Acid" by Robert N. Stoller. *The Physics Teacher* (January 1976). Describes a procedure similar to the demonstration suggested in this chapter.

7

The Atomic Structure of Matter

INTRODUCTION

Many textbooks treat atomic physics at the end of their survey of physical knowledge. There are several good reasons for this. It is consistent with a historical treatment since this is one of the "newest" topics covered in high school texts. Also, much of the thinking required to understand atomic phenomena is based on other physical studies such as conservation of momentum, spectra, and electrical charges. This area is much more abstract than the mechanical concepts treated earlier. Atomic phenomena deal with indirect evidence (similar to molecular concepts), but the phenomena displaying the evidence are themselves somewhat specialized, and thus not as familiar to pupils in terms of daily experiences. Students, for example, can cite diffusion of perfume through the air as evidence for the existence of something like a molecule, but very few will be familiar with protons ejected from some paraffin and detected by an ionization chamber as evidence for the existence of a neutron.

There is some logic, however, for inclusion of atomic theory earlier in your course. One possibility is almost the reverse of the argument for closing with this area. It is reasonable to assume that a good concept of the atom and its structure will aid students in subsequent instruction in electricity, magnetism, light, and so on, since the atomic structure of matter is basic to such phenomena.

Consider the instructional value of a "change of pace" for your pupils. Ideas in atomic physics are usually treated descriptively, whereas more math is applied to areas in mechanics. It also makes sense to provide your students with a broad view of what physics is about earlier than the last several weeks of the course.

This chapter is background for atomic (and other) studies but not necessarily a prerequisite. The emphasis is on process rather than subject matter. Your pupils all know about atoms. Much of this knowledge will have come from earlier science courses. The approach is to consider *how* some of this very basic knowledge was attained. The historical discoveries and experiments which led to current atomic conceptions were characterized by indirectness and a great deal more inference than research in mechanics. This chapter stresses how we have come to know what we understand about atoms. The application of this knowledge and effects on daily living is the focus of Chapter 8.

CONTENT OVERVIEW

Relating student experiences to the physics underlying the activity is an instructional approach emphasized throughout this book. In this chapter, however, the experiences are not as direct. Use diagrams, models, and analogy as alternatives to direct experience. The general approach is to start with the familiar, to strengthen these concepts by exploring processes which led to basic knowledge of atomic structure, and then to expand into new atomic concepts.

Safety note: Several of the demonstrations suggested in this chapter involve cathode ray tubes. X-radiation produced by collisions of electrons with the tube structure should be limited by keeping the voltage from the coil at low levels or by using power supplies that automatically limit the operating voltage and keep this radiation within acceptable levels. Check your state and federal guidelines for specific recommendations.

OBJECTIVES

As a result of the learning experiences in this chapter, students should be able to:

1. Interpret atomic symbols and relate these symbols to the structure of a particular atom.

2. Use the term "isotope" correctly.

3. Summarize some of the experiments and theories which contribute to our current understandings of atomic structure.

4. Calculate the binding energy per nucleon for a nucleus given appropriate information.

5. Describe the operating principles of several different particle accelerators.

LEARNING EXPERIENCES

Topic I: Atomic Symbols and Structure

1. *Activity.* Poll the knowledge your students already possess regarding the structure of an atom and summarize class contributions on the board or overhead. Usually this activity will produce a sketch similar to this one.

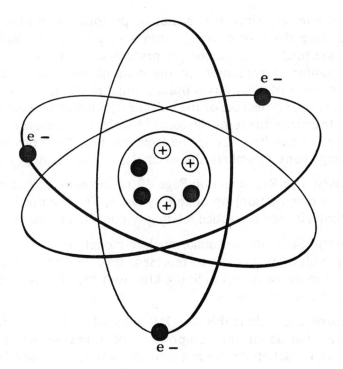

Students are aware of a nucleus containing positively charged protons and electrically neutral particles, neutrons. They also will relate negatively charged electrons orbiting around this central core. Pupils are aware that all things are made up of atoms and that these "building blocks of matter" are too small to be seen even with the most powerful microscope.

Point out that atoms are composed of electrons and a nucleus. The nucleus is composed of protons and neutrons. They in turn appear to be composites of quarks. The idea of a "particle" is very fuzzy at this level. The forces acting between the particles also have certain "particle-like" manifestations, although this quickly gets beyond the realm of this level of physics.

2. *Teacher Presentation.* Explain that atomic symbols are used to describe atoms and their structure. These symbols consist of a letter representing the name of the atom and, more importantly, superscripts and subscripts—numbers that convey information about the structure of the atom. It is necessary to introduce the atomic mass unit, the A.M.U., as the unit of matter measurement appropriate for the small domain of things atomic. One A.M.U. equals $\frac{1}{12}$ of the mass of the most abundant carbon atom, carbon-12. Relating the A.M.U. to kilograms: 1 A.M.U. = 1.66×10^{-27} kg. You may wish to introduce the units for distance, angstroms (°A), as equal to 10^{-10} meters at this point. Emphasize the smallness of both measures by expressing them as decimal values on the board.

Explain that the subscript in atomic symbols represents the charge on the nucleus in elementary charges. Since a proton has a charge of +1, it also tells the number of protons in the nucleus. This number, called the "atomic number," determines the chemical properties of the substance. The top number, the "mass number," is the atomic mass of the atom, in A.M.U.'s, rounded off to the nearest whole number. Since the masses of protons and neutrons are near 1 A.M.U. each (and since the mass of an electron is very small in comparison), the mass number tells the total of the number of protons and neutrons in the atom. By subtracting the number of protons from the mass number, the neutron count is determined. The number of electrons is usually equal to the number of protons, since the entire atom is neutral because of the balance of numbers of equal but opposite charges.

Introduce the term "isotopes" to refer to members of the same atomic "family"; that is, to members having the same number of protons but different masses due to varying neutron numbers. Put examples of a few isotopes on the board.

3. *Activity.* Use Reproduction Page 49 to summarize your presentation (or as a basis for the presentation) on atomic symbols. The last portion of this page provides the student with some practice relating symbols to atomic structure.

4. *Activity.* Students can make nuclear models in relation to symbols by using ping pong balls of two colors to represent protons and neutrons or, better yet, borrow some models or model building kits from the chemistry department. You also can order models of your own.

5. *Discussion.* Conclude this description by asking how we are able to provide so much information about the composition of atoms—structures so infinitesimally small that individual atoms are not directly observable, much less their composite parts. Also ask how we know such detailed information about those parts. The answers to such questions will be partially disclosed in the next topic.

Topic II: Experimental Evidence and Theories Related to Atomic Structure

1. *Demonstration.* Replicate some of the experiments leading to the discovery of the electron by using a large tube such as the one used to show that a coin and a feather accelerate equally due to gravity in a vacuum. Connect this tube as shown below:

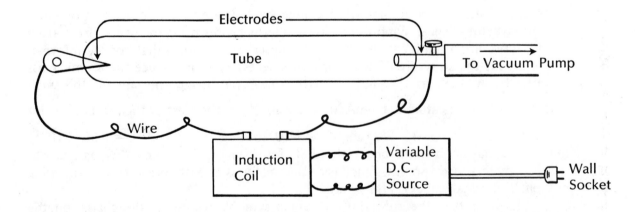

Physicists used similar tubes to study conduction of electricity in gases. The discovery of the electron was a by-product of such studies. With the vacuum pump off, raise the voltage on the power supply; no effects will appear in the tube. Now start the pump and evacuate some of the air. As the pressure inside drops, students will see purple "fingers" appear at each electrode. As the pressure drops lower, the "fingers" will form into a band of purple light across the entire length of the tube. Show that this glow is not "regular light" by bringing a magnet near the beam. The magnet will cause deflection of the beam.

2. *Demonstration*. Scientific supply companies provide several different types of tubes for demonstrating cathode rays. One of the most common has a shield with a slit in it near the cathode. The beam in this tube strikes a fluorescent screen along the length of the tube which makes it visible. The direction of cathode rays (from (−) to (+)) is demonstrated with such a device through noting which side of the shield is struck. Check the apparatus ahead of time to be sure the cathode is connected to the correct end of the tube for this demonstration. You can show that the cathode rays travel out in straight lines with a Crookes tube, which casts a sharp shadow due to a metal cross placed in the beam. The fact that the beam is due to mass moving is shown by using a tube with a "paddle-wheel" mounted on a track above the beam. Spinning of this wheel when the beam hits the paddles is an indication of the presence of a moving mass.

Numerous other cathode ray tubes are in catalogs from scientitic supply houses. Various properties of cathode rays are shown by each one.

3. *Discussion*. Ask your class to infer what cathode rays consist of from the observations made during the previous demonstration. A small, negatively charged particle could produce the effects observed. (If you have studied electromagnetism prior to this demonstration, the magnetic deflection should be discussed as being consistent with negative charge moving from cathode to the positive terminal.)

Relate to your class that J. J. Thomson observed that the nature of these negative particles did not change as the cathode material was varied or when the gas in the tube changed. These tiny negative particles, electrons, might be present in all matter. If they are, some sort of positive charge also must exist in all things, since matter is normally neutral. This observation started the search for the particle we now call the proton.

4. *Activity*. Since it is not practical to replicate all of the experiments that had a bearing on atomic structure, student research and reports may offer a good compromise. The experimental work of Jean Perrin, Sir William Crookes, and J. J. Thomson are appropriate topics relating to electrons and protons. James Chadwick's discovery of the neutron also would fit here.

5. *Demonstration*. Cathode ray tubes used as oscilloscopes and as T.V. picture tubes are a high interest topic. Use your oscilloscope and manual controls to show how the electron beam is deflected electrically and magnetically. Emphasize that the formation of the spot of light is due to a single beam of electrons striking the phosphor-coated screen. Show that the brightness of the spot is influenced by varying the applied voltage. With the sweep still off, show that the spot can be made to move rapidly enough by manually turning the horizontal position control to give the appearance of a horizontal line across the screen. Next set the sweep to automatic and show that the entire screen can be illuminated with the single electron beam by rapidly rotating the vertical control. Explain that this rapid zig-zag pattern is what is used in television; the picture is formed by alternating

light and darker regions in conjunction with light patterns in the studio. If light and color have been studied previously, the theory of color T.V. using three types of phosphors and electron guns is a logical topic for discussion.

If you choose to explore this application in detail, some old picture tubes that are cut away will be useful for your descriptions. Take some care with the phosphor coatings since they may be poisonous.

An interesting homework assignment is to have the students explain the physics of a T.V. picture tube to a parent or guardian and then have the parent put his or her understandings in writing. The student can submit his parent's report to you for evaluation.

6. *Activity*. Use Reproduction Page 50 as a student guide to Thomson's famous experiment to determine the charge to mass ratio of an electron. Details of this experiment can be obtained from several of the sources listed at the end of this chapter.

7. *Laboratory*. Students can perform the above experiment with reasonable success in a laboratory setting. Commercial apparatus is available from most scientific supply houses along with specific instructions for operation. This experiment and another showing the behavior of electron beams are described in detail, using a "home made" version of the apparatus, in Units 4 and 5 of the *Project Physics Course Text and Handbook* (listed in the references). If this experiment is chosen, Reproduction Page 50 will provide good theoretical background.

8. *Activity*. Use Reproduction Page 51 to help with the description of the Millikan Oil Drop Experiment. Students should be aware of the reasoning used by Millikan in determining the elementary charge, the charge on one electron, and how this relates to the apparatus and data analysis. Details of this experiment are available from several sources listed in the references. Point out that Millikan did not measure the charge of an electron directly; he measured the charges on oil drops and deduced the electronic charge from his data. The analogy presented in Reproduction Page 51 will be helpful in illustrating Millikan's reasoning.

9. *Laboratory*. Students can replicate the Millikan Oil Drop Experiment with some modern improvements. Apparatus for this experiment is available from many supply houses. Latex spheres now substitute for oil. They offer the advantage of being of uniform weight and size, thus eliminating the calculations Millikan had to perform to determine weight by timing the terminal velocity of his droplets. If you choose this experiment, you will also need a D.C. power supply that can provide about 300 volts, plus a voltmeter to measure voltages up to that value.

Since a large number of spheres must be balanced in order to check Millikan's conclusions, consider having each student record balancing voltages for several drops and contributing this data to a class composite. The results of this summary are shared for analysis.

The results can be used in at least two different ways: It reinforces that groupings of balancing voltages indicate similar quantization of charge on the spheres and the idea that electrical charge comes only in certain discrete quantities. Secondly, measurements that allow for the actual calculation of the charges on the spheres (and thus the charge on an electron) are possible from this apparatus. This offers the student the opportunity to go through some of Millikan's calculations (though results are often off by a power of ten or more from the accepted value for the elementary charge, 1.6×10^{-19} coulombs). The option depends on your judgements of the class and time.

10. *Activity.* Spectra produced by excited gases are said to be like fingerprints of an atom. Have students observe spectra with a hand held diffraction grating. Use a show case bulb in the front of the room as an incandescent source producing a continuous spectrum. Contrast this with the bright line spectrum produced by excited gases from spectrum tubes or by introducing various salts into a flame. Relate the frequency of the lines to the Bohr model of electron energy levels in atoms. The different spectra produced by different excited atoms is evidence of the energy level transitions made by the electrons in each gas. Explain that this type of evidence is related to Bohr's model of the atom.

11. *Laboratory.* Students can observe the hydrogen spectrum and gather data for the calculation of energy levels for that atom. The positions of the various bright lines are recorded directly in °A, if a spectroscope with a scale is available. If you do not have spectroscopes, set up the hydrogen tube with a meter stick below it. One student observes the spectrum through a diffraction grating of spacing d at some distance, l, away from the tube. The observing student directs another who is near the tube to move his finger in space until it is just over the bright line to be measured. The distance of this line from the tube, x, is recorded; the wavelength, λ, is approximated by:

$$\lambda = \frac{xd}{l}$$

Photographing the arrangement above has advantages over the preceding method because all the lines are recorded at once and some of the faint lines become visible through longer exposure time. These lines might be overlooked with the naked eye. A double exposure will place the meterstick in the picture, and x is calculated for each line as above. Once the wavelengths are known, students calculate the energies of the photons of each line using $E = \frac{hc}{\lambda}$, where E is the energy, c the speed of light, and h is Planck's constant. Pupils then can use these energies to construct their own energy level diagrams or for comparison with such diagrams in textbooks.

A shortened version of this laboratory is to choose only one or two lines for measurement and compare the energies with an energy level diagram. In any case, stress the indirect nature of this evidence about atomic structure.

12. *Teacher Presentation.* Use Reproduction Page 52 in conjunction with an explanation of the Rutherford Scattering Experiment. This page shows the essential apparatus involved. Spaces are left for students to enter each of the three observations Rutherford made as you describe them and for conclusions about the results of each observation.

Observations	Conclusions
1. Most of the alpha particles went straight through.	1. An atom is mostly space.
2. A few alpha particles were deflected at various angles.	2. A positive charge is present.
3. On rare occasions, an alpha particle came almost straight back.	3. A small, massive particle is present.

The following analogy may be helpful to your explanation. You may try to parallel your description of Rutherford's experiment with the analog and develop both at the same time.

Ask your class to imagine that they are on the stage of a large, completely dark auditorium and that you have placed some "targets" somewhere in the space above the seats. Your students are to tell you as much as they can about the targets without seeing them and without leaving the stage. (Rutherford could not see or touch individual atoms either.) When your class recognizes the futility of this task as described so far, ask what aids they would like to help with the problem, and how each might provide the information needed. Eventually, agree to provide the students with an unlimited supply of projectiles which they can throw into the darkness and listen for effects. (The scattering experiment used alpha particles and a phosphor coated screen for observation of effects.) A good imaginary projectile is a positively charged tennis ball or similar object. Once the experiment is set up, describe the following observations, and ask what information each provides about the targets:

a. The first 1,000 tennis balls encounter nothing. (Most of the alpha particles went straight through the gold foil.)
b. Occasionally, a tennis ball is deflected to the side but does not contact a target. (Some of the alpha particles were scattered.)
c. Very rarely, a tennis ball comes straight back to the stage. (You may have to model some crude collisions to lead the class to the mass relationship required for this behavior. Rutherford concluded that his targets, nuclei, were very massive compared to alpha particles from analogous observations.)

Several other points should occur in discussion. Students may ask what happened to effects produced by electrons, since Rutherford's observations supported the concept of a small, massive, positively charged nucleus. Ask what effect some mosquitoes flying around in the auditorium would have produced on the thought experiment results. The tiny mass of electrons would not affect Rutherford's alpha particles either.

Pose this question to your class: How did Rutherford know that his observations were due to individual nuclei and not to the effects of many nuclei bunched together? (You can't find out about an individual brick by bouncing a ball off a brick wall six feet thick.) The answer to this question involves the choice of gold foil as the "target." The following demonstration will help explain this choice.

13. *Demonstration.* Explain that of all possible materials, gold can be made very thin and still hold together as a solid sheet that is only a few hundred atoms thick (which is not a very large number in atomic considerations). Obtain some gold foil

and remove one sheet (about seven centimeters square) from the paper separations of the packet. Students will immediately notice the effects of air friction on this very thin material. If you let the sheet "float" onto your hand, pupils can see that the metal conforms to the texture of your skin, since fingerprints can be observed in the gold as it rests on your hand. Final proof of the extreme thinness of this foil comes when a student questions the cost of this gold. Cite the current market value per ounce and tell the student that he may have this sheet; it is no longer valuable to you because you cannot return it to the package. Explain that you will roll it up first. You can make the sheet "disappear" by working the foil into the crevices of your fingerprints and thus put final emphasis on the very tiny amount of gold in the thin sheet.

14. *Activity.* Students can construct models of the Rutherford nuclear atom by using a large magnet to represent the nucleus. This magnet is fastened to a low-friction surface such as an air table or glass tray with tiny plastic spheres sprinkled on it. Smaller magnets (representing alpha particles) are directed near the "nucleus" at various distances from it. If the polarity of the magnets produces repulsion, the alpha magnets will be scattered much like Rutherford's alpha particles were.

   If a low-friction surface is not available, similar effects result when a magnet suspended from a string (a pendulum) swings near a fixed magnet on a table.

15. *Activity.* Students may construct (or you may purchase) a potential hill, meaning a flat surface that has a "hill" built into the middle. Metal balls rolled toward this hill will be deflected from their straight line paths as a function of how directly they approach the incline. This produces results similar to Rutherford's scattering.

16. *Laboratory.* If students construct an appropriate launching device (a rubber band or inclined ruler with a groove down the center), the potential hill or magnet models can produce data of scattering angle versus distance from the target. The launching device is to allow for numerous repeats with projectiles having the same speed. Varying the type of interaction (changing the hill shape or using hard non-magnetic discs) will show contrasting scattering-angle distributions.

17. *Activity.* Several other activities are appropriate for this topic. Some are experimental and involve calculations from data while others emphasize the idea of inference from indirect evidence. Here are some additional suggestions (detailed instructions are in the references cited at the end of the chapter):
   a. See how much students are able to find out about a small object sealed in a cigar box or similar enclosure without opening the box. They should list what they did, their observations, and conclusions.
   b. Students can use a thyratron 885 tube to demonstrate the ionization energy of an atom—the Franck-Hertz effect.
   c. Planck's constant can be calculated through experiments with the photoelectric effect.
   d. Electrolysis of water is easy to do and has implications for this topic.
   e. Dalton's work leading to the periodic table is modeled by using several different weight metal spheres. If you place various numbers of these balls in lightweight containers, students can figure out the "structural formulas" for each container by knowing the masses of the constituent spheres and measuring the total mass of the container.

    f. Have students calculate the mass of an individual atom from data obtained from electrolysis of copper sulfate solution by comparing the electricity used with the mass of one of the products.

18. *Activity.* Student (or teacher) presentations on the following scientists and their contributions to atomic structure are appropriate for this topic. The references at the end of the chapter provide good starting points for these investigations:
    a. Dalton's atomic theory
    b. Mendeleev's periodic table of the elements
    c. Davy and Faraday's work with electrolysis
    d. Hertz on the photelectric effect followed by Einstein
    e. Max Planck on quantum theory
    f. Wilhelm Röntgen on X-rays
    g. Johann Balmer on lines of hydrogen
    h. The Thomson atom

Topic III: Atomic Masses, Mass Defect, and Binding Energy

1. *Teacher Presentation.* In this section, students will make calculations using atomic masses that are known very accurately. It is reasonable to expect questions concerning how such small quantities are measured, especially in the atomic domain where the quantities are so small that they were not even detected until recently. Keep to the "How do we know?" theme of this chapter by describing the mass spectrograph, a device that provides for the measurement of atomic masses. Use Reproduction Page 53, a diagram of one type of a mass spectrograph, in conjunction with the following description:

    The operation of this device depends on slight differences among the masses of the particles measured. The particles are ionized and projected through the region of crossed electrical and magnetic fields. These fields deflect particles in such a way that only those having a specific velocity pass through the slit. Others are deflected and blocked by the chamber walls. As the ions which do pass through the slit enter the top chamber, they are deflected by another magnetic field causing them to move in an arc. Ions with the same mass and charge describe the same arc but less massive ones are deflected more and ions having greater mass describe a wider arc. The respective masses are calculated through knowledge of their speeds, the field strength, and the size of the arc. Photographic plates are often used to detect where the ions end up. Collecting vessels at different locations are used if the device is used for separating isotopes.

2. *Activity.* Students can demonstrate the principles employed in a mass spectrograph by building a model. Different size steel balls represent isotopes of different masses. The velocity of each ball is controlled by starting it from the top of a launching ramp made from two rulers or a grooved piece of wood. The balls roll down the ramp and onto a flat surface. Mount a magnet on this surface so the moving steel balls pass near it. Smaller masses will be deflected more than larger ones as in the mass spectrograph. Isotope separation is demonstrated if students arrange "catching bins" in appropriate positions. These can be small boxes placed on their sides or enclosures made from strings of putty open on one side. After final adjustment of this model, balls can be released in any order and they will end up in the pre-

determined location. Do not release them too close together since the induced field on one ball will affect the path of the next one.

3. *Teacher Presentation.* Follow the mass spectrograph instruction with an application of this information—mass defect and calculation of binding energy. Reproduction Page 54 is a sketch representing mass defect (the mass of a nucleus is less than the sum of the masses of its constituent particles) and a sample calculation of binding energy for a nucleus.

Note that the end calculation is for the binding energy per nucleon. Explain that one of the reasons for this calculation is not to find out how much energy is holding the core together but to know how much energy is required to break it apart. Biologists dissect frogs to understand their internal structure; physicists "dissect" nuclei to gain similar knowledge. The units for expressing binding energy, Mev's (mega electron volts), are a consequence, partially, of the electrical dissecting devices used for this study, particle accelerators or "atom smashers."

The conversion factor used to relate mass defect to energy (1.A.M.U. = 931 Mev) is a direct result of the application of $E = mc^2$, Einstein's famous equation. It symbolizes that energy and mass are different forms of the same thing. If mass, m, disappears, a predictable amount of energy, E, results. (c is the speed of light.) Reproduction Page 55 shows the derivation of the conversion factor. It is important that students relate their calculations of energy to this basic formula, even though they will probably use the conversion factor as a timesaving short cut for most calculations of nuclear energy.

You may want to conclude your presentation by discussing how the law of conservation of energy from classical physics has been adjusted to the law of conservation of mass and energy to take mass-energy conversions into account. This demonstrates the tentative nature of scientific knowledge. As we learn new things, we adjust our descriptions of the physical world to accommodate the newer discovery.

4. *Activity.* Pass out Reproduction Page 56 to your class. Assign each student one element from the list and have pupils do a binding energy per nucleon calculation for their element (note that helium, carbon, and oxygen are not the most common isotopic forms). If the calculated binding energies per nucleon are plotted, a definite maximum results in the middle of the periodic table. Any reaction that proceeds toward this maximum (fission and fusion) must lose mass and release energy as a consequence. This class graph activity will provide practice in binding energy calculations and a resource for later studies on fission and fusion.

5. *Demonstration.* Show the electrical principles employed in particle accelerators using a Van de Graaff generator. A neutral pith ball suspended near the sphere will be attracted, pick up the same charge as the sphere, and then repel away with considerable speed. This demonstrates the electrical acceleration of particles that can be directed toward "target" atoms.

Similar repulsion and resultant acceleration of particles is shown if some small styrofoam balls are placed on the dome of a Van de Graaff. They will "fly away" quickly when the machine is turned on.

6. *Activity.* Divide your class into several small groups. Each group is to investigate one of the following topics, work up a presentation, and report their findings to the rest of the class. Topics fall under the general area of particle accelerators.

- Careers in high energy physics
- Cyclotron
- Betatron
- Synchro cyclotrons
- Synchrotrons (bevatron, cosmotron)
- Linear accelerators
- Mev, Bev, Gev

Reports should stress the basic operating principles used for accelerating particles and how some of the devices are used in research.

7. *Activity.* Many colleges and universities have accelerators which they use in studies and research. If such a facility is nearby, arrange a field trip to the installation. Check on what the school is doing and relate appropriate background to your students before the visit.

ASSESSING ACHIEVEMENT OF OBJECTIVES

Ongoing Evaluation

The extent to which students have mastered each topic in this chapter is measured through several quizzes given at appropriate points in the instructional sequence. Laboratory and other reports will provide additional evaluation material.

Final Evaluation

Construct an essay or short answer unit test directly from the list of objectives for this chapter. Such a test will certainly require atomic symbol interpretation and the calculation of mass defect and binding energies. The nature of questions on historical contributions to our understanding of atomic structure and particle accelerators will depend on the emphasis of your instruction. These questions can range from requesting a general description of how we know what we do about atomic structure, to specific and detailed identification of one (or several) key experiments.

Resources for Teaching Atomic Structure

Below is a selected list of resources useful for teaching concepts of atomic structure. The list is divided into audio-visual materials and print. If a source is especially useful for teachers only or students only, this is noted with the citation. Addresses of publishers can be found in the alphabetical list at the end of this book.

Audio-Visual Materials

Cosmic Rays. Film. McGraw-Hill. Presents the development of modern concepts of atomic structure and cosmic radiation. Discusses the contribution of cosmic ray research to the understanding of the basic structure of matter.

The Coulomb Force Constant. Film. P.S.S.C. Shows a large scale version of the Millikan experiment.

Electrons in a Uniform Magnetic Field. Film. P.S.S.C. An experiment to determine the mass of an electron.

The Mass of an Electron. Film. P.S.S.C. A demonstration by Eric Rogers to determine the mass of an electron.

The Millikan Experiment. Film. P.S.S.C. Shows a simplified Millikan experiment using plastic spheres instead of oil.

The Nature of Matter: An Atomic View. Film. McGraw-Hill. Discusses various theories on the nature of the atom. Research using linear accelerators, bubble chambers, and photographic emulsions is reviewed.

The Rutherford Atom. Film. P.S.S.C. Uses a simple alpha particle scattering experiment to illustrate Rutherford's famous work. Uses models to show the nuclear atom and Coulomb scattering.

The Spectrograph. Film. McGraw-Hill. Demonstrates principles of the spectrograph and use of this device for industrial purposes.

The Structure of Atoms. Film. McGraw-Hill. Provides experimental evidence for our concept of the atom. Rutherford's experiment, the charge on an electron, and the charge to mass ratio are shown.

Mass of an Atom. Filmloop. Ealing Corp. Presents data from which the mass of a copper atom can be determined.

Mass Spectrometer: Behavior of Particles in Magnetic and Electric Fields. Filmloop. Encyclopedia Britannica Corporation. Introduces the basic components of the mass spectrometer and describes how magnetic and electric fields influence the motion of ions in the mass spectrometer.

Rutherford Scattering. Filmloop. Ealing Corp. Uses computer simulation to show scattering of alpha particles as a function of distance from nucleus.

Thomson Model of the Atom. Filmloop. Ealing Corp. Shows a model in which ping pong balls with magnets in them form various patterns in a tub of water with a radial magnetic field.

Measuring the Electron Charge by Millikan's Technique. Sound filmstrip. H. M. Stone Productions. This visual shows Millikan's original technique as well as current laboratory methods using plastic spheres. A teacher's guide and student worksheets accompany the filmstrip.

Measuring the Electron Mass by e/m Method. Sound filmstrip. H. M. Stone Productions. This filmstrip shows how the mass of an electron is found by the application of electrical and magnetic forces. A teacher manual and student worksheets accompany the filmstrip.

Print

Elementary Modern Physics by R. T. Weidner and R. L. Sells. Allyn and Bacon, 1980. Chapter 10 on nuclear structure is good teacher background. Chapter 12 on subatomic particles is also appropriate.

Accelerators by Robert Wilson and Raphael Littauer. Doubleday Anchor, 1960. A good discussion of important tools of nuclear physics.

"Exotic Light Nuclei" by J. Cerny and A. M. Poskanzer. *Scientific American* (June 1978). Unusual combinations of neutrons and protons are created in a laboratory. These unstable configurations last long enough to be studied.

"Heavy Leptons" by M. L. Perl and W. T. Kirk. *Scientific American* (March 1978). The addition of a new member of this group which includes electrons and muons.

"Resonance Particles" by R. D. Hill. *Scientific American* (January 1963). A summary of some of the important aspects of the physics of fundamental particles.

Rutherford—Recollections of the Cambridge Days by M. Olephant. Elsevier Press, 1972. Rutherford's former student recalls some of his work.

The Sub-Nuclear Zoo by S. Engdahl and R. Roberson. Antheneum, 1977. The story of how and why studies in particle physics (high energy physics) are carried on and what the world may hope to gain by them.

"Isabelle" by P. Schewe and P. Wanderer. *The Physics Teacher* (October 1979). Description of a proposed new high energy accelerator and the experiments it will be used for. Good teacher reading for background.

"The Two-Neutrino Experiment" by L. M. Lederman. *Scientific American* (March 1963). An account of a fundamental experiment in particle physics.

The Restless Universe by M. Born. Dover, 1951. Chapter 4 has a good explanation of the electronic structure of the atom.

Mr. Tompkins Explores the Atom by G. Gamow. Cambridge University Press, 1945. A novel approach to atomic structure and the behavior of atoms.

J. J. Thomson by G. Thomson. Doubleday Anchor, 1966. A biography on the discoverer of the electron. Much material on his experiments.

Invitation to Physics by K. Greider. Harcourt, Brace, Jovanovich, 1973. A very readable account of elementary particles in Chapter 20.

"The Atomic Nucleus" by R. Heofstrater. *Scientific American* (1956). An account of how we measure the size and shape of the nucleus.

The Rise of Robert Millikan by Robert H. Kargon. Cornell University Press, 1982. Covers many incidents in the life of Robert Millikan. It includes a discussion of important events in physics that took place during the time of Millikan's work. A good teacher reference; also useful for a student report.

"Unraveling the Mysteries of the Atom" by Leon Lederman. *The Physics Teacher* (January 1982). Describes the work at the Fermi National Accelerator Laboratory and some implications of that research. Good teacher reading. Also appropriate for interested students.

8

Nuclear Energy

INTRODUCTION

Radiation and atomic energy have always been fascinating topics for students. Current energy-related problems and the use of nuclear energy in dealing with them make this chapter extremely important to young men and women for several reasons. First, atomic energy is a major portion of the background required to be a scientifically literate person. This background is usually acquired as a direct result of schooling. Second, students must know some of the facts related to nuclear energy to be enlightened citizens. They will have to make decisions as voters, and many of these decisions will be related to topics introduced in this chapter. Today's knowledge about nuclear energy has much to do with the priority given to development programs by various governments. Third, topics in this chapter represent a major area of physics. Numerous educational specialities and occupations are available in the nuclear area. Finally, all of us live in an age where total destruction of life is possible through thermonuclear warfare. Scientifically accurate information will not change this state of affairs, but it can serve to dispell unnecessary anxiety by eliminating horror stories that are not possible, and it can impress an accurate picture of the seriousness and extent of this world political problem.

Scientists have taken different political stands on issues related to nuclear energy, especially following World War II. Numerous physicists are speaking out on political issues related to topics in this chapter. Include some of these issues in your instruction. Perhaps some members of the class will be interested in researching them.

Regardless of your personal position on nuclear energy—pro, con, or someplace in the middle—you should present both sides of the issue. It seems that the informational and entertainment media have focused on the negative features of atomic energy more than its benefits, so your students may have information in this area that is biased toward the negative. Provide balance by discussing some of the lesser known positive effects of radiation and nuclear energy. Discuss uses of this knowledge related to healing, agriculture, world food supply, pest control, manufacturing, and quality control.

Some concerned citizens have already provided input on world destruction. Balance that possibility with an alternate one: the possibility of a world of abundant energy provided by fusion. If this nuclear process is applied on a large scale, it can mark an end to the scarcity of energy and materials (and pollution).

Considering the curiosity of students about topics in this chapter, and the wide range and seriousness of controversial applications of atomic energy, your students should view this material as extremely interesting and important to their lives. The nuclear process is of concern not only to physicists; it affects economists, ecologists, political scientists, psychologists, and citizens of the entire world community.

CONTENT OVERVIEW

Many students will know of alpha, beta, and gamma radiation from earlier science studies. Use this knowledge as a starting point for your instruction. Broaden concepts of radiation to include other nuclear emissions and maintain the "How do we know?" theme from the previous chapter by replicating some early experiments in radiation detection and discussing the operation of several measuring devices.

Half-life is another concept students have heard of before. Several half-life measurement exercises and an explanation of the statistical nature of the concept are an important addition to students' understandings.

The use of atomic symbols in writing nuclear equations and the calculation of mass-energy relationships in this chapter should be fairly easy for your pupils. If they were successful in the previous study of atomic structure, a brief review in this area should suffice.

Once students have some familiarity with the descriptors, they are ready for an expanded study of fission and fusion. You may want to first present the physics of each process and then engage your class in some of the applications and controversies. An alternate strategy is to use the controversies as a starting point (a motivation) and approach the fission and fusion processes from that angle.

Safety note: Check regulations applying to your area on the allowable strength of radiation sources. Remember, when working with radiation (even very weak sources), you are a model your students will emulate. Follow good safety procedures such as limiting exposure to short times through careful planning. Maintain distance from sources by setting up experiments so that the radiation source is far away from people. Use tongs when handling sources. In the case of liquids, wear gloves or wash your hands following exposure; spill protection procedures also are appropriate. Of course, food consumption during lab work of this kind is not allowed.

OBJECTIVES

As a result of the learning experiences in this chapter, students should be able to:

1. Discuss the properties of radiation.

2. Name and describe alpha, beta, and gamma radiation and how they are detected and measured.

3. Determine the half-life of a radioactive sample and use half-life in problem solving.

4. Write and interpret nuclear equations.

5. Calculate the energy involved in nuclear reactions.

6. Describe the fission process including concepts of critical mass and chain reaction.

7. Name several uses of radiation.

8. Explain radioactive dating.

9. Describe the fusion process.

10. Describe the basic principles of fission as they are applied in the construction of a nuclear reactor for production of electricity.

LEARNING EXPERIENCES

Topic I: Radiation—Properties, Detection and Uses

1. *Activity.* Reproduce Henri Becquerel's discovery of radioactivity. Use laboratory sources of alpha, beta, and gamma radiation. Tape the sources to a Polaroid film pac which has been removed from the foil wrapper but still has the light shield in place. After enough exposure time (one hour to one day—depending on the sources), place the film pac in a camera, remove the light shield, and develop the film. Gamma radiation will leave a fuzzy area exposed on the film. Exposures due to beta particles are more clear in outline, while the alpha particles will not produce an effect on film because their penetration power is not sufficient to go through the film pac covering. Subsequent development of film deeper in the pac will provide the evidence on the relative penetration of the beta and gamma radiation.

2. *Activity.* If you can find an old clock face that glows in the dark due to emitted radiation, it will take its own picture if you place the exposed face against a film pac. Some gasoline lantern mantels which contain thorium will also work for this activity. Somewhat longer exposure times may be required depending on the activity of the source, distance from the film, and sensitivity of the film.

3. *Activity.* A variation of the above experience uses a metal object such as a coin between the radiation source and the film. The developed film will show the outline of such an object.

4. *Teacher Presentation.* Explain that radiation consists of rays and particles coming from unstable nuclei as those nuclei change. Radiation cannot be detected directly with our senses so we make use of several properties in the detection and measurement of radiation:
   a. It affects film.
   b. It ionizes gases.
   c. It produces fluorescence in certain substances.
   d. It can produce physiological effects on living organisms.

The first three properties are used by most detection devices, while the fourth is of special interest because of its application in the healing professions and its potential as a pollution problem. All of these applications will be examined in more detail in subsequent activities.

5. *Activity.* A simple foil leaf electroscope will show the ionization effect of radiation on air. Charge an electroscope and then note its discharge rate. When a radiation source is placed near the knob of the electroscope, the device will discharge at a greater rate. A lighted flame will cause an increase in the discharge rate, too. This is due to the ions produced by the flame. If an alpha source is used, a couple of sheets of paper between the source and the electroscope will produce a "normal" rate of discharge showing the low penetration of alpha particles. Further experimentation with alpha particles will show no effect beyond about 4 cm distance, giving an indication of the range of such radiation in air.

6. *Demonstration.* After explaining the operation of a Geiger-Müller tube, you can model how a single ionization caused by radiation produces an avalanche of electrons in the tube. A plywood board with small depressions in it made with a drill will hold marbles in position. The board is now tipped at an angle to represent the electric field. The angle is just short of making the marbles leave their original positions. A single marble in the top row, if removed from its position and let go, will cause a cascade of marbles to arrive at the bottom of the board analogous to the electrons which reach the central wire of a Geiger-Müller tube.

7. *Activity.* A group of interested students may wish to build a Geiger counter. Numerous plans exist, from simple (and inexpensive) to more elaborate (and expensive) circuits. Plans for construction can be found in several popular science magazines or in the references at the end of this chapter. Kits for the construction of Geiger counters are on the market as well.

8. *Laboratory.* Determining the plateau and operating voltage for a Geiger-Müller tube. If you have Geiger counters with variable voltage adjustments, some students may want to perform an experiment to determine the operating voltage of a Geiger-Müller tube. With a radiation source near the tube, raise the voltage on the tube until counting begins. Subsequent small increments in voltage will produce corresponding increases in the count rate. Data of count rate versus voltage should be plotted as they are measured. Data will look like this.

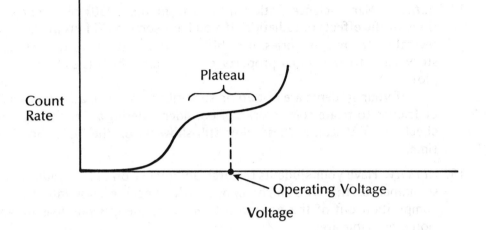

The flattened portion is called the plateau. The operating voltage is in the middle of this range. Be careful not to raise the voltage too high—just enough to determine the end of the plateau.

9. *Demonstration.* Cloud formation flasks are available from supply houses that sell earth science equipment. These flasks, with rubber bulbs, show the formation of clouds when a gas is cooled below its dewpoint by sudden expansion. Smoke particles provide the condensation nuclei needed. In the Wilson cloud chamber, the condensation nuclei are ions formed by radiation passing through the chamber.

10. *Activity.* Have students make a cloud chamber and observe radiation tracks with it. Various versions of continuous-acting diffusion cloud chambers are available from supply houses or you can have pupils make their own. The device is essentially a glass or plastic enclosure illuminated from the side and viewed from above. The bottom often has a black blotter paper surface saturated with alcohol. This alcohol forms a vapor inside which is cooled by placing the entire set up on a dry ice-alcohol mixture. When conditions are right, cosmic radiation will produce visible cloud traces. If you desire, place an alpha source inside the chamber before cooling.

11. *Activity.* Several of the audio-visual suppliers listed at the end of this book provide film loops of tracks in a cloud chamber. This would be a good substitute for Activity #9.

12. *Activity.* Students can see light flashes produced in a commercial spinthariscope if it is used in a light shielded environment and the observer's eye is used to the dark. A home-made device uses a light tight box with zinc sulfide on one wall with a radiation source adjacent to it. The opposite wall has a cardboard tube through a hole. Inside the tube is a magnifying lens that you can adjust for maximum magnification for viewing the light flashes produced on the zinc sulfide as radiation impinges on it.

13. *Activity.* Use Reproduction Page 57 as a summary of radiation detection devices and their operation. If you prefer more detailed study, assign groups of students to

research and report on one method. These reports can include schematic drawings, explanations, and models.

14. *Activity.* Many science fiction movies from the 1950s represent some exaggerations of the effects of radiation. If you have some sci fi fans in class who can relate several of the movie stories, use this as a discussion base. In each case, relate the story back to the actual property of radiation which is exaggerated to make the plot.

   If your students are not up on such films, they can ask other teachers, family, or friends to relate some stories or consider ordering a film for class viewing. Also, check the T.V. guide—these films still show up on the "late show" from time to time.

15. *Activity.* Have your students research and report on uses of radiation. The uses are so numerous that you might consider dividing the class into teams and make a competition out of this assignment. Some of the general areas in which information is available are:
   a. Food preservation
   b. Radioisotopes in industry
   c. Radioisotopes in medicine
   d. Radioisotopes in research
   e. Non-destructive testing
   f. Neutron-activation analysis
   g. Tracers

16. *Laboratory.* Use Reproduction Page 58, which shows the effects of a magnetic field on alpha, beta, and gamma radiation, as an introduction to the following experiment. Arrange the set up as shown in the sketch but without the magnet. The reading on the counter should be nearly background level. Now bring in and adjust the magnet until it causes the particles to bend around the shield and into the counter causing a dramatic increase in the reading.

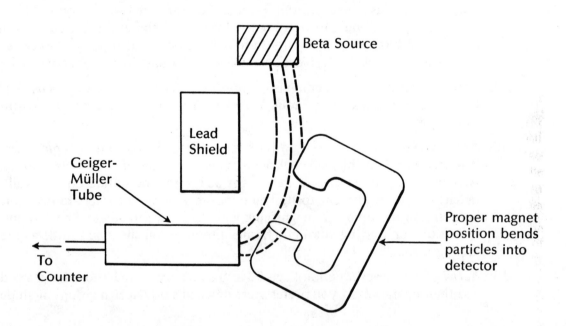

17. *Laboratory.* Use a Geiger counter and a point source of radiation. Measure the radiation per unit time as a function of distance from the source. Such data will show that doubling the distance reduces the counts to $\frac{1}{4}$; tripling the distance produces $\frac{1}{9}$ the reading. This is the inverse square law. Note: If a low count rate is used, be sure to measure and subtract background radiation. Also, do not get too close to the source with the detector because the distances to the ends of the counter tube are significantly different from the distance to the center of the tube. This will cause results to vary from the inverse square relationship.

18. *Laboratory.* In a lab on radiation shielding, students compare the absorbtion of various materials for both beta and gamma radiation.

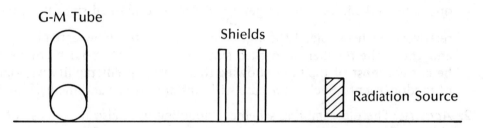

Data are recorded to plot a graph of radiation reaching the counter as a function of thickness of various shielding materials. Choose materials such as cardboard, aluminum, sheet metal, glass, or lead. If all the shield samples are cut from stock of the same thickness, data are kept in terms of "number of shields"; if not, individual thicknesses are measured with calipers.

Results are often described in "half thicknesses" of various materials; that is, the thickness required to reduce the radiation to one half its original value.

Topic II: Nuclear Equations

1. *Teacher Presentation.* Reproduction Page 59 summarizes data on several commonly emitted forms of radiation. Use it as a basis for a lecture on nuclear equations. Emphasize the balancing of charge and mass (to the nearest whole number). Be sure to include alpha and beta decay in your presentation. Nuclear bombardment equations also are appropriate here. Choose examples from references at the end of this chapter.

2. *Activity.* Use Reproduction Page 60 as practice, homework, or evaluation of student work with nuclear equations. A periodic table is needed in conjunction with this assignment.

Topic III: Half-Life and Radioactive Dating

1. *Teacher Presentation.* Introduce the statistical nature of measurements of radioactive decay. Obtain some dice (either conventional ones or twenty- or eight-sided dice

available from most supply houses). Take one die and let it represent an unstable nucleus. Explain that it could decay instantly or a million years could go by and it might still be in its original condition. There is no way to predict when any one unstable atom will decay. It is a *random* event.

Now mark one side of the die. The marked side will represent the decay of this atom when it comes "up" on a roll. Time is measured in rolls. Record the roll number on which the marked side comes up. After several recordings, ask the class to predict the next roll number on which the marked side will come up. This prediction cannot be made with certainty—another indication that the event is random.

You now can show that large numbers of random events often are predictable: Take 160 (or a similarly large number) of the dice you are using, each one having markings like the single die used earlier. Predict the number of marked sides which will come up through probability. For example, if twenty-sided dice are used, with one side marked, you should get $\frac{1}{20} \times 160 = 8$ marked sides up. (Because of the relatively small sample, ±2 is a good error estimate.) Now actually roll all 160 dice and count the number of marked sides that come up. Your prediction, 6–10, will be correct most of the time, showing that there is predictability with large numbers of random events. Such is the case with unstable atoms and the half-life concept.

2. *Activity.* The old gambling scheme, "doubling up," also makes use of the predictability of large numbers of random events. If a coin is flipped 100 times, odds are it will come up heads 50 times and tails the other 50 times. The object is to be wagering more on the times it comes up heads than when it comes up tails.

Have pairs of students keep a record of imaginary wagers, wins, and losses over 100 tosses of the coin. The wagerer starts with $1.00. If the player wins, he keeps the bet at $1.00; if he loses, he doubles his bet and continues doubling until he wins; then the bet is reduced to $1.00 again, and the process is repeated.

Reproduction Page 61 is a tally sheet. Use it to combine results from the entire class. The coin should come up "heads" about half of the time, and all groups should show a profit. Be sure to instruct pupils to continue the process if the one hundredth toss is a "loss." In this case, play is extended until the next "win."

3. *Laboratory.* The arrival of cosmic radiation at a Geiger-Müller tube is a random event. Have each student take counts for, say, 15–30 seconds, and plot each result on a frequency versus counts/time graph. If each pupil does several repeats, a bell-shaped curve will result from the class composite. The highest frequency is the most probable reading. Compare this value to one obtained by counting for a long time and then dividing the "total counts" by the time.

4. *Laboratory.* Dice radioactivity analog. Use dice as in Teacher Presentation #1 in this section to model radioactive decay. Students record the number of "unstable" dice remaining versus time in "throw number." Each time a marked side comes up, that die is replaced with some other object that represents a stable atom (commercial kits include balls for this function). This does not affect results but it helps the student understand that the radioactive substance does not "disappear" as it decays. Half-life, the time required for half of the original sample to change, is found from a graph of the data. Students may plot either "number unstable left" versus "time in throws" or log N versus time, where N is the number left.

If commercial dice analog kits are not available, a large number of coins will substitute, although a relatively short half-life results. A cigar box with a mark on the bottom is another way to generate data. Objects such as washers or coins are placed in the box; then the box is shaken, placed on a table, and opened. Any coin touching the mark is removed and replaced with a "stable" representative.

5. *Laboratory.* Radioactive dating analog. Arrange whatever model was used in Laboratory #4 in some stage of decay before lab time. The student must analyze the stage of decay (count the number of unstable atoms remaining), go to the previously determined decay curve, and, from the curve, determine the time (age) required for the sample to have reached that condition. Students may verify their results by repeating the earlier experiment to see if their "ages" are reasonable.

6. *Activity.* Student research and reports on radioactive dating using carbon-14 and uranium would be appropriate at this point.

7. *Laboratory.* If commercial dice are available, more advanced students may wish to repeat Laboratory #5. However, replace the original unstable die with a second unstable "daughter," rather than a stable form. Instructions for this procedure are included in the kits.

8. *Laboratory.* Half-life of a short-lived isotope. Commercially available "mini-generators" are excellent sources of short-lived isotopes for lab work. In one such kit, Barium 137-m is provided by a long half-lived parent. Barium 137-m decays to stable Barium 137 with a half-life of about 2.6 minutes through the emission of a gamma ray. Students can calculate this half life by measuring the activity (in counts/min. or counts/30 sec.) versus time and graphing.

9. *Laboratory.* The discharging of a capacitor through a resistor will produce a curve similar to the decay curves of radioisotopes if one plots voltage versus time. Circuits for this experiment are listed in the references at the end of the chapter.

Topic IV: Fission and Fusion

1. *Teacher Presentation.* Use Reproduction Page 62 to illustrate the fission of uranium. Several points should be emphasized:
   a. The mass of the products is less than the reactants. The difference in mass has been converted into energy according to Einstein's equation, $E = mc^2$. Reproduction Page 63 sets up this calculation. Have your students complete it.
   b. The product nuclei shown represent two of the most common fission fragments. Actually, a great variety of products is produced, each product having *roughly* half of the mass of the U-235 nucleus.
   c. The product nuclei fly apart with very high velocities and they are usually unstable. Most of the energy released is manifested as heat.
   d. Often additional neutrons are freed during this process. These neutrons can impinge on other U-235 nuclei, making a chain reaction possible.

2. *Activity.* Have students make and demonstrate several models of a chain reaction. Dominoes will illustrate both a continuing and an increasing chain reaction. Wooden match heads also will serve as a model. Mouse traps in a box covered with a trans-

parent lid make an especially dramatic model. Corks, rubber stoppers, or ping pong balls represent the neutrons. Each trap has two "neutrons" on it which are released when the trap is triggered. In this model, the trap springs, critical size, effect of the box cover, and control of the reaction are all aspects that you can relate to an operating nuclear reactor.

3. *Activity.* Have your class help you to illustrate critical mass. On a fairly large expanse of blackboard, represent some U-235 nuclei with small circles about 2 cm. in diameter and 10 cm. apart. Now walk by this area making a chalk line on the board without looking at the circles. Have the class indicate when you contact a target nucleus. During the first few trials, either no contact will occur or, if it does, two lines representing released neutrons will probably not encounter another circle. Gradually, add more circles to the board space (if this is to be a good model, you can add more circles but they cannot be closer together). Eventually, you will have enough circles on the board so that contact is virtually guaranteed and released neutrons also have a great likelihood of making contact—the concept of critical mass.

4. *Activity.* Use Reproduction Page 64 in a discussion of nuclear reactors and the production of electrical energy. You can elaborate on each of the components or assign research projects to different groups in the class who will discuss specific functions and components of a reactor. In this case, Reproduction Page 64 will tie the individual reports together.

5. *Demonstration.* Show the need for using substances such as hydrogen, deuterium, and carbon as moderators of neutrons in reactors. The neutron will lose the greatest portion of its energy when it collides with a particle of nearly its own mass. Show this with collisions of various massed discs on an air table or other smooth surface. Collisions between steel balls suspended by string also will demonstrate the moderator material choice.

6. *Activity.* Your local electrical utility may provide you with a speaker, program, and/or materials on nuclear reactors and electricity. Be sure to check this local resource.

7. *Activity.* Nuclear energy is a controversial topic. Have students contribute material to make up two bulletin boards, one pro and the other against nuclear power plants. Instead of a bulletin board, your pupils may wish to have a debate as a way of concluding research into the controversy.

8. *Activity.* Use Reproduction Page 65 to elaborate on breeder reactors—another controversial aspect of nuclear energy.

9. *Activity.* Reproduction Page 66 is a summary of various fusion processes. In discussing this process, you should touch on the following points:
   a. Fusion requires special conditions of extremely high temperatures.
   b. Energy released from this process is due to mass conversion, like fission, and the amount is predicted by $E = mc^2$.
   c. Two main research approaches to developing large scale, controlled fusion involve using magnetic bottles and lasers to produce the conditions needed.

d. If fusion is developed, it will provide abundant energy from low cost fuel and no pollution. (Note the reactants and products.)

10. *Activity*. Have pupils write a story about the effects of cheap energy via fusion on world economy, politics, and/or cultures.

11. *Activity*. Some pupils may wish to investigate the possibility of a "fusion torch" recycling device.

12. *Activity*. This chapter provides an especially varied and long list of topics suitable for a research project. Some of these topics are listed below. Many are large enough for group work, while others are appropriate for individuals:
    a. The Manhattan Project
    b. Enrico Fermi
    c. The decision to bomb Japan
    d. Effects of radiation from atomic bombs
    e. Uses of atomic energy
    f. Plowshare
    g. Nuclear energy for desalting
    h. The Atomic Energy Commission
    i. Oppenheimer
    j. I. I. Rabi
    k. Nuclear rocket engines
    l. Disposal techniques for radioactive wastes
    m. Madame and Pierre Curie
    n. Röntgen

13. *Activity*. Have students calculate the energy released in beta decay, alpha decay, fission, and fusion processes using a method similar to the one outlined in Reproduction Page 63. Once the calculations are made, compare the energy released from *equal amounts of fuel* for each process.

ASSESSING ACHIEVEMENT OF OBJECTIVES

Ongoing Evaluation

The extent to which students have mastered the concepts covered in this chapter should be measured with quizzes inserted at appropriate points in the instruction. Various research projects submitted by pupils as well as class presentations can be graded.

Final Evaluation

Construct an essay or short answer unit test directly from the objectives stated at the beginning of this chapter. Reproduction Page 67 provides some questions which may be useful for such a final evaluation.

Resources for Teaching Nuclear Energy

Below is a selected list of resources useful for teaching concepts in nuclear energy. The list is divided into audio-visual materials and print. If a source is especially useful for teachers only or students only, this is noted with the citation. Addresses of publishers can be found in the alphabetical list at the end of this book.

Audio-Visual Materials

Long Time Intervals. Film. P.S.S.C. Emphasizes the use of radioactive decay of uranium to measure time.

Marie Curie—A Love Story. Film. Chatsworth Film Productions. The story of the life and work of the Curies, including their discovery of polonium and radium. Available from Syracuse University Film Rental Center.

The Mass of Atoms. Film. P.S.S.C. Shows various laboratory techniques and precautions necessary for taking measurements of a sample of polonium.

Nuclear Radiation: Fallout. Film. John Colburn Associates. Discusses fallout and how it affects living matter. Explains what is being done to solve problems associated with nuclear radiation.

The Atom: A Closer Look. Four filmstrips and sound cassettes. Walt Disney Educational Media Company, 1981. Discusses the structure of the atom and the atomic energy controversy. Radioactivity and its detection are also described. A good general introduction to the atom and its parts; also a review of the basic structure and function of nuclear power plants.

Random Events. Film. P.S.S.C. Uses several demonstrations to show that large numbers of random events are predictable. Relates this to the predictable nature of radioactive decay.

Nuclear Energy. Sound filmstrip. C. Clark Co. Examines nuclear power from a factual and objective point of view. Discusses the history and future of nuclear energy.

The Mighty Atom. Film. McGraw-Hill. Presents nuclear energy as a source of power. Discusses uses in food preservation, cancer treatment, and research.

U-238 Radioactive Series. Film. McGraw-Hill. Traces the decay of U-238 into lead. Alpha and beta emission and the statistical nature of the process are emphasized.

Atom in the Hospital. Film. Handel. Shows research, diagnosis, and treatment in hospital settings using nuclear science.

Atom Underground. Film. Handel. Shows an application of atomic explosions for vast underground engineering jobs.

Scintillation Spectrometry. Filmloop. Ealing Corp. Shows the assembly of the device and the gamma ray spectrum of Mn 56, photopeak, Compton edge, and backscatter.

Chain Reaction—Controlled Chain Reaction. Filmloop. Encyclopedia Britannica Corporation. Two sections use animated diagrams to show various stages of a chain reaction and a controlled chain reaction around a U-235 nucleus cluster.

Radioactive Decay. Filmloop. Ealing Corp. Gamma rays from Cu 64 and Mn 56 are collected and displayed with a scintillation counter. Half-lives are determined and compared.

Print

Elementary Modern Physics by R. T. Weidner and R. L. Sells. Allyn and Bacon, 1980. Chapter 11 on nuclear reactions and radiation detectors is good teacher background reading.

"The Cosmic Background Radiation and the New Aether Drift" by R. A. Muller. *Scientific American* (May 1978). Observation of the cosmic radiation left over from the "big bang" shows that our galaxy is moving at high speed.

"Fusion Power with Particle Beams" by G. Yonas. *Scientific American* (November 1978). One approach to fusion power by bombarding a pellet of fuel with beams of electrons or ions from high voltage electric pulses.

The New Age in Physics by H. Massey. Harper and Row, 1960. Chapters 7 and 8 are devoted to nuclear physics.

"Nuclear Fission" by R. B. Leachman. *Scientific American* (August 1965). An important aspect of nuclear research.

Restless Atom by A. Romer. Doubleday Anchor, 1960. A historical account of nuclear physics.

"Semiconductor Particle Detectors" by O. M. Bilaniuk. *Scientific American* (October 1962). A new technique of great importance to nuclear physics.

Physics as a Liberal Art by J. S. Trefil. Pergamon, 1978. Chapter 14 has some good material on nuclear reactors and the safety-energy question.

Nuclear Science and Society by B. L. Cohen. Anchor Doubleday, 1974. Discusses uses of nuclear energy, atomic structure, and the reactor controversy.

The End of Affluence by P. R. Ehrlich. Ballantine Books, 1974. Presents the environmentalist point of view on nuclear reactors.

Nuclear Energy: Its Physics and Social Challenge by D. R. Inglis. Addison-Wesley, 1973. A detailed description of the nuclear reactor and the physics of its operation.

"Current Physics Research" by P. E. Schewe. *The Physics Teacher* (September 1980). This article summarizes high energy particle accelerators and fusion reactors as well as several other current developments.

"How Old Is It" by R. Gannon. *Popular Science* (November 1979). A good overview of radiodating methods, useful dating ranges, and the types of material suited for the various processes.

Nuclear Power Without Tears by F. Hoyle and G. Hoyle. W. H. Freeman, 1980. A brief work presenting the case for nuclear energy. Makes good introductory reading and may lead to further investigations.

"Fast Neutron Radio Therapy" by P. H. McGinley. *The Physics Teacher* (February 1973). Good teacher reading in this review of the work done to establish the clinical value of fast neutron beams.

Geigy Scientific Tables by C. Lentner, editor. Medical Education Division, Ciba-Geigy Corporation, 1981. Provide information about measuring the physiological effects of radiation on humans. See the section on radioactivity and radiation dosimetry.

"New A-Bomb Studies Alter Radiation Estimates" by Eliot Marshall. *Science* (May 1981). The physiological effects of radiation and new analysis of data from Hiroshima are the topics in this article.

Common Sense in Nuclear Energy by Fred Hoyle and Geoffrey Hoyle. W. H. Freeman, 1980. An excellent introductory book for readers open to an unapologetic overview of the case for nuclear energy.

How Safe is Nuclear Energy? by Sir Alan Cotrell. Heinemann, 1981. In the highly emotional atmosphere generated by fears of nuclear weapons and radiation, the intelligent general reader can obtain authorative and balanced answers to many questions about safety and dangers of nuclear energy from this book.

"Reflections (Nuclear Arms)" by Jonathan Schell. *New Yorker* (February 1982). Summarizes the physics of fission and fusion and describes nuclear weapons and detonation. Environmental effects, moral, philosophical, political, and social consequences are discussed.

"Cosmic-Ray Record in Solar System Matter" by R. C. Reedy and J. R. Arnold. *Science* (January 1963). Expands on man-made radiation detectors by discussing the observation of cosmic rays with detectors nature has provided—the moon, meteorites, and the earth. Good teacher reading if you want to expand your presentation of radiation detectors.

Nuclear Energy, Nuclear Weapons Proliferation, and the Arms Race edited by Jack Hollander. American Association of Physics Teachers, 1982. A brief but authoritative introduction to many of the main arguments in nuclear energy and nuclear weapons debates, this booklet can be useful to a wide range of readers, from high school students to teachers.

The Physicists by C. P. Snow. Little, Brown, 1981. Mainly a presentation of the first half-century of particle physics, starting with J. J. Thomson and the electron, and continuing through arguments on the H-bomb. An appendix presents a plea for scientists to involve themselves in extending the benefits of science and curtailing the dangers. Good teacher reading. Some students may be interested in portions of this work.

"Catastrophic Releases of Radioactivity" by S. A. Fetter and K. Tsipis. *Scientific American* (April 1981). Compares radioactivity released from the detonation of a thermonuclear weapon, a core melt down, a reactor containment vessel bursting, and a thermonuclear warhead exploding. Both teachers and students will find these comparisons informative.

9

Waves

INTRODUCTION

There are various ways in which energy is transferred. Gross movement of materials, heat going from higher to lower temperature regions, or electricity moving through a conductor are examples of such transfers. Wave motion is also an energy transfer process. Sounds are heard due to disturbances traveling from the source to our ears. Wave theory deals adequately with some properties of light. In fact, radio waves, light, untraviolet and infra red waves, X-rays, and gamma radiation are all fundamentally similar—they are all electromagnetic waves. Quantum theory descriptions of the universe use wave properties applied to matter, a very unusual way of looking at the physical world compared to classical views. Perhaps we will find that such things as gravity, E.S.P., and other psychic phenomena produce their effects through waves. Future discoveries may provide such knowledge. Current descriptions of the universe using the wave concept will provide students with insights into many phenomena they experience regularly.

CONTENT OVERVIEW

The basic concept of a wave involves some quantity or disturbance (energy) that changes regularly in magnitude with respect to time at some location and also changes regularly in magnitude from place to place. The standard illustration involves pebbles on the surface of a pond creating regular wave patterns. Reproduce this in class to be sure that all pupils have the idea clearly in mind at the beginning of this study.

The order of presentation in this chapter is as follows:

1. Wave descriptors
2. Types of waves

3. Properties
   a. Reflection
   b. Refraction
   c. Diffraction
   d. Interference
4. A quantum view of light

These topics are presented in most textbooks. The order, of course, is not dictated by this presentation—pick the topics you wish to use and present them in the order chosen for your course. In most instances, one topic is not pre-requisite to another. The general approach has been to go from concrete to more abstract and from familiar to unfamiliar.

OBJECTIVES

As a result of the learning experiences in this chapter, students should be able to:

1. Identify wave characteristics such as amplitude, period, frequency, wavelength, and phase.
2. Use the relationship $v = f\lambda$ in problem solving.
3. Apply the law of reflection to predict wave paths and optical effects.
4. Discuss refraction in terms of speed change and make predictions using the law of refraction and Snell's law.
5. Describe diffraction and conditions necessary to produce it.
6. Discuss interference of waves in terms of the superposition principle.
7. Relate sound phenomena to the waves underlying them.
8. Relate the Doppler effect to motion.
9. Explain the photoelectric effect as it relates to light and the quantum theory.

LEARNING EXPERIENCES

Topic I: Characteristics of Waves

1. *Demonstration.* Since most waves and their descriptors cannot be seen, it is helpful to use a model to make wave characteristics visible. A slinky stretched across the classroom floor, suspended from the ceiling, or on a long table top will serve to demonstrate several wave characteristics for your class.

   Show that energy is transferred, but not mass, by sending a couple of pulses down the spring. If you mark one coil with some paper or string, students will see that the disturbance moves across the room but the paper moves only a very small amount.

Show that the velocity of a pulse depends on the medium by sending two pulses along the slinky—the first with a lot of tension in the coils and the second (slower) with less tension in the spring. Relate this to the speed of sound waves and the *elasticity* of the medium (not the density as many people think).

Pulses of different amplitudes should be related to the energy of the source (your hand and the work it does on the slinky).

Time related characteristics, frequency, and period will require a series of pulses. Combine the frequency demonstration with examples of wavelengths and show the inverse relationship between them. Relate this to the wave equation: $v = f\lambda$.

Phase and interference phenomena also will show in the model.

2. *Activity.* Use Reproduction Page 68 in conjunction with the preceding demonstration or as an assignment.

3. *Activity.* Reproduction Page 69 is a summary of characteristics of longitudinal and transverse waves. Use it in conjunction with the slinky demonstration or as a review sheet.

4. *Demonstration.* Many of the characteristics of waves visible with a slinky demonstration also can be viewed when demonstrated with a ripple tank. Mount the tank on an overhead projector and display the various effects on a screen for the entire class to see. Of course, some care is required for balance and to avoid spills. The light effects produced by a ripple tank are themselves applications of refraction of light waves (discussed later in this chapter).

5. *Laboratory.* Use a slinky to verify the wave equation, $v = f\lambda$. Stretch the device out on the floor, measure v, the speed of a pulse, by timing it over a measured distance (the length of the spring). Adjust the frequency to produce standing waves in the slinky. For a half wave, λ, the wavelength equals two times the length; for a full wave, λ equals the length. In each case, frequencies are measured by counting waves generated and the time required to produce them. Use Reproduction Page 70 with this lab.

6. *Activity.* Students can measure the speed of sound waves in air by timing how long it takes a sound to travel a fixed distance such as the length of an athletic field. After the distance is measured, a hammer striking a metal bar produces the sound. Students start their stopwatches by observing when the hammer strikes and stop them when the sound is heard. Correction for reaction time in stopping is needed. Larger distances are available if pupils use sound that is reflected from a surface such as a building.

7. *Activity.* Pupils can plot the course of a thunderstorm or determine its distance from them by timing how long it takes for the thunder to sound after a lightning flash. Sound travels through air at a rate of approximately one mile every 5 seconds.

8. *Activity.* Play the Bell Telephone record, "The Science of Sound," but tap off the external speaker connections of the phonograph and connect to the vertical input of an oscilloscope. With proper adjustment of sweep and gain, students will see

transverse representations of the sounds they hear. Relationships between loudness and amplitude, pitch and wavelength (frequency), and pure tones versus overtones should be pointed out.

The record, listed in the references, presents several topics normally covered in student texts on the science of sound (acoustics).

Topic II: Reflection

1. *Activity.* Mount a piece of mirror on the front demonstration table so that members of the class can see each other in the mirror. Ask pupils to identify who they see in the mirror. Ask students to record the name of the people involved and their location in the room on Reproduction Page 71.

    Pupils should represent the rays of light as leaving from the "seen" person, going to the mirror, and then leaving the mirror and traveling to the person who did the seeing. After several pairs of paths are drawn, draw in normal lines and show that, for each reflection, $\angle I = \angle R$.

2. *Demonstration.* Virtual image in a plane mirror. Mount a sheet of glass (or remove a glass panel from a cabinet) in front of the class as shown. Prior to the class meeting, arrange two candles or two light bulbs—one in front of the glass (on the class

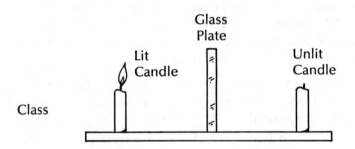

side) and the second in the location of the mirror image of the first. Ask if pupils can see both objects. Next light the front candle or bulb; the back candle or bulb also will appear lit since it is aligned with the virtual image of the first. Later move the rear object to show that there is only one position where the trick will work— the location of the virtual image when the glass acts like a plane mirror.

3. *Laboratory.* Use Reproduction Pages 72 and 73 for some laboratory work on formation of images by plane mirrors through an application of rays, wave fronts, and the law of reflection. These instructions will let each student proceed at his own rate and leave you free to give additional help and explanations as needed.

4. *Demonstration.* Show reflection of water waves in a ripple tank, first from a plane barrier and then from curved reflecting surfaces.

5. *Activity.* Ask students how large a mirror is required for a person to see the entire length of her body in it. If some debate results, there are several ways to lend insight into this standard textbook question. Pass our small mirrors and ask pupils to adjust them so that the top of their (image) head just touches the top of the

mirror. Students then note how far down on their bodies they can see. Moving the mirror farther away and readjusting will produce no change in the portion of a student's body which is visible in the mirror.

A second procedure is to bring in a full length mirror and cover the bottom half as pupils observe their images. No change in the observed image will result.

6. *Activity.* Investigate spherical reflecting surfaces and images through ray diagrams. Project some individual rays onto spherical or parabolic reflecting surfaces to show the reflection of individual rays used in the ray diagrams.

7. *Activity.* Some students may wish to apply the information obtained from curved mirror images to fun house mirrors. They should be able to describe how a short, fat image and a long, thin image are produced.

8. *Demonstration.* Use parabolic mirrors to show their effect on sound waves. After aligning two such devices, have one pupil speak softly at the focus of one parabola. If the mirrors are large enough and aligned properly, a second student with her ear at the focus of the second parabolic reflector will hear the words clearly across the room.

A similar demonstration using an iron will cause a significant increase in the temperature of a thermometer located at the focus of the second mirror, thus showing reflection of infra red radiation.

9. *Activity.* Student research and reports on radio astronomy and the role played by reflection would be appropriate here. Other groups may investigate radar, sonar, navigation by bats, and reflection of radio waves by the ionosphere.

10. *Demonstration.* Students will see multiple reflections in the following arrangements:
    a.

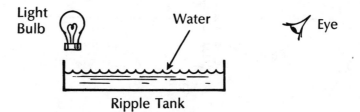

Ripple Tank

   b. Mount two mirrors vertically with edges touching. As the angle between these mirrors is varied, multiple reflections of an object placed between them are seen.

11. *Evaluation Activity.* Use Reproduction Page 74 as a short quiz on reflection of waves.

Topic III: Refraction

1. *Activity.* After explaining the theory of refraction with blackboard and textbook aids, try the following exercise as a way to clarify why the direction of a wave front changes when it encounters a boundary between two different optically dense media: Make a line on the floor to represent the media boundary. Let four

or five students represent portions of a wave front by wrapping their arms over each other's shoulders. The rule is to walk at normal speed on one side of the line but walk heel to toe once on the other side. With two such groups (wave fronts) encountering the boundary along a normal line, shortening of the wavelength (distance between groups) is demonstrated. When an oblique angle of incidence is used, bending toward the normal occurs. Reversing the direction of travel produces bending away from the normal.

2. *Laboratory.* Students can trace rays of light through a glass plate by aligning two pins in the ray. The laws of refraction will be demonstrated as well as the necessity for an oblique angle. If the definition of index of refraction as a speed ratio is combined with Snell's law and some measured angles, the students will be able to calculate the speed of light in the glass. Specific instructions for this lab are available in several of the references at the end of this chapter.

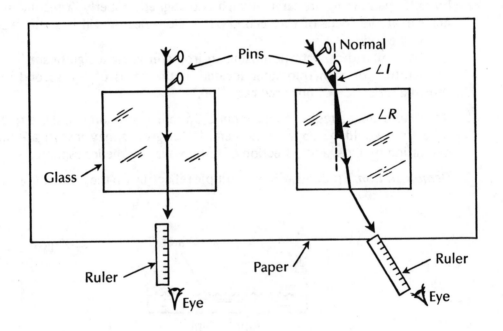

3. *Laboratory.* Indicies of refraction of liquids may be determined by using a semicircular, clear plastic container.

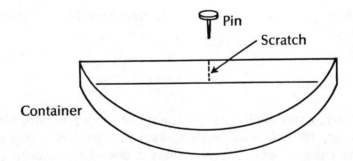

Students sight through the curved side of the container and line up the scratch mark with the pin. When the container is removed, the sight lines and normals are drawn, angles are measured, and the index of refraction is calculated using Snell's law. Several liquids are used as long as they are transparent and do not dissolve the plastic.

4. *Demonstrations.* Show total internal reflection by using a semi-circular piece of glass and an optical disk. Stress the necessity of exceeding the critical angle in order for this phenomenon to occur. Other demonstrations of total internal reflection:

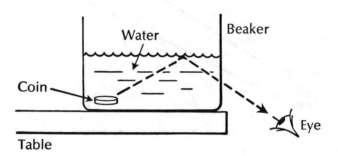

a. The coin can be seen through total internal reflection.
b. A beam of light will follow a stream of water emerging from an opening of a can, if the light beam is directed into the can.
c. Use a light pipe or some plastic light fibers to show the application of total internal reflection.

5. *Teacher Presentation.* Instruct your students in the construction of ray diagrams to predict the nature and location of images formed with lenses. It is better that pupils learn a method for such diagrams rather than memorizing each of several drawings. Use the optical disk to show that two rays are always affected by a lens in the same way—any ray parallel to the principal axis goes through the focal point after exiting the lens, while a ray through the center of the lens is not bent at all.

6. *Laboratory.* Students can use Reproduction Page 75 as a guide for constructing several ray diagrams and then duplicating these diagrams in a laboratory setting with actual lenses. The data sheet (Reproduction Page 76) essentially parallels the ray diagrams. Once pupils know the focal length of their lens, each of the distances is converted from multiples of F to an actual number of centimeters. Students can then proceed to verify the ray diagram predictions.

   Formulas relating object, image, and focal length distances and sizes also are verified through measurements in this lab.

7. *Activity.* Students can use a convex lens as a burning glass to cause some paper to smolder.

8. *Activity.* Invite a local optometrist or ophthamologist as a guest speaker on refraction, the human eye, and corrective lenses.

9. *Activity.* Students can study and set up working models of a telescope, a microscope, a movie projector, and so forth.

10. *Demonstration.* Show dispersion of white light with a prism. Discuss this phenomenon as an example of variable refraction.

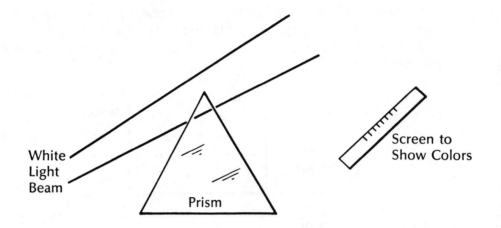

11. *Activity.* Students may want to research and demonstrate the production of rainbows at this point in the study. Chromatic aberration in lenses is another topic that would be appropriate at this time.

12. *Demonstration.* Show that refraction of water waves in a ripple tank occurs when the speed changes due to changing depth.

13. *Activity.* Use Reproduction Page 77 as an assignment for small groups, homework, basis for discussion, or evaluation device. Several refraction phenomena are presented for explanation.

14. *Evaluation Activity.* Reproduction Page 78 is a short quiz on concepts related to the study of refraction of waves.

Topic IV: Diffraction and Interference

1. *Demonstration.* Show and define diffraction of waves using a ripple tank with a barrier placed in it. The pattern will look like this:

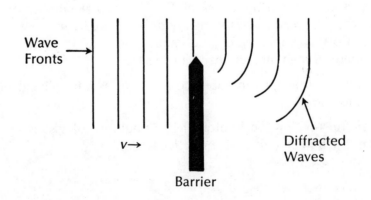

2. *Demonstration.* Project a laser beam onto a screen for class viewing. Slowly bring the sharp edge of a razor blade into the beam near the laser. The edge will cause the spot on the screen to spread as a result of diffraction (similar to the ripple tank). Insert the razor from several different angles and note the effect on the spot. Now with the razor blade in position, bring in a second blade from the opposite side of the beam. Alternate bands of light–dark fringes will appear on the screen. Show that this is an interference phenomenon by first removing one blade and then the other (one at a time). The pattern will go back to the diffraction spread, since interference is only observed when both blades are used to diffract the beam.

3. *Laboratory.* Use Reproduction Page 79 to outline the theory behind Young's double slit experiment. When students feel comfortable with the theory, they can use it to make measurements and calculate the wavelengths of light. Details of the experiment are outlined in several of the resources at the end of this chapter. The apparatus is arranged as follows:

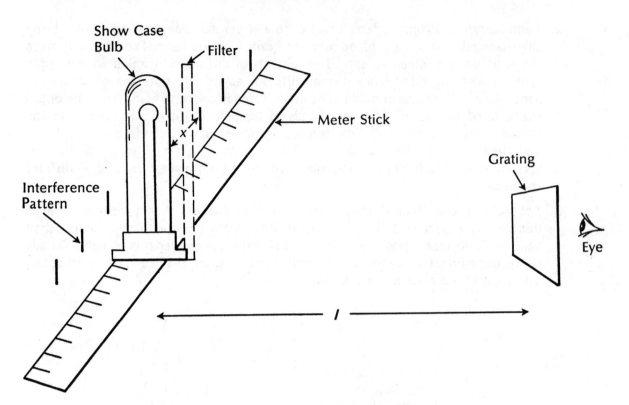

4. *Activity.* Newton's Rings. Students can observe interference of light waves through the following arrangements:

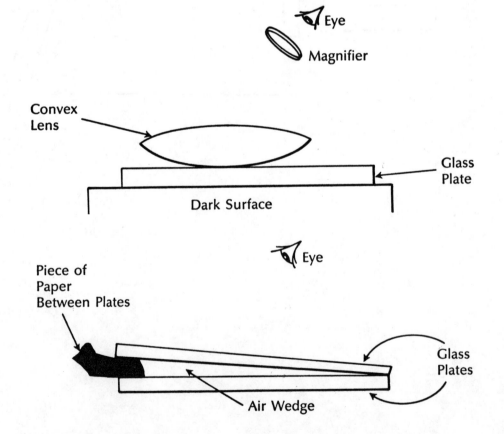

Both set ups require monochromatic light to produce alternate light and dark fringes.

5. *Demonstration.* Use a ripple tank to show interference patterns with water waves. Use either a double slit arrangement or two wave sources in phase—the latter produces a more visible effect. You can show the effects of changing some of the variables in the Young's double slit experiment by varying the wavelength and then the slit spacing. Have pupils record the effects on the interference pattern in each case.

6. *Activity.* Interference of sound waves/beats. Two similar tuning forks can be made to produce slightly different frequencies by "weighting" one of them. This decreases one of the frequencies, and when both are sounded at the same time, alternate loud and soft sound results. This is called beats. It is due to alternate constructive and destructive interference. The beat frequency is equal to the difference between the two tuning fork frequencies. This is used by musicians as a very accurate way to tune stringed instruments.

7. *Demonstration.* Make a model to help pupils understand what is happening in Activity #6 above:

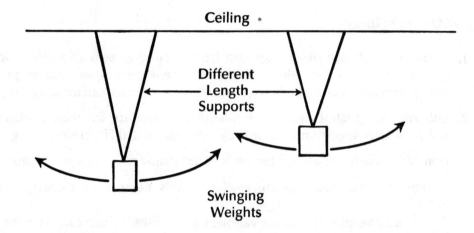

If both weights are started swinging in phase (together), they will alternatively go in first the same direction (constructive interference) and later in opposite directions (destructive interference). Then the weights will go back in phase again, over and over. If you choose to make frequency measurements on this model, you can show that the "beat frequency" equals the difference in the individual frequencies of the swinging weights. This is analogous to the tuning fork pattern.

8. *Activity.* Color by interference. If white light from a showcase bulb passes through a diffraction grating, color patterns will result due to interference of various wavelengths. Pupils can figure out how this happens if you aid them by placing red and blue filters on the top and bottom portion of the bulb. The filters enable students to see the separate red, blue, and multicolored patterns at the same time for comparison and analysis.

9. *Activity.* There are several other convenient ways for students to see colors and interference patterns.
   a. The colors in a soap film are formed the same way as those from gasoline or oil

spilled on water; that is, by the interference of light reflected from the two surfaces. If a soap film is held in a vertical orientation, a wedge-shaped layer forms due to water draining downward. Horizontal fringes are seen when white light from a large white surface is reflected by the film.

b. Many supply houses have a wedge filter that produces colors by interference of reflected and transmitted light.

c. The grooves in an L-P phonograph record will produce several orders of spectra if pupils view reflected light from a showcase bulb. The filament and grooves should be in the same line.

d. Two razor slits in a piece of cardboard will produce interference patterns.

e. If pupils squint at a monochromatic light source, an interference pattern due to the students' eyelashes will result.

10. *Demonstration.* Various beautiful interference patterns are the result of passing light from a laser through irregular pieces of glass and projecting the pattern on the wall or screen. Glass bowl covers and crystal work well. Slight movements of the glass will produce corresponding changes in the displayed pattern.

Topic V: Quantum Ideas

1. *Activity.* Pupils can observe spectra from excited gases with a diffraction grating in a dark room. They should note that different gases when excited produce bright line spectra characteristic of each element. These spectra can identify the gas involved.

2. *Laboratory.* Spectral Analysis. Students can calculate the wavelengths of several of the hydrogen spectrum lines through the use of a diffraction grating and the relationship used in an earlier lab on wavelength, $\lambda = \frac{xd}{l}$ (Reproduction Page 79). If commercial spectroscopes are available, λ is determined directly from the scale in °A.

   Once the student has the various wavelengths, he can calculate the energy level transitions for the excited hydrogen atom by using $E = hf = \frac{hc}{\lambda}$. h is Planck's constant (6.6 × 10^{-34} joule − s); c is the speed of light in a vacuum $\left(3 \times 10^8 \frac{m}{s}\right)$.

   The energy of the emitted photon is the difference in energy between the initial and final Bohr energy levels for hydrogen. Pupils can now draw an energy level diagram.

3. *Teacher Presentation.* A good way to introduce the photoelectric effect is to set up a relay connected to a photocell so that a light or counter operates each time the light beam to the cell is broken, either by students as they enter the room or by the teacher during a lecture.

   Analysis of such an "electric eye" set up should start with the idea that electrons are emitted from certain materials when light is incident. The nature of this emission has important implications for the nature of light.

   Use Reproduction Page 80 to summarize the photoelectric effect and its implications for a particle theory of light.

4. *Laboratory.* Several of the references cited at the end of this chapter provide details for a student laboratory on the photoelectric effect. In this experiment, pupils should gather data to show that current in the tube depends on intensity of the incident light. Through the use of filters, pupils can gather data on the "stopping potential" (kinetic energy of the photoelectrons) and frequency of incident light. If these data are plotted, a straight line will result, and the slope will be Planck's constant. The equation of this line is the photoelectric equation proposed by Einstein: E (photoelectron) $= hf - W$, where hf is the energy of a photon of frequency, f, and W is the work function of the photoelectric material.

5. *Activity.* Interested students might research the work of Einstein on the photoelectric effect and report to the class.

6. *Demonstration.* Use a thyratron 885 tube to demonstrate the Franck-Hertz effect. Specific directions are in the references at the end of this chapter. Essentially, the electron current will increase linearly with voltage until the electrons achieve the ionization energy of argon. As soon as the argon gas ionizes, current will increase dramatically. The point is that ionization takes place in any gas at a particular energy characteristic of that gas. This is a special case of Bohr's energy levels.

7. *Activity.* Use Reproduction Page 81 as the basis for a summary discussion on the properties of light and their implications for either a wave or particle model. Conclude with a quantum description using De Broglie's equation for "particle waves," $\lambda = \dfrac{h}{mv}$. This relationship is derived in Reproduction Page 82.

ASSESSING ACHIEVEMENT OF OBJECTIVES

Ongoing Evaluation

Use the several quizzes on Reproduction Pages at appropriate points to measure the extent to which students have mastered the various concepts in this chapter.

Final Evaluation

Construct a unit test directly from the list of objectives for this chapter. In addition, laboratory reports, research assignments, and responses to several Reproduction Pages provide material for inclusion in a final assessment.

Resources for Teaching Waves

Below is a selected list of resources useful for teaching wave concepts. The list is divided into audiovisual materials and print. If a source is especially useful for teachers only or students only, this is noted with the citation. Addresses of publishers can be found in the alphabetical list at the end of this book.

Audio-Visual Materials

Electromagnetic Waves. Film, P.S.S.C. Shows interference, polarization, and origin from accelerated charges for four different regions of the electromagnetic spectrum: X-ray, light, microwaves, and radio waves.

The Frank-Hertz Experiment. Film. P.S.S.C. Explains that the kinetic energy of a stream of electrons is transferred to atoms only in discrete packets of energy.

Interference of Photons. Film. P.S.S.C. Presents an experiment where light shows both particle and wave properties.

Introduction to Optics. Film. P.S.S.C. Starting with the idea that light travels in straight lines, this film shows bending by diffraction, scattering, refraction, and reflection.

Laser Light. Film. Scientific American. Describes the nature of light and how laser light is produced. Types of lasers and holography also are discussed.

Laser—The Light of the Future. Film. N.E.T., Indiana University. A working model of atoms shows how ordinary light and laser light are produced. Dr. Arthur Shawlow's part in working out the physics of the first laser is discussed.

Matter Waves. Film. P.S.S.C. Presents a modern version of the original experiment that showed the wave behavior of the electron. Electron diffraction patterns are shown.

The Nature of Color. Film. Coronet. Shows Newton's explanation of the rainbow. Reflection, absorption, and color mixing are discussed.

Photoelectric Effect. Film. P.S.S.C. Shows demonstrations of the photoelectric effect and an experiment to measure the kinetic energy of emitted photoelectrons.

Photons. Film. P.S.S.C. Uses photomultiplier tubes and an oscilloscope to show that light shows particle behavior.

Principles of X-Rays. Film. McGraw-Hill. Brief history of the X-ray. Shows experiments in the development of radiography and applications in research.

Progressive Waves: Transverse and Longitudinal. Film. McGraw-Hill. Demonstrates the two types of waves. Relates velocity, wave length, and frequency.

Simple Waves. Film. P.S.S.C. Shows elementary characteristics of waves by means of pulses in ropes and slinkys. Slow motion sequences help clarify wave properties.

Sound Waves and Stars: The Doppler Effect. Film. Film Associates. Discusses the Doppler effect as applied to a moving source. Applies the effect to light to discuss investigations about stars and the universe.

Sound Waves in Air. Film. Modern Learning Aides. Investigates sound transmission. Uses experiments in reflection, refraction, diffraction, and interference in a ripple tank to show characteristics.

The Speed of Light in Air and Water. Film. Modern Learning Aides. Several experimental techniques for speed measurement are shown using photocells, oscilloscopes, and high speed rotating mirrors.

Standing Waves and the Principle of Superposition. Film. E.B.E.C. Introduces, defines, and illustrates the superposition principle. Shows how standing waves are formed.

"The Concept that Shook Physics" Quantum Theory. Sound filmstrip. C. Clark Co. This program deals in detail with Max Planck and his work.

"The Science of Sound." Record. Folkway Records, 1960. Discusses acoustics in several parts: How we hear, frequency, pitch, intensity, Doppler effect, and more.

"Computer Speech" by D. H. Van Lenten. Record. Bell Telephone Laboratories, Inc., 1963. Contains samples of synthesized speech produced by programming a computer.

Interference. Filmloop. Encyclopedia Britannica. Demonstrates interference and shows the pattern produced by combining the waves from two similar generators.

The Photoelectric Effect. Filmloop. Encyclopedia Britannica. Uses charged electroscopes and ultraviolet light in four experiments illustrating the photoelectric effect.

Doppler Effect. Filmloop. Eye Gate. Scenes demonstrate the Doppler effect in a ripple tank.

Light and Electrons. Filmloop. Encyclopedia Britannica. Illustrates how light can expel electrons from a metal, control the flow of electrons, and give rise to a voltage.

Absorption Spectra. Filmloop. Ealing Corp. A spectrometer is used to show absorption patterns produced by sodium, hemoglobin, and didymium glass.

Superposition. Filmloop. Ealing Corp. Explains that the amplitudes and wavelengths of two waves add up algebraically as the waves are varied. Presents a display in three colors on the face of a cathode ray tube.

Vibrations of a Rubber Hose. Filmloop. Ealing Corp. A long vertical rubber hose is agitated at one end by a variable speed motor. The frequency is adjusted to show a succession of modal patterns.

Vibrations of a Wire. Filmloop. Ealing Corp. Modes of vibration.

Vibrations of a Drum. Filmloop. Ealing Corp. Modes of vibration.

Vibrations of a Metal Plate. Filmloop. Ealing Corp. Modes of vibration.

Standing Waves in a Gas. Filmloop. Ealing Corp. Nodes produced by a loudspeaker in a glass tube are made visible using cork dust and by the cooling of a hot wire inside the tube.

Standing Waves on a String. Filmloop. Ealing Corp. Uses animation to show how standing waves are produced by interference of oppositely moving equal waves.

A New Reality. Film. International Film Bureau. A treatment of quantum ideas in absorption and emission of energy by atoms.

Single Slit Diffraction. Filmloop. BFA Educational Media. This loop shows water waves which are diffracted. The waves are photographically slowed down and effects of changing several variables illustrated.

Interference of Waves. Filmloop. BFA Educational Media. Water waves illustrate interference patterns produced when plane waves pass through two slits. Effects of changing *d* and *r* are shown. Interference areas are marked on the film and thus easily observed.

Multiple Slit Diffraction. Filmloop. BFA Educational Media. Shows that the interference pattern from two slits is similar to the pattern for two point sources. Successive patterns using 2, 3, 4, and 8 slits are illustrated.

Holography. Transparencies. Lansford Publishing Company. This set is designed for use with groups having very little scientific background or with students who have a familiarity with optics.

Michelson Interferometer. Filmloop. Ealing Corp. Shows patterns produced when an interferometer is illuminated with a sodium arc. Fringes are related to other variables in the apparatus.

The Spectrum of the Hydrogen Atom. Filmloop. Encyclopedia Britannica. Shows how a line spectrum results from the transfer of discrete quantities of energy when an electron moves through energy levels.

Tacoma Narrows Bridge Collapse. Filmloop. Ealing Corp. Classic footage of the vibration of a bridge and its eventual collapse fits topics in this chapter.

Print

Elementary Modern Physics by R. Weidner and R. L. Sells. Allyn and Bacon, 1980. Chapters 4 and 5 on quantum effects and Chapter 6 on spectra. Chapter 9 on lasers and holography. This material is good teacher background or suitable for a more advanced student.

"Advances in Optical Lasers" by A. L. Schalow. *Scientific American* (July 1963). The theory of lasers and a discussion of the various types.

Electrons and Waves by J. P. Pierce. Doubleday Anchor, 1966. An excellent treatment of the applications of modern physics.

"The Luminescence of the Moon" by Z. Kopal. *Scientific American* (May, 1965). A study on moonlight shows that it is not all reflected light.

"The Michelson-Morley Experiment" by R. S. Shankland. *Scientific American* (November 1964). This article describes the Michelson interferometer and its relation to light and to relativity.

Michelson and the Speed of Light by B. Jaffe. Doubleday Anchor, 1960. An account of Michelson's work.

"Moiré Patterns" by Gerald Oster and Yasunori Nishiyima. *Scientific American* (May 1963). An effect similar to interference with experiments and observations that students can make.

"The Amazing Mirror Maze" by Walter Wick. *Games* (September/October 1981). Shows a maze in which the walls are floor to ceiling mirrors. This can make an interesting physics assignment because it requires an understanding of plane-mirror images.

"Resource Letter L-1, Lasers" by Donald O'Shea and Donald C. Peckham. *American Journal of Physics* (October 1981). An excellent source of information on lasers and applications. The listing includes articles, texts, demonstrations, and historical references.

Laser Age in Optics by L. V. Tarasov. Imported Publications, 1981. A good resource book for teachers. Topics include propagation, interference, superposition, polarization, Bohr theory, coherence, and holography. The explanations, examples, diagrams, and applications are worthwhile additions to class presentations.

"Demonstrating the Image in a Mirror" by Frank G. Karioris. *The Physics Teacher* (October 1982). A short article describing a way to measure the image distance in a plane mirror.

Quantum Electronics by J. P. Pierce. Doubleday Anchor, 1966. Another treatment of the applications of modern physics.

"Light-Emitting Semiconductors" by F. F. Morehead, Jr. *Scientific American* (May 1967). Discusses the possibilities of solid state lasers.

A Source Book in Physics by W. F. Magie. Harvard University Press, 1963. Huygen's principle; speed of light determinations by Römer, Bradley, Fizeau, and Foucault; interference and polarization selections from Grimaldi, Newton, Young, and Malus.

"Atmospheric Halos" by D. K. Lynch. *Scientific American* (April 1978). Explains some interesting optical effects in the atmosphere.

"The Bright Colors in a Soap Film Are a Lesson in Wave Interference" by Jearl Walker. *Scientific American* (September 1978). Excellent photographs and useful technical details.

"Experiments with Goggles" by I. Kohler. *Scientific American* (May 1962). Some modern experiments in human vision.

"Eye and Camera" by G. Wald. *Scientific American* (August 1950). A comparison of the two similar optical instruments.

"The Interaction of Light with Light" by J. A. Giordmaine. *Scientific American* (April 1964). New optical effects with intense beams of light from lasers.

"The Moon Illusion" by Lloyd Kaufman and Irvin Rock. *Scientific American* (July 1962). Experiments in vision including some that students can do.

The Nature of Light and Color in the Open by M. Minnaert. Dover Publications, 1954. Mirages and other out-of-doors optical effects.

"The Optics of Long Wavelength X-Rays" by E. Spiller and R. Feder. *Scientific American* (November 1978). Applications of soft X-rays in the laboratory and effects on technology.

"The Perception of Neutral Colors" by H. Wallach. *Scientific American* (January 1963). Experiments in human vision.

"Photography by Laser" by Emmett N. Leith and Juris Upatnieks. *Scientific American* (June 1965). Describes the new photographic process and its potential.

Scientific American. The September 1968 issue is devoted to light. Many of the aspects of light and effects on other areas of science are presented.

"Side Looking Airborne Radar" by H. Jensen et. al. *Scientific American* (October 1977). A discussion of "seeing" at wave lengths outside the visible range.

"Three-Pigment Color Vision" by E. F. MacNichol, Jr. *Scientific American* (December 1964). Experiments with human vision and cells on the retina.

Echoes of Bats and Men by D. Griffin. Doubleday Anchor, 1959. Applications of sound reflections in industry and nature.

Horns, Strings and Harmony by A. H. Benade. Doubleday Anchor, 1960. Basic wave theory as it applies to musical instruments.

Moments of Discovery. George Schwartz and Philip Bishop, editors. Basic Books, 1958. The original account of Huygen's work on his wave theory.

The Physics of Music by Carleen M. Hutchens. W. H. Freeman and Co., 1968. A collection of articles on various aspects of sound and music.

Sound Waves and Light Waves by W. E. Kock. Doubleday Anchor, 1965. An approach to the fundamentals of wave motion.

"Oscilloscope Measurement of the Velocity of Sound" by R. H. Johns. *The Physics Teacher* (December 1972). Description of an experimental determination of the speed of sound.

"The Longest Electromagnetic Waves" by J. R. Heirtzler. *Scientific American* (March 1962). Discusses electromagnetic waves in general and those of very long wavelength.

Thirty Years that Shook Physics by G. Gamow. Doubleday Anchor, 1966. The story of the quantum theory.

The Physics of Television by D. G. Fink and D. M. Lutyens. Doubleday Anchor, 1960. Chapter 2 is appropriate for this section.

Waves and Beaches by W. Bascom. Doubleday Anchor, 1964. A good introduction to ripple tank work.

Look How Many People Wear Glasses by R. Brindze. Antheneum, 1975. Presents information about eyes, vision, and eyeglasses in a straight forward, uncomplicated manner.

The Speech Chain by P. B. Denes and E. N. Pinson. Bell Telephone Laboratories, 1963. The physics and biology of spoken language.

Introduction to Photographic Principles by L. Larmore. Dover Publications, 1965. Applies the principles of physics to this area of modern technology.

Light, Color and Vision by Y. LeGrand. John Wiley and Sons, 1958. Presents a thorough and broad discussion of these topics.

"Light-Wave Communication" by S. Boyle. *Scientific American* (August 1977). Describes how messages are transmitted by light through glass fibers.

"Teachers' Pets IV: Mirrors in Air and Water" by Robert Gardner. *The Physics Teacher* (February 1976). Describes a procedure which modifies the plane mirror experiments suggested in this chapter. The modification will introduce students to the refraction of light.

"Beat Analogy Using Pocket Combs" by Peter Melzer. *The Physics Teacher* (February 1976). A short article describing Moiré patterns by pocket combs. This provides an analog to develop interference concepts.

"Polarization Effects with Pendulums" by Bruce H. Morgan. *The Physics Teacher* (November 1982). Describes an apparatus employing two pendulums attached to threads crossing over an overhead projector. This apparatus is used to demonstrate effects observed with polarized light.

Laser: Super tool of the 1980's by Jeff Hecht and Dick Tersi. Ticknor and Fields, 1982. Reviews and evaluates lasers—past, present, and future. This comprehensive book is well developed and contains some humor and personal experiences that make good reading for teachers and students.

10

Static Electricity

INTRODUCTION

Electrical energy is critical to our society. Consider the dramatic effects on people when power lines are down or when temporary blackouts occur. Fortunately, most of these interruptions are short lived, but they do illustrate the major role that electricity plays in our culture. Without such energy, we can imagine an existence much closer to a primitive lifestyle than the relatively advanced, technological style to which we are accustomed.

Students are generally eager to study electricity, perhaps because of its importance to our society, perhaps because of the mysterious (almost magical) image people have of electrical energy. Your task is to help make electricity understandable to your students and to illustrate how knowledge leads to control and to the many beneficial applications we enjoy.

CONTENT OVERVIEW

Once again in this chapter, start your presentation with electrical phenomena that are already a part of each pupil's experience. The crackling of a comb going through hair on a dry day; the sticking together of clothes when they come out of a drier; the shock resulting from touching a metal door knob after walking across a rug or sliding over plastic seat covers; balloons sticking to a wall after being rubbed against some hair—these are just a few experiences that your pupils have had with electrostatic effects. The main thrust in the instructional sequence is to reproduce these or other phenomena and to review them with an eye toward the electrical nature of matter. If atomic structure has already been presented (Chapter 7), students will need very little review in order to conceptualize electrostatic effects as being produced by the redistribution of electrons in the atoms of the materials involved. If atomic structure is not yet a part of your students' backgrounds, some instruction on the neutrality of atoms, positive protons, negative electrons, and the arrangement of these charged particles in the atom will aid pupils in forming a broad concept of the electrical nature of matter, which they can apply in atomic and electrical studies.

Once charge production and transfer are covered and applied to familiar phenomena, you can introduce additional experiences to reinforce concepts and provide some insights that your pupils may not have had prior to this study. Safety procedures during lightning storms and the use of pointed conductors are two examples of electrical phenomena that pupils probably have heard of but do not fully understand.

Although a thorough background in atomic structure is not required for this study, it might be advantageous for students to have some awareness of structure. This will aid in conceptualizing what happens to charges in matter to produce electrostatic phenomena used in this chapter. This study should precede the one on current electricity, since the idea of charge transfer is basic to the concept of current. Also, the notion of electric fields introduced here is essential for a thorough understanding of moving electrical charges (current) and concurrent effects.

If there is a time of year when the weather is especially dry, you might consider that period for instruction on electrostatics. Conversely, many of the demonstrations and laboratory procedures will not work very well during humid weather.

Many of the demonstrations will require alternate ways to produce positive charge. The standard procedure (rubbing a glass rod with silk) very often will not produce sufficiently large charges for the activities outlined. Charging devices should be free from grease and oil from hands. Electrostatic effects often will be enhanced if materials are washed and dried with heat prior to use.

OBJECTIVES

As a result of the learning experiences in this chapter, students should be able to:

1. Produce two kinds of electric charge in a laboratory setting using several different methods.

2. Describe the operation of an electroscope and use this device to detect charge.

3. Explain charging by conduction and induction.

4. Use Coulomb's Law to solve problems for the force between charges.

5. Illustrate and interpret electric fields with lines of force.

6. Describe charge distribution on a conductor and point discharge.

LEARNING EXPERIENCES

Topic I: Charge Production, Transfer, and Distribution

1. *Teacher Presentation.* Develop the idea that all charge is the result of the electrical nature of matter. Also convey that atoms contain positive protons and negative electrons, and that under normal conditions, the numbers of these particles are balanced. This is neutrality. A charged condition is produced by somehow disturb-

ing this balance. Since electrons are held less tightly to an atom than the positive protons, most charge is the result of disturbing the electrons; that is, negative charge is due to an excess of electrons, while positive charge is due to a deficiency of electrons. Use this simple rule and the fact that like charges repel and unlike charges attract in the analysis of several charging phenomena.

2. *Laboratory.* Electric charges are detected through forces which they exert. Students are supplied with fur and rubber rods as well as glass rods and silk. (Vinyl and acetate rods with wool and cotton cloth or other charging materials also will work.) Pupils also have two pith balls hung from separate supports. The following procedures and explanations are involved:
   a. Charge one rod and touch both pith balls with it. Now bring the balls near one another. Explain what happens.
   b. Discharge the balls by rubbing them with your finger. Explain the effect.
   c. Charge one ball with the rubber rod and the other with the glass rod. Explain what you see.
   d. Discharge one ball and then bring it near the other one. Explain what happens.
   e. Charge other objects and investigate the charge with the pith balls. Try rubbing a variety of materials with different cloths. Keep a record of effects.

3. *Demonstration.* You can do the activity above as a demonstration. Substitute balloons sprayed with metallic paint for the pith balls, which are too small for such a demonstration.

4. *Demonstration.* Describe the operation of a leaf electroscope for your class. Charge the electroscope by conduction and explain the charging process and the operation of the device as well as the charge distribution on the leaves and stem of the electroscope. Blackboard diagrams accompanying each step will make your presentation more clear. Also, some electroscopes have a small bulb which attaches to the knob and indicates the passage of charge with a flash of light. This accessory will aid pupils with their analysis of the process.

5. *Activity.* Students can use Reproduction Page 83 as a set of instructions to follow in order to charge a leaf electroscope permanently by induction. You may have to supplement the instructions with some discussion on the process of grounding and what it means. This Reproduction Page also will serve as a model of how to describe the distribution of charge and resulting effects on devices listed in the next activity.

6. *Laboratory.* Provide students with a variety of materials for charging. In each case, pupils are to operate (charge) the device and then produce sketches similar to Reproduction Page 83, which describe the charges underlying the observed effects. In some of the cases, you may wish to provide additional descriptions of operation or have pupils do some independent research.
   a. Produce and verify (+) and (−) charge.
   b. Charge a pith ball by conduction.
   c. Charge a leaf electroscope (+) by conduction.
   d. Charge a leaf electroscope (−) by induction.
   e. Charge and operate an electrophorus.
   f. Operate and describe a Wimshurst machine.

g. Show the effect of bringing a charged object near a leaf electroscope that is already charged.
h. Make the leaves of a charged electroscope collapse and then diverge again by bringing a charged object near it.

7. *Demonstration.* Several effects similar to those in Activity 6 are good for further student analysis but require the control of a teacher-demonstrator:
   a. Use a Van de Graaff generator, an insulated stand, and a student volunteer with long, dry, clean hair to show the repulsion of the charges on that pupil's hairdo when she is charged up with the Van de Graaff.
   b. Describe the charging of a second grounded sphere brought near the dome of the Van de Graaff. Use this as an introduction to the charging of a Leyden jar and a brief discussion on capacitors. Caution: The amount of charge involved when a Leyden jar is electrified in this manner is relatively large and potentially dangerous. Use proper safety precautions and discharge the device when the demonstration is completed.

Topic II: Coulomb's Law of Electrostatics

1. *Teacher Presentation.* Explain to your class that the attractive and repulsive forces discussed thus far are more thoroughly described by a relationship known as Coulomb's Law. Use Reproduction Page 84 with your presentation. Students should understand what each of the variables in the equation represents and how each affects the magnitude and direction of the force as highlighted by questions on that page.

   Note that this form of the Coulomb's Law equation is a good predictor only if the size of the charged objects is small compared to the distance between the bodies.

2. *Activity.* Students should get some practice in problem analysis and solution using Coulomb's Law. Assign several textbook problems in this area. Most texts have many such questions, but if yours does not, choose some from the references at the end of this chapter.

3. *Demonstration.* Review several of the earlier electrostatic effects with an analytic eye toward Coulomb's Law. In general, the dependence on amounts of charge and the inverse relationship with distance can be verified qualitatively.

4. *Laboratory.* Several of the references cited at the end of this chapter describe the details for construction of various "balances" to measure the effects of distance and of charge on electrostatic force. Choose one or several alternate versions for more quantitative verification of Coulomb's Law.

Topic III: Electric Fields

1. *Teacher Presentation.* Define an electric field as a region around a charged body where the force effects due to that charge can be detected. The force is described by Coulomb's Law in terms of magnitude and direction. A second charged object is needed to detect the field through the force. By convention, this second charge

is positive and small since its function is to detect the field but not contribute to the field itself. All this gives rise to graphic descriptions of electric fields (which have direction and, therefore, are vector quantities) through "lines of force." These lines represent the *direction* of force on a small, *positive* test change. They also represent the relative field strength by their density—the closer together they are, the stronger the field.

2. *Demonstration.* Reinforce the lines of force idea with a concrete experience by using a positively charged pith ball (test charge) near the dome of a Van de Graaff generator. The direction and magnitude of the field at various points will show from the force effects on the pith ball.

    If a second, oppositely charged, dome is near the Van de Graaff, the resultant field also will show with the pith ball.

3. *Activity.* Use Reproduction Page 85 to help your pupils understand and interpret electric fields through the lines of force construct.

Topic IV: Charge Distribution on Conductors

1. *Activity.* Students may introduce this section by reporting on Michael Faraday's experiments with the distribution of charge on conductors. These reports may include demonstrations such as Faraday's silk bag and the ice pail experiment, which show that charge resides only on the outside of a conductor.

2. *Demonstration.* The absence of electrical effects inside a closed conductor is demonstrated with the metal cylinder and pith balls shown below:

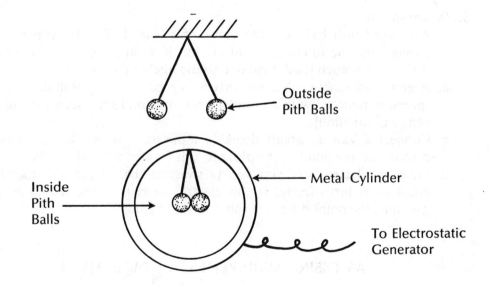

When the metal cylinder is charged, the outside pith balls diverge but the pair inside show no effect. This demonstrates that there is no electrical effect inside of the cylinder.

3. *Activity.* Discuss implications of the above behavior for the topic of electrical shielding. This discussion can range from metal wire covering, to wire cages around electrical installations, to why a person is safe during an electrical storm if inside an automobile.

4. *Teacher Presentation.* Most student texts have a sketch similar to the one below, which represents that electrical charge density is greatest at the point of greatest curvature of a conducting surface.

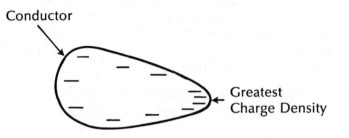

Extend this idea to include maximum curvature as being a point. The great concentration of charge on such points produces very intense electric fields—fields strong enough to ionize the surrounding air which discharges the conductor. This *slow* leakage of charge is called brush or corona discharge.

5. *Activity.* Extend the idea of point discharge through a class discussion or individual research projects on the following topics:
   a. St. Elmo's fire
   b. "Pigtails" attached to aircraft wings
   c. Lightning rods

6. *Demonstrations.*
   a. A charged pith ball near the dome of a Van de Graaff generator will show a strong field due to charge build up, but if a pin is taped on the dome, the pith ball shows a much lesser field due to the discharging effect.
   b. A grounded sphere will draw fairly heavy sparks with a Van de Graaff, but if the sphere is replaced with a grounded pin, no sparks are seen (lightning rod "prevention" function).
   c. Connect a Van de Graaff dome to a pin using some wire. If a candle flame is placed near the point of the pin, the ions formed will deflect the flame.
   d. Pivot an electrostatic pinwheel (a swastika shaped piece of metal with sharp ends) so it turns freely. If this electric whirl is connected to an electrostatic machine, the point discharge will cause it to spin.

ASSESSING ACHIEVEMENT OF OBJECTIVES

Ongoing Evaluation

The extent to which students have mastered the concepts under each topic can be measured during the instructional sequence with Reproduction Pages 86, 87, 88, and 89. These are quiz questions on topics in this chapter and related ideas. Insert them at appropriate stages of the instruction.

Final Evaluation

You may choose to combine the questions from Reproduction Pages 86–89 with additional questions to form a unit test on this chapter. Refer back to the objectives for an overall guide to constructing such an evaluation device. Reports, class discussion, and lab work should also be included as part of a final assessment.

Resources for Teaching Static Electricity

Below is a selected list of resources useful for teaching concepts in electrostatics. The list is divided into audio-visual materials and print. If a source is especially useful for teachers only or students only, this is noted with the citation. Addresses of publishers can be found in the alphabetical list at the end of this book.

Audio-Visual Materials

Coulomb's Law. Film. P.S.S.C. Eric Rogers demonstrates the inverse square relationship and the dependence of force on charge.

Electric Fields. Film. P.S.S.C. Experiments demonstrate the vector addition of fields, the shielding effects of closed conducting surfaces, and the electric force which drives current in a conductor.

Electric Lines of Force. Film. P.S.S.C. Shows how to produce electric field patterns using grass seeds that align to form various patterns.

Electrostatic Charges and Forces. Film. Coronet. Discusses insulators, conductors, electric fields, Coulomb's Law, Faraday's ice pail experiment, and Van de Graaff generators.

Electrostatics. Film. E.B.E.C. Uses animation to explain electrification, charging, electroscopes, lightning, and lightning rods.

Coulomb's Law. Filmloop. Encyclopedia Brittanica Corporation. Illustrates variables in Coulomb's Law with an experiment using a balance. Data is provided.

Variation of Charge with Curvature. Filmloop. Encyclopedia Britannica Corporation. Shows the pear shaped conductor and discharging effect of points. Uses animation to explain phenomena.

Print

A Source Book in Physics by W. F. Magie, McGraw-Hill, 1935. See extracts from Coulomb's work in 1785, pages 408–420.

The Scientific Revolution 1500–1800 by A. R. Hall. Beacon Press, 1954. Has a good description of the early work in electricity.

Physics, The Pioneer Science by L. W. Taylor. Dover Publications, 1959. An excellent treatment of the historical evolution of electrostatics.

Benjamin Franklin's Experiments by I. B. Cohen, editor. Harvard University Press, 1941. Some additional history on electricity.

Electricity One-Seven by H. Mileaf, editor. Hayden Book Co., 1978. The first portion of this comprehensive work on electricity deals with topics in this chapter.

"Computing E-Field Lines" by D. E. Kelly. *The Physics Teacher* (September 1980). Discusses a computer program which computes the electric lines of force for several charges.

"The A.B.C.'s of Lightning Protection" by D. Logan. *Ham Radio Horizons* (September 1980). An informative article for the layman who wants to understand the principles of lightning and protection plans.

"Milli-Can Experiment" by J. H. Nelson. *The Physics Teacher* (January 1980). Presents an experimental analog using gravitational force as a means of identifying a "quantum" of mass compared to electrical force as a means of identifying a "quantum" of electrical charge.

"Coulomb's Law on the Overhead Projector" by J. B. Johnston. *The Physics Teacher* (January 1979). Describes a technique for the Coulomb's Law experiment that reduces some of the errors associated with traditional approaches.

"Demonstration of Gauss' Law for a Metal Surface" by T. W. Haywood and R. C. Nelson. *The Physics Teacher* (December 1979). Uses a Van de Graaff, styrofoam buttons, a can, and a plastic container to demonstrate that charge resides on the outer surface of a conductor.

"Is a Swimmer Safe in a Lightning Storm" by Bobby N. Thurman. *The Physics Teacher* (May 1980). An answer to this often asked question.

Electrostatics by W. Yurkewicz. Spring Educational Associates, 1984. A programmed instruction booklet designed to teach analysis of various charging processes with an electroscope. Field tested to meet the 90–90 criteria. 39 panels.

11

Current Electricity

INTRODUCTION

This chapter deals with physical concepts that underlie one of our most important and dominant energy forms, electricity. Consider the degree to which our lives are affected by the technology developed from our knowledge and resultant control of this area of physics. Once again, you, the teacher, have a wide variety of student experiences with current electricity that will provide a concrete base for pupils—a base which will help them assimilate and organize the physical descriptions in this chapter. It is safe to assume that your students have already had experiences (and, therefore, formed some initial concepts) with circuits, electrical energy, magnets, motors, generators, switches, fuses, and circuit breakers. Formal instruction provides an opportunity to unify these various and separate conceptions. Such unification (and resultant simplification) is possible through our understandings of electrical current, the associated magnetic effects, and other energy relationships.

CONTENT OVERVIEW

Start this area with definitions and clarifying examples of the three basic descriptors for current electricity: current, voltage, and resistance. Some special emphasis will help students differentiate voltage from current, two concepts often held as similar by introductory students. The relationships among these three descriptors can be clarified through Ohm's Law and by using series and parallel circuits to describe power and energy in electrical terms.

The second portion of this chapter explains that a moving charge (current) produces a magnetic field. This basic concept is applied to help unify electromagnetic phenomena such as magnetism, motors, and generators.

Explain to your pupils that this study will not allow them to wire a new home or build a T.V. set in their basements. It will enable them to understand the common base for both of these activities and other electrical technology—a reasonable starting point for any application of the physics of current electricity.

OBJECTIVES

As a result of the learning experiences in this chapter, students should be able to:

1. Define the terms current, voltage, and resistance and use these words correctly in describing electrical phenomena.

2. State Ohm's Law verbally and mathematically and use this relationship in problem solving.

3. Describe effects of length, cross sectional area, and resistivity on the resistance of wire.

4. Build and analyze series and parallel circuits and solve problems employing current, voltage, and resistance relationships for these circuits.

5. Calculate energy and power in electrical circuits.

6. Describe magnetism as a property of moving charges.

7. Represent magnetic fields with flux lines and apply Ampere's rule for determining the direction of fields.

8. Predict and explain the interaction of magnetic fields as applied to electromagnets, generators, and motors.

9. Use Lenz's Law in explaining conservation of energy in a generator.

LEARNING EXPERIENCES

Topic I: Current, Voltage, and Resistance in Circuits—Ohm's Law

1. *Teacher Presentation.* Electrostatics deals with effects of stationary charges. Current electricity describes phenomena associated with migrating (moving) charges. Current is defined as the time rate of charge transfer. In symbols, $I = \frac{Q}{t}$, where I is the current in amperes; Q is the amount of charge (in coulombs) passing a point in a circuit in time, t, in seconds. An ampere, then, is equal to a coulomb/second. Point out that variations in current magnitude are due to changing the amount of charge, Q, and *not* by increasing or decreasing the time it takes for the effect to happen. Refer back to some of the activities in the previous chapters such as grounding a charged electroscope or discharging a Van de Graaff for examples of charge transfer-current.

2. *Activity.* Use Reproduction Page 90 to summarize definitions of current, voltage, resistance, and a simple circuit. The analogy with a water system goes beyond the simple diagrams. Note that when the pump is working, water circulates through the entire system because of a potential energy differential; in electrical circuits, charges migrate because of an electrical potential difference, an E.M.F. (electromotive force).

   Discuss potential difference using Reproduction Page 91 as an aid.

3. *Activity.* Students can investigate the different resistance offered to current by different materials by using the circuit below:

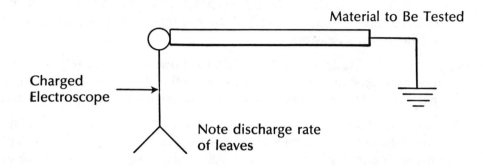

Material to Be Tested

Charged
Electroscope →

Note discharge rate
of leaves

Students should try several common materials, wires, string (first dry and then wet with a salt solution). A slight modification will allow the testing of liquids. Try water with and without ionizing materials in it.

4. *Demonstration.* Use a student volunteer, a D.C. voltage supply, and a galvanometer to show that human skin changes resistance with the emotional state of an individual. Use about six volts of E.M.F. Connect the student's fingers and galvanometer in series as shown:

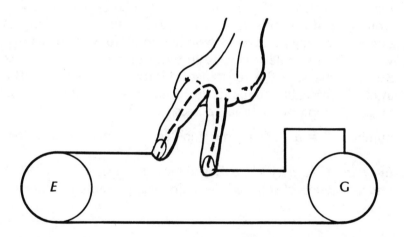

It is helpful to use a large galvanometer or a projection model on an overhead projector for good visibility.

Current reading on the galvanometer will be large at first, showing low skin resistance due to student anxiety. When the pupil sees he will not be electrocuted by this circuit, he will calm down and the current will decrease due to increased skin resistance. You can lower the resistance and increase the current again by telling the class that this is part of a lie detector device and threatening to ask the "wired" student some embarrassing questions. Don't actually embarrass the volunteer.

5. *Activity.* Student research and reporting on the lie detector and galvanic skin response is appropriate here.

6. *Laboratory.* Reproduction Page 92 is a laboratory guide sheet for replication of Ohm's experimental determination of resistance of a circuit. Have your students build the circuit described but wait until you have checked and approved the circuit before plugging in the power supply. Choose E.M.F.'s and resistances that will produce currents in the milliamp range, to reduce problems associated with overheating the resistors.

7. *Laboratory.* Students can take data to show the inverse relationship between current and resistance in a circuit by using the above circuit with the E.M.F. fixed, inserting various resistors in place, and noting the corresponding current.

8. *Demonstration.* Show the temperature dependence of the resistance of a wire by winding a coil on a tube which will not burn. If this coil of wire is placed in a circuit with either an ammeter or a light bulb, your students will see the current decrease in the circuit as you heat the coil with a bunsen flame. Cooling the coil will decrease its resistance and current will increase again.

9. *Laboratory.* Students can take data of E.M.F. versus current through a lamp up to and slightly above the lamp's rated voltage. The resulting graph will not be linear like the plots from the Ohm's law laboratory (Activity #6 above). Students should explain the curve. It might be helpful to plot the calculated resistance of the filament versus current. The results will support the fact that resistance increases with temperature.

10. *Laboratory.* Coils of wire of varying thickness, length, and material are available from scientific supply houses or make your own for this lab. Appropriate wire samples are wound around wooden cores (dowels or empty thread spindles will work). Each sample is labeled in terms of length, type of wire, and guage number. Students measure the resistance of each of the coils. Sufficient coils should be available to enable pupils to determine that the resistance of wire, R, depends on length, l, type of material, p (resistivity), and cross sectional area, A (via guage number). $R = \rho \dfrac{l}{A}$. Reproduction Page 93 is a guide sheet for this activity.

11. *Evaluation Activity.* Use Reproduction Pages 94 and 95 to check on student understandings of some of the main ideas presented in this section.

Topic II: Series and Parallel Circuits

1. *Teacher Presentation.* Explain that electrical connections can be made either in series or parallel. Sketch some sample circuits on the board or overhead and differentiate these circuits based on a single current path (series) or alternate paths (parallel). Introduce the idea that electrical quantities (current, voltage, and resistance) are combined in different ways for each of these circuits.

2. *Activity.* Use Reproduction Pages 96 and 97 to present and summarize current, voltage, and resistance relationships in series and in parallel. The mathematical derivations using Ohm's law should be followed, but students will get a better "feel" for the relationships from some of the activities listed below.

3. *Activity.* Have students use a rope model to show the total resistance and voltage drop relationships in series circuits:

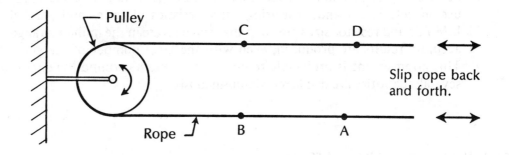

In the above arrangement, one person represents the E.M.F. by pulling the rope back and forth. As this happens, other students, one at a time, grasp the rope at points A, B, C, and D respectively, to represent added resistors. The person working the rope can immediately "feel" the additional resistance. He will note also that the energy put into the pulling is dissipated through the friction in each of the "loads." People serving as the resistors should not grasp too tightly or rope burns will result.

4. *Activity.* Students usually can follow the derivation for total resistance in a parallel circuit but find it difficult to accept that as more resistors are added in parallel, the total resistance *decreases.* Ask your class to participate in the following scenario: Students in the classroom represent charges and the marking of the end of class time will represent an E.M.F., in the sense that there will be a potential difference between the classroom location and the hallway. At the end of class, there is a tendency to migrate to the lower potential position—the hallway. If there is only one doorway (representing one current path), a certain amount of resistance is manifested by pupils bumping into one another and the sides of the passage way as they exit. If, however, several other doorways to the hall (alternate paths) were constructed, it would be easier (less resistance) to make the migration from the classroom.

5. *Demonstration.* A standard series and parallel circuit demonstrator consists of five light bulb sockets connected with four switches as shown:

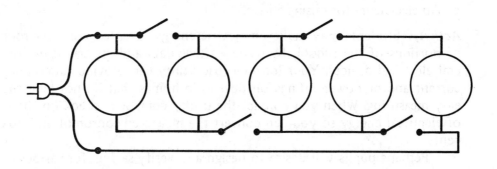

Use light bulbs of the same wattage initially to show characteristics of pure series and parallel circuits. The equal voltage drops in parallel and the single current path in series are the most obvious. Arranging several different wattage bulbs will provoke discussion about circuit characteristics for series and parallel.

6. *Laboratory*. Reproduction Pages 98 and 99 are guide and data sheets for students to use in setting up and measuring characteristics of series and parallel circuits. If E.M.F.'s and resistor sizes are such that currents are in the milliamp range, reasonably accurate results are produced, even with the large number of meters in the circuit. This arrangement is preferable to moving two meters around the circuit because the several quantities are displayed simultaneously.

Topic III: Energy and Power Effects

1. *Teacher Presentation*. Use Reproduction Page 90 to supplement and summarize your derivation of electrical quantities and their combination into expressions for energy and power relationships in circuits. Emphasize the conceptual relationships before expressing those relationships with the standard equations: Energy = VIt, I^2Rt, or $V^2\frac{t}{R}$; Power = VI, I^2R, or $\frac{V^2}{R}$.

2. *Demonstration*. Show heating effects in series and parallel by using equal lengths of copper and nichrome wire. Connect both in series and measure which one becomes hotter by having pieces of wax attached to both wires. The larger resistance wire will become hotter. In parallel, however, the lower resistance wire becomes warmer. Students should be able to explain this.

3. *Laboratory*. Students can verify that 4.19 watt-seconds = 1 calorie by measuring current and voltage supplied to a heating coil in a calorimeter with water in it for a measured period of time. If values are adjusted so that the water temperature changes by about 10°C in ten minutes, a reasonable comparison between experimental and accepted values will result.

4. *Laboratory*. The efficiency of several devices that are operated electrically can be determined from laboratory measurements. Here are a few suggestions:
   a. A hot plate heating up some water.
   b. An operating model of a steam engine raising a weight with a pulley system.
   c. An electric motor raising a load.

5. *Activity*. Students may make an electric energy inventory of their rooms, homes, or portions of the school, by using wattage data and estimated use times for several electrical devices. Your local electric utility can provide data on average use or current and/or power ratings on devices in homes that do not lend themselves to easy measuring. When you contact the utility company, check on the current cost of electrical energy so you can convert the measured consumption into dollars and cents.

   Perhaps pupils will desire to design and verify savings for various conservation programs.

6. *Activity*. Assign pupils the task of observing the electric meter in their homes during various times of the day. Ask them to relate rate of rotation with electrical use at a

particular time. Students should equate rate of rotation with power and total number of turns with energy.

7. *Evaluation Activity.* Use Reproduction Page 100 for assessing student progress on power and energy calculations in electric circuits.

Topic IV: Electricity and Magnetism

1. *Demonstration.* Your pupils probably think of electricity and magnetism as two separate phenomena. Your purpose in the initial presentation is to show that magnetism is related to electric current.

   Arrange a wire in a north-south orientation. Place a large magnetic needle on a low friction pivot point (free to swing in a horizontal plane) below the wire. Students will observe deflection of this compass needle when current passes through the wire. Reversing the current reverses the direction of deflection of the needle. Record the deflection and current direction on a sketch on the board and repeat the process with the needle on top of the wire. Again sketch the directions involved.

2. *Demonstration.* Reinforce the previous demonstration with a second. In this case, use many small compasses arranged on a horizontal platform around two wires that pass through the support in a vertical orientation.

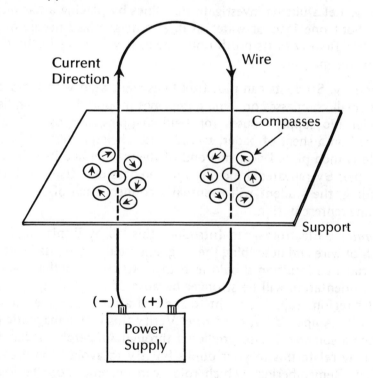

With no current in the wire, the small compasses align pointing in a northward direction. When the current is turned on as shown, the compasses take on a circular orientation around each wire. Record the current and compass directions, reverse the current, and again make a record of the magnetic field direction as associated with the current direction.

3. *Teacher Presentation.* Explain to your class that magnetic fields are associated with moving charges—currents. These fields are described through a flux line construct. Flux lines are similar in nature to the lines of force used to describe electrical fields. The direction of the flux lines represents the direction of magnetic force on a north magnetic pole (the points of the compasses); the density of the lines represents the field strength at a point.

   Relate Ampere's left-hand rule for predicting the direction of flux lines associated with charge migration: If the thumb of your left hand represents the direction of negative charge motion through a conductor, then your fingers will point in the direction of the flux lines when grasping that conductor.

   Go back to the records kept on the first two demonstrations to validate and apply this rule.

4. *Demonstration.* Show flux line orientations associated with permanent magnets by placing a magnet on the stage of an overhead projector. Place a piece of clear plastic over the magnet and then sprinkle some iron filings onto the plastic. Slight tapping of the plastic will cause the filings to align with the magnetic field of the permanent magnet. Use this arrangement to investigate fields due to bar magnets, horseshoe magnets, attraction between two unlike poles, and repulsion between similar poles. The effect of a high permeability "keeper" across the poles of a horseshow magnet also is clearly shown with this arrangement.

5. *Activity.* Let students investigate flux lines by placing a bar magnet on a glass dish with about one inch of water in it. If a magnetized needle or small magnet is arranged to float with its north pole down, it will move in the direction of the flux lines of the magnet.

6. *Laboratory.* Students can plot flux lines associated with various magnetic fields by using small compasses or some compasses mounted on a handle designed and sold by scientific supply houses for field mapping purposes. The magnet(s) is (are) replaced on a sheet of paper, traced, and labeled in terms of polarity. The compass needle is then placed near one end of the magnet and its orientation is recorded on the paper. By repeatedly moving the compass one diameter farther away and again recording, the student will eventually connect each of the recordings to form the flux line representation.

7. *Laboratory.* Electromagnet. Introduce this lab by displaying a three or four meter length of wire and describing the magnetic field around its length. Now coil the wire up. Student's intuition should lead them to conclude that the magnetic field in the coiled orientation will be stronger because of the "piling up" of the flux lines in a smaller region. Supply current to the coil after predicting the direction of the flux lines with Ampere's left-hand rule. Verify this with a magnetic needle. The polarity of such a solenoid is also predicted through Ampere's left-hand rule for a solenoid. You may relate this to your pupils but try to avoid "too many" hand rules in this section. Remembering "which rule" can become more tedious than the analysis of the phenomena the rules are supposed to help clarify.

   If pupils are provided with several core materials such as wood, glass, and iron, they can show that an electromagnet's strength depends on the permeability of the core. "Strength" is measured by the number of paper clips, tacks, and the like the magnet will hold. Using the iron core, students also can show the strength dependence on length of wire and current. Direction of flux lines associated with current direction also is demonstrated.

8. *Activity.* Several research topics are associated with this study. Students can research and report (with demonstrations) some of the work done by Oersted, Ampere, Faraday, and Henry. Other reports might investigate the properties of ferromagnetism, diamagnetism, and paramagnetism.

Topic V: Effects of Interacting Fields

1. *Demonstration.* Suspend a wire from a tall support between the poles of a strong magnet. An alnico magnet is good for this demonstration. If the wire and magnet are arranged as shown, students will observe deflection of the wire in the magnetic field when current is in the wire. Reversing the current direction reverses the deflection:

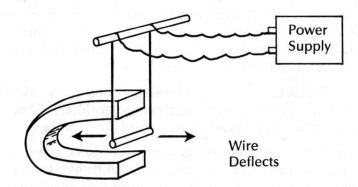

Note the polarity of the magnet and the current direction.

2. *Demonstration.* Repeat the demonstration outlined in Chapter 7 that shows that a beam of electrons in a cathode ray tube is deflected when a magnet is brought near. This time students should carefully record the polarity of the magnet, the direction of the beam, and the direction of deflection.

3. *Teacher Presentation.* Use Reproduction Page 101 in conjunction with student notes from the preceding demonstrations to describe the force on a charge moving through a magnetic field. Different student texts describe the behavior in various ways. This reproduction page uses a resultant field approach. In any case, pupils should be able to analyze and predict the direction of the force given information on the charge motion and the field through which the charge moves.

4. *Activity.* Give pupils a magnetic needle on a pivot (horizontal) and a bar magnet. Ask them to see if they can make the needle turn continuously by using the magnet. When your students obtain continuous turning of the needle by alternating attraction and repulsion or by attracting or repelling at just the right point in a turn, inform them that they are demonstrating the operation of an electric motor.

5. *Teacher Presentation or Laboratory.* St. Louis Motor. Use this working model of a D.C. motor as an application of the principles discussed in the previous four

activities. Pupils should investigate the commutator and relate its operation to reversing current direction in the coil every half turn. Effects of the amount of current supplied to the device and the strength of the permanent magnetic field should be demonstrated, explained, and related back to basic principles of electricity and magnetism.

6. *Activity.* Some of your students may be interested in constructing a motor of their own. Several of the resources at the end of this chapter provide directions for such a project.

7. *Activity.* Student investigations into the construction and multiple types and uses of electric motors are appropriate at this point. Several of the references at the end of this chapter are good starting points.

8. *Laboratory.* Pupils can use a current balance available from most supply houses to gather quantitative data which will show that the force of deflection depends directly on the current magnitude, the length of the conductor, and the field strength. This current balance also is useful to describe forces between two current carrying wires. Current magnitudes, distances apart, and length effects are measurable. Details for the operation of this device are included by most suppliers. Several of the references at the conclusion of this chapter describe the experimental procedure in detail.

9. *Activity.* Students may wish to investigate and apply principles discussed in this section to the construction of a galvanometer. Modification of this device into an ammeter and voltmeter makes a good small group project.

10. *Demonstration.* Use several coils of wire, magnets, and a demonstration galvanometer to produce induced currents. You can demonstrate the effects of speed of movement, field strength, amount of wire in the coil, dependence of current direction on direction of movement, and the necessity of cutting across flux lines.

11. *Activity.* Two students can use a very long length of wire (50m or so) and the flux lines of the earth's magnetic field to generate a current which is measurable with a galvanometer. If the pupils face each other and spin the wire like a jump rope, current will register on the meter. Try to notice (and explain) differential effects when the pupils are oriented east-west and north-south.

12. *Teacher Presentation.* Use Reproduction Page 102 as a student guide and summary on induced E.M.F. and current. Include your preferred way of determining the direction of the induced current. Use this direction to continue the presentation of Lenz's Law in terms of energy conservation and direction of the induced current.

13. *Activity.* Have pupils build, operate, and explain the motor-generator system shown below.

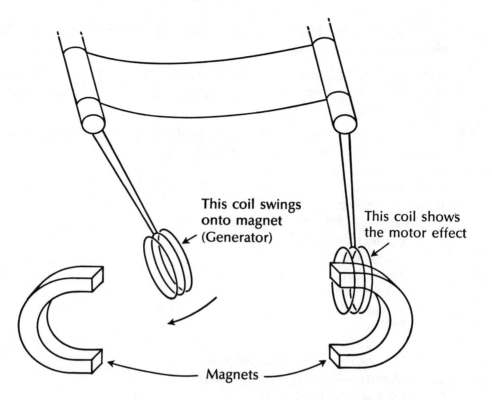

This coil swings onto magnet (Generator)

This coil shows the motor effect

Magnets

Both coils are connected to form one continuous conducting path. You need strong magnets and many loops in the generator coil for this activity.

14. *Activity.* Have pairs of students get a "feel" for Lenz's Law by using a hand generator and a light bulb. One pupil cranks the hand generator at a fairly rapid, steady speed with the light bulb loosened in its socket so as to create an open circuit and no current. When this condition is achieved, the other pupil tightens the light bulb in its socket, completing the circuit. The current delivers energy to the light bulb and it lights. At the same time, the pupil turning the crank of the generator feels the increased resistance to turning and becomes aware of the greater amount of work he must do to keep supplying energy to the bulb.

Students should then switch places. Try to notice and explain effects of using various wattage bulbs.

15. *Demonstration.* Use a St. Louis motor to make a D.C. generator. Connect a galvanometer to the terminals of the motor. Spin the coil and note the effects of speed and direction of spin and magnetic field strength on the current magnitude and direction.

16. *Demonstration.* Eddy currents and Lenz's Law. Set a metal dish spinning on a pivot point and have the class note the rate of slowing down. Repeat the process but hold a horseshoe magnet so that its poles straddle the dish. Note and explain the more rapid deceleration. Discuss the "magnetic brake."

17. *Activity.* Local utility companies usually are very cooperative in arranging field trips to their generating stations. If such a facility is nearby, a trip would provide a good opportunity for application of concepts studied in class. If a field trip is

not possible, your local utility might provide a guest speaker and/or an audio-visual display at no charge.

18. *Activity.* Students can bring in, demonstrate, or research generators used in bicycle lighting systems, automobiles, lawn mowers, chain saws, and many other ignition systems.

19. *Activity.* Various additional topics are available for student research and reporting/demonstrating in this area. Some of these are:
    a. Induction coils
    b. Transformers
    c. Inductors in electronics
    d. Other ways of producing E.M.F.:
        1. photoelectric
        2. thermoelectric
        3. piezoelectric
        4. primary cells
        5. storage cells
        6. fuel cells
        7. solar cells
        8. magnetohydrodynamic generators
    e. Microwave ovens and their operation
    f. The operation of antennas

20. *Evaluation Activity.* Reproduction Page 103 is a quiz on concepts included in Topics IV and V. Use it at appropriate points in the instruction.

ASSESSING STUDENT OBJECTIVES

Ongoing Evaluation

The extent to which students have mastered the individual concepts covered under each topic can be measured by using the several reproduction pages listed under "Evaluation Activity" that appear throughout the chapter. Several other activities such as laboratory work and reports and research can be submitted for grading.

Final Evaluation

For an overall evaluation of a student's understanding, you can construct a unit test, either short answer or essay, directly from the objectives at the beginning of this chapter, or you may choose to use the several evaluation reproduction pages all at once as a portion of a final test.

This final assessment also should include evidence and judgements of student participation and involvement with classroom activities and homework over the time period spent on topics in this chapter.

Resources for Teaching Current Electricity

Below is a selected list of resources useful for teaching concepts in current electricity. The list is divided into audio-visual materials and print. If a source is especially useful for teachers only or students only, this is noted with the citation. Addresses of publishers can be found in the alphabetical list at the end of this book.

Audio-Visual Materials

Counting Electrical Charges in Motion. Film. P.S.S.C. Shows the calibration of an ammeter during an electrolysis experiment through the counting of elementary charges.

Electrical Potential Energy and Potential Difference. Film. P.S.S.C. Shows how a battery establishes an electric field in a circuit and how to measure the potential energy. Analyzes energy transformations via potential difference and current.

Electrodynamics. Film. E.B.E.C. Traces electricity from Galvani to electromagnetic induction. Shows industrial application of electricity.

Electromagnetic Induction. Coronet. Explains the production of an induced EMF and investigates generators, motors, and transformers.

Solving Basic D.C. Circuit Problems. Filmstrip/cassette in four parts with matching slides. Prentice-Hall Media. The lessons enable students having no prior experience with D.C. systems to understand fairly complicated circuits, including heating and magnetic effects. A student workbook/study guide with problems is included.

Electricity and Magnetism. Filmloop. Eye Gate. Shows how electricity is produced when a coil of wire is moved through a field. It also recreates some of Faraday's original experiments.

Print

Conductors and Semiconductors by A. Holden. Bell Telephone Laboratories, 1964. Discusses all aspects of electricity.

"The Conservation Laws of Physics" by Gerald Feinberg and Maurice Goldhaber. *Scientific American* (October 1963). Provides new insights into everyday aspects of physics. Conservation of charge is relevant to this chapter.

"High Voltage Power Transmission" by L. O. Barthold and H. G. Pfeiffer. *Scientific American* (May 1964). Applying electrical theory to the solution of an engineering problem.

"Intense Magnetic Fields" by Henry H. Kolm and Arthur J. Freeman. *Scientific American* (April 1965). Describes the uses of strong fields in many areas of science. Effects of such fields and their production are discussed.

"Microelectronics." *Scientific American* (September 1977). This issue is devoted to detailed but readable articles on the topic. Many concepts of circuits are developed.

"Teaching Electrical Resistance" by M. Iona. *The Physics Teacher* (May 1979). A summary and comparison of the various ways in which resistance is discussed by various textbook authors.

"Fusion Power with Particle Beams" by G. Yonas. *Scientific American* (November 1978). A complete, well-illustrated discussion that will enhance lessons and is readable by students.

"The Search for Electromagnetic Induction" by S. Devons. *The Physics Teacher* (December 1978). Some historical insights on Ampere, Faraday, and others. Good teacher background.

Electricity One-Seven by H. Mileaf, editor. Hayden Book Co., 1978. Clear presentations on individual topics in this chapter with good diagrams.

A Source Book in Physics by W. F. Magie. Harvard University Press, 1935. See sections on Ampere, Ohm, Lenz, and Oersted.

"Mysterious Lights in Series and Parallel" by C. Keller. *The Physics Teacher* (September 1980). Teachers can follow the directions to make a "black box" designed to test understanding of series and parallel circuits.

"A Simple Magnet Force Experiment" by J. M. Piowaty. *The Physics Teacher* (November 1980). A description of an experiment to measure the magnetic field of a strong horseshoe magnet.

"Electrical Conductivity" by P. B. Allen. *The Physics Teacher* (September 1979). Some good theoretical summaries on the topic of conduction. Appropriate for teacher background.

Electricity, Today's Technologies, Tomorrow's Alternatives by the Electric Power Research Institute. William Kaufmann, Inc., 1981. Provides timely data and thoughtful perspectives on existing and proposed sources of electricity.

"Teaching Electricity with Batteries and Bulbs" by James Evans. *The Physics Teacher* (January 1978). Describes a way of introducing students to direct-current electricity. The approach is to extend methods used at the elementary level to more advanced students. The technique and philosophy warrant teacher reading.

Appendix A

Addresses of Producers of Resources

Distributors of Audio-Visual Materials

Audio Visual Services
Kent State University
Kent, Ohio 44242

BFA Educational Media
2211 Michigan Avenue
P.O. Box 1795
Santa Monica, California 90406

Boston University Film Rental Center
765 Commonwealth Ave.
Boston, Massachusetts 02215

CRM/McGraw-Hill Films
110 Fifteenth Street
DelMar, California 92014

Charles W. Clark Co., Inc.
546 Smith Street
Farmingdale, New York 11735

Coronet
65 East South Water Street
Chicago, Illinois 60601

Ealing (Holt/Ealing)
Holt, Rinehart and Winston, Inc.
Media Dept.
383 Madison Avenue
New York, New York 10017

Encyclopedia Britannica Corp.
425 North Michigan Avenue
Chicago, Illinois 60611

Eye Gate
146-01 Archer Avenue
Jamaica, New York 11435

Folkways Records
701 Seventh Avenue
New York, New York 10036

H M Stone Productions
6 East 45th Street
New York, New York 10017

International Film Bureau, Inc.
332 S. Michigan Avenue
Chicago, Illinois 60604

Instructional Support Center
Learning Systems Institute
Florida State University
Tallahassee, Florida 32306

John Colburn Associates
P.O. Box 187
Lake Bluff, Illinois 60044

Modern Learning Aids
3 East 54th Street
New York, New York 10022

Prentice Hall Media
150 White Plains Road
Tarrytown, New York 10591

Spring Green Multimedia
P.O. Box 9015
Washington, D.C. 20003

Syracuse University Film Rental Center
1455 East Colvin Street
Syracuse, New York 13210

Visual Aids Service
University of Illinois
Champaign, Illinois 61820

Walt Disney Educational Media Company
500 S. Buena Vista Street
Burbank, California 91521

Publishers

Addison-Wesley Publishing Co.
Jacob Way
Reading, Massachusetts 01867

Allyn and Bacon, Inc.
7 Wells Avenue
Newton, Massachusetts 02159

American Association for the Advancement of
  Science
1515 Massachusetts Ave. N.W.
Washington, D.C. 20005

American Association of Physics Teachers
S.U.N.Y. at Stony Brook
Stony Brook, New York 11794

Appleton-Century-Crofts
25 Van Zant Street
East Norwalk, Connecticut 06855

Atheneum Publications
597 5th Avenue
New York, New York 10017

Ballantine Books, Inc.
201 E. 50th Street
New York, New York 10022

Basic Books, Inc.
10 E. 53rd Street
New York, New York 10022

Beacon Press, Inc.
25 Beacon Street
Boston, Massachusetts 02108

Bedminster Press
Vreeland Avenue
Totowa, New Jersey 07504

Bell Telephone Laboratories
Contact local Bell System office

Cambridge University Press
32 E. 57th Street
New York, New York 10022

Center For Applied Research in Education, Inc.
c/o Prentice-Hall
Englewood Cliffs, New Jersey 07632
Orders to: P.O. Box 130
          W. Nyack, New York 10994

Center for Curriculum Research and Service
63 North Gate Road
Albany, New York 12203

Central Scientific Co.
2600 S. Kostner Avenue
Chicago, Illinois 60623

Charles W. Clark Co. Inc.
546 Smith Street
Farmingdale, New York 11735

Chemical Rubber Publishing Co.
18901 Cranwood Parkway
Cleveland, Ohio 44128

Medical Education Division
Ciba-Geigy Corporation
West Caldwell, New Jersey 07006

Collier Books
866 3rd Avenue
New York, New York 10022

Committee on Assessing the Progress of Education
Room 201A Huron Towers
2222 Fuller Road
Ann Arbor, Michigan 48104

Cornell University Press
124 Roberts Place
P.O. Box 250
Ithaca, New York 14850

Doubleday Anchor
501 Franklin Avenue
Garden City, New York 11530

Dover Publications, Inc.
180 Varick Street
New York, New York 10014

E. P. Dutton and Co. Inc.
2 Park Avenue
New York, New York 10016

Elsevier Press
52 Vanderbilt Avenue
New York, New York 10017

Exploritorium Publishers
Marina Blvd. and Lyon Streets
San Francisco, California 94123

F. W. Faxon Co. Inc.
15 Southwest Park
Westwood, Massachusetts 02090

Fearon-Pitman Publishers
Pitman Learning Inc.
6 Davis Drive
Belmont, California 94002

W. H. Freeman and Co.
660 Market St.
San Francisco, California 94104

Games
P.O. Box 10145
Des Moines, Iowa 50340

Halstead Press
605 Third Avenue
New York, New York 10158

Harcourt, Brace, Jovanovich
757 Third Avenue
New York, New York 10017

Harper and Row, Publishers, Inc.
10 East Fifty-Third Street
New York, New York 10022

Harvard University Press
79 Garden Street
Cambridge, Massachusetts 02138

Hayden Book Co., Inc.
50 Essex Street
Rochelle Park, New Jersey 07662

D. C. Heath and Co.
125 Spring Street
Lexington, Massachusetts 02173

Heinemann Ed. Books Inc.
4 Front Street
London-Exeter, N.H. 03833

Holt, Rinehart and Winston
383 Madison Avenue
New York, New York 10017

Houghton Mifflin
2 Park Street
Boston, Massachusetts 02107

Physics Department
Indiana University of Pennsylvania

c/o Dr. David Reban
Indiana, Pennsylvania 15705

Imported Publications
320 W. Ohio Street
Chicago, Illinois 60610

Insight Press
614 Vermont Street
San Francisco, California 94107

William Kaufmann
95 1st Street
Los Altos, California 94022

Kendall/Hunt
2460 Kerper Boulevard
Dubuque, Iowa 52001

Lansford Publishing Company
P.O. Box 8711
San Jose, California 95155

MacMillan and Co. Inc.
866 Third Avenue
New York, New York 10022

McGraw-Hill Book Co.
1221 Avenue of the Americas
New York, New York 10020

Mentor Book Co.
1301 Avenue of the Americas
New York, New York 10019

Julian Messner
1230 Avenue of the Americas
New York, New York 10020

Metrologic Publications
143 Harding Avenue
Bellmawr, New Jersey 08030

Minnesota Mining and Manufacturing Company
St. Paul, Minnesota 55101

National Aeronautics and Space Administration
821 15th Street N.W.
Suite 430
Washington, D.C. 20005

National Science Teachers Association
1742 Connecticut Avenue
Washington, D.C. 20009

New American Library
1633 Broadway
New York, New York 10019

New Yorker
25 W. 43rd Street
New York, New York 10036

Newsweek Inc.
10100 Santa Monica Boulevard
Los Angeles, California 90067

New York Times
229 West 43rd Street
New York, New York 10036

Ontario Assessment Instrument Pool
The Minster of Education
Toronto, Ontario, Canada M7A1N8

Oxford University Press
200 Madison Avenue
New York, New York 10016

Park Lane Press
Saw Mill Road
West Haven, Connecticut 06516

Pergamon Press, Inc.
Maxwell House, Fairview Park
Elmsford, New York 10523

The Physics Olympics Subcommittee
c/o Mrs. Jean Brattin, Chairman
3146 Warrington Road
Cleveland, Ohio 44120

Princeton University Press
41 William Street
Princeton, New Jersey 08560

Reinhold Books
383 Madison Avenue
New York, New York 10017

Research and Education Association
505 Eighth Avenue
New York, New York 10018

Rodale Press
33 E. Minor Street
Emmaus, Pennsylvania 18049

Richard Rosen Press Inc.
29 E. 21st Street
New York, New York 10010

Ronald Press Co.
605 Third Avenue
New York, New York 10158

Sampson Low, Marston Co.
U.S.A. Distributor: Ginn and Co.
191 Spring Street
Lexington, Massachusetts 02173

Science
1515 Massachusetts Avenue N.W.
Washington, D.C. 20005

Science Teacher's Association of Ontario
The Ontario Institute for Studies in Education
252 Bloor Street, West
Toronto, Ontario, M5S1V6

Science Digest
The Hearst Corporation
244 W. 57th Street
New York, New York 10019

Science News
by Science Service Inc.
1719 N. Street N.W.
Washington, D.C. 20036

Scientific American
415 Madison Avenue
New York, New York 10017

Scott Graphics, Inc.
Holyoke, Massachusetts 01040

Charles Scribner's Sons
597 Fifth Avenue
New York, New York 10017

Sigma Books
London, England

Signet
New American Library
1633 Broadway
New York, New York 10019

Spring Educational Associates
40 Pinewood Avenue
Saratoga Springs, New York 12866

State Education Department of New York
Albany, New York 12224

Sterling Publishing Co. Inc.
2 Park Avenue
New York, New York 10016

Ticknor and Fields
383 Orange Street
New Haven, Connecticut 06511

Time
by Time Inc.
3435 Wilshire Blvd.
Los Angeles, California 90010

University Books
120 Enterprise Avenue
Secaucus, New Jersey 07094

University of South Carolina Press
Department of Physics
Columbia, South Carolina 29208

University Press of New England
3 Lebanon Street
Hanover, New Hampshire 03755

U.S. Government Printing Office
Washington, D.C. 20402

Van Nostrand Reinhold Co.
Division of Litton Ed. Pub. Inc.
135 W. 50th Street
New York, New York 10020

J. Weston Walch, Publisher
Box 658
Portland, Maine 04104

Ward-Whidden House
The Hill
Portsmouth, New Hampshire 03801

John Wiley and Sons, Inc.
605 Third Avenue
New York, New York 10158

Appendix B

Answers to Selected Problems

Reproduction Page 8

1. vector—a force acting downward
2. scalar—no direction
3. scalar—an amount of matter
4. scalar—no direction
5. scalar—(energy) no direction
6. vectors (displacements)—distances and direction
7. vector—a force; direction is opposite to motion
8. scalar—no direction

Reproduction Page 9

Line A is at 58°

Line B is at 207°

Problems

1st arrow represents 40N

2nd arrow represents 55N

Student's scales determine correctness of remaining problems

Reproduction Page 10

1. $\overline{R} = 10.5N$ at 161.5°
2. $\overline{R} = 539N$ at 248°

Reproduction Page 11

Student answers will vary somewhat depending on drawing accuracy.

1. $\overline{R}$ = 228N at 149°
2. $\overline{R}$ = 35N at 165°

Reproduction Page 12

Student answers on these will vary depending on their graphic accuracy.

1. 113N at 78.5°   4. 660N at 315°
2. 2,925N at 242°   5. .167N at 125°
3. 5.0N at 113°

Reproduction Page 13

Rope Pulling Sled

horizontal component—pulls sled to the left

vertical component—tends to lift sled upward

Lawn Mower

horizontal component—moves mower to the left

vertical component—pushes mower downward

Car's Weight on a Hill

component down the incline—tends to make car go down the hill

component perpendicular to the incline—pushes normal to the road

Hammock Rope

horizontal component—pulls hammock to the left

vertical component—pulls upward

Guy Wire

horizontal component—pulls tower to the left

vertical component—pulls tower downward

Reproduction Page 16

1. reduced μ
2. increase μ
3. increase μ
4. increase N
5. decrease μ
6. larger μ uphill; smaller μ downhill

7. low μ
8. μ decreases when wet
9. sliding friction is less than starting friction
10. starting friction is greater than sliding friction
11. increase N

Reproduction Page 17

At 4 s, the paint thickness is $\frac{1}{16}$; at 5 s, there are 25 areas and the paint thickness is $\frac{1}{25}$; at 10 s, there are 100 areas and the thickness is $\frac{1}{100}$.

Weight of Object at Various Distances from the Earth

3 s	$\frac{1}{9} \times 100N = 11.1N$
4 s	$\frac{1}{16} \times 100N = 6.25N$
5 s	$\frac{1}{25} \times 100N = 4N$
6 s	$\frac{1}{36} \times 100N = 2.78N$
7 s	$\frac{1}{49} \times 100N = 2.04N$
8 s	$\frac{1}{64} \times 100N = 1.56N$

Reproduction Page 19

I 1. Student examples—use Reproduction Page 7 as a guide for correcting.

II 1. Scalar quantities have magnitude but vector quantities have both magnitude and direction. Use Reproduction Page 8 as a guide for student examples.

   2. (a and b) Lengths according to student scale; check directions with a protractor (see Reproduction Page 9).

III 1. $\overline{R} = 40.2$N at 60.5°

    2. $\overline{R} = 35$N at 175° (approximately)

IV 1. parallel component = 450N

    perpendicular component = 779N

V 1. If it is in equilibrium, it will not change its motion; if it is not in equilibrium, its motion (speed and/or direction) will change.

    2. Rope 1 = 100N   (These are approximate
       Rope 2 = 68.5N   depending on accuracy of
       Rope 3 = 85.0N   student drawing.)

VI 1. $\overline{F} = 15$N

    2. Either change the surface employing a greater coefficient or increase the normal force.
Employ a device to lower the coefficient.

    3. Coefficient is the slope of the graph = .1.

VII 1. Two earth radii above the *surface* will place the mass three times as far away, making the gravitational force $\frac{1}{9}$ as great or 10N.

    2. Force on the 20 kg mass is toward the 10 kg mass. Force on the 10 kg mass is toward the 20 kg mass.
Magnitude of the mutual force is 3.34×10^{-9} N

Reproduction Page 20

B, E, and F are moving at the same speed (5 km/hr).
    C and D are moving at the same speed (12 km/hr).
    B and F are moving at the same velocity.

Reproduction Page 22

1. Average speed = $2.08 \frac{m}{s}$.

   In one hour, she will go 7,488 m.

2. Acceleration = $3.13 \frac{m}{s^2}$.

   Distance traveled = 100 m.

3. Bridge height = 11 m

   Speed of rock when it hit the water = $14.7 \frac{m}{s}$.

4. Time to fall 100 m = 4.52 s.

   Speed at 100 m mark = $44.3 \frac{m}{s}$.

Speed 1 s later = 54.1 $\frac{m}{s}$.

5. Height = 11 m.

Speed when ball left hand = 14.7 $\frac{m}{s}$.

Reproduction Page 24

1. a and d
2. b and c
3. a and d; b and c
4. A—uniform acceleration
   B—constant velocity
   C—constant velocity (the object is stopped)
   D—uniform acceleration
   E—constant velocity
   F—uniform acceleration (deceleration)

5. – 6.

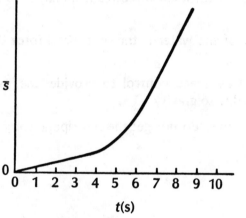
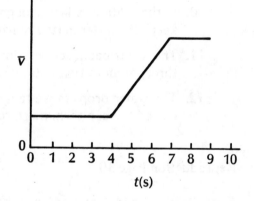

Reproduction Page 25

1. 1.67 $\frac{m}{s^2}$

2. 29.4 $\frac{m}{s}$

3. 44.1 m

4. 9.8 $\frac{m}{s^2}$

5. (b) a scalar; the others are vectors

6. 2s

7. (c)

8. 5 $\frac{m}{s^2}$

9. parabolic

10. (b)

Reproduction Page 29

1. The banking provides an inward component of the track's push. This inward component provides some (or all) of the required centripetal force.

2. A proper speed of the satellite determines a match between the centripetal force required and the amount provided by gravitation.

3. Too great a satellite speed requires a centripetal force greater than that provided by gravity. As a result, the orbit radius increases until there is a match.

4. In this case, more centripetal force is provided by gravity than required by the motion. This greater force causes the satellite to spiral toward the earth.

5. The high speed produces centripetal force requirements greater than those provided.

6. The smaller mass requires less centripetal force.

7. Suspended masses move toward the outside of the circle (larger r) until the bottom of the test tube provides the required centripetal force.

8. Essentially, the tub with holes in it provides the required centripetal force on clothes but not on water, which travels tangentially outward and eventually drains.

9. The increased scale reading illustrates the additional force (centripetal) required when the mass goes in a circle.

10. If the motion is fast enough, the weight of the water is the centripetal force that keeps the water in its circular path.

11. The centripetal acceleration is adjusted by speed control to provide one, two, three, or more times normal acceleration due to gravity.

12. The water drops move tangentially when they do not get the centripetal force required to keep them in a circular path.

Reproduction Page 30

Note: "action" and "reaction" may be interchanged.

1. The action force is by the gun on the bullet. This accelerates the bullet, forward. The reaction is by the bullet on the gun, accelerating the gun backward.

2. The action is on the air in the combustion chamber of the engine. It accelerates the air backwards. The reaction force is exerted by the air on the engine, accelerating the engine forward.

3. Same as #2, except propellant replaces air.

4. Action force is by the foot backward against the floor (no noticeable acceleration of the floor since it is attached to the earth—too great a mass). The floor exerts a reaction force on the foot, moving it forward.

5. Sprinter's foot pushes backward on blocks (similar to #4). The reaction is by the blocks on the sprinter, accelerating him forward.

6. Action force is by the earth on the object, downward, producing the acceleration due to gravity. The object exerts the reaction force on the earth, upwards, but the earth's acceleration is negligible due to its large mass.

7. The tire exerts an action force on the gravel, accelerating some stones backward. The parking lot surface exerts a reaction force on the tires, and thus the car, accelerating it forward.

8. Similar to #1.

9. The propeller pushes water backwards, accelerating the liquid. The reaction force is exerted by the water on the propeller, driving the motor (and the boat) forward.

10. The balloon exerts an action force on the air inside, accelerating the air out the back. The air exerts a forward reaction force on the balloon, causing it to fly around.

11. The sprinkler confinement pushes water outward. The water exerts the reaction force on the sprinkler, moving it in the opposite direction.

12. Similar to #11.

Reproduction Page 31

1. In the first case, a large force acts for a small time; in the latter case, a smaller force acts for a longer time to produce the same change in momentum.

2. The barrier uses a very large force for a very short time to produce the same change in momentum.

3. The "sudden" stop implies a very short time; therefore, very large forces are involved in changing the momentum to zero.

4. The cushion is to increase the time of the catch, thus reducing the force to stop the ball.

5. If she did not have a net (which increases the stopping time), very large forces coupled with the short time would produce the momentum change.

6. The moving bumpers increase the time and thus decrease the force required to produce the momentum change in a collision.

7. In a "belly whopper," a diver stops quickly with large forces; in a head first dive, the same momentum change happens over a longer time involving smaller forces.

8. The smaller engine exerts less force and thus requires more time to produce the same change in momentum.

9. Producing the same momentum change more slowly means using smaller forces for longer times.

10. The greater mass of the larger planes means more momentum change to stop. Longer runways provide more time to produce this change with the same amount of force.

Reproduction Page 32

I 1.	b	II 1.	b	III 1.	b	IV 1.	a
2.	a	2.	d	2.	c	2.	d
3.	d	3.	a	3.	a	3.	d
4.	b	4.	c	4.	b	4.	b
5.	d	5.	c			5.	d
		6.	d			6.	d

Reproduction Page 33

1. lever—multiplies force
2. inclined plane (wrapped around)—multiplies force
3. pulley—usually to multiply force
4. lever—multiplies force
5. inclined plane—multiplies force
6. inclined plane—multiplies force
7. lever—lower gears multiply force; higher gears multiply distance
8. lever—multiplies force
9. lever—multiplies force
10. lever—multiplies distance (speed)
11. lever—multiplies distance (speed)
12. inclined plane—multiplies force
13. pulley—multiplies force
14. inclined plane (wrapped around)—multiplies force

Reproduction Page 35

1st curve: 60 J
2nd curve: 5 J
3rd plot: 6 J
4th plot: 40 J

Reproduction Page 38

1. $PE = 2,965$ J

2. $KE = 81.6$ J

3. $h = 5.10$ m

4. $v = 19.8 \frac{m}{s}$

5. $v = 7.67 \frac{m}{s}$

6. A $PE = 490$ J; $KE = 0$J; $v = 0$

   B $PE = 245$ J; $KE = 245$ J; $v = 9.9 \frac{m}{s}$

   C $PE = 0$; $KE = 490$ J; $v = 14 \frac{m}{s}$

   D $PE = 343$ J; $KE = 147$ J; $v = 7.67 \frac{m}{s}$

Reproduction Page 39

1. b	13. d	25. a
2. b	14. c	26. d
3. a and c	15. d	27. b
4. b	16. a	28. b
5. a	17. b	29. d
6. b	18. c	30. b
7. a	19. c	31. c
8. c	20. a	32. c
9. d	21. b	33. c
10. a	22. a	34. d
11. c	23. a	35. d
12. c	24. d	

Reproduction Page 40

1. Heat leaves the body to the cooler floor at a greater rate with the tile because tile is a better conductor of heat. This gives a cooler sensation than the rug.

2. Sunbathing raises the skin temperature, making the difference in temperature between skin and water greater. This produces a greater rate of heat loss and the colder sensation.

3. "Once you get in" means that the skin temperature is lower, the temperature difference with the water is less, and the swimmer loses heat at a lesser rate—producing a less cold feeling.

4. The ill person will have a higher temperature than the healthy one. Heat will transfer to the healthy person and produce a warm sensation.

5. If you feel your own forehead, there will be no sensation of warm or cold since there is no temperature difference and resultant heat transfer.

6. Cool skin temperature at first produces a large temperature difference with the air in the room, a larger rate of heat transfer, and a very warm feeling. Later, as the skin temperature rises, the temperature difference decreases, and the rate of heat transfer also decreases.

7. At night, your skin temperature is lower. The difference between skin and water temperature is less, and thus the rate of heat loss is less—reducing the cool feeling.

8. The wind helps to remove heat from your body at a greater rate, thus the cooler feeling.

9. Dry socks are better insulators than wet ones. Heat loss to the cooler environment is reduced and the sensation is less cool.

10. Clothing reduces heat loss in the winter when you do not want to lose a lot of body heat. In the summer, the temperature of the air is not as low, so clothing is removed to compensate for the reduced temperature difference and to produce the same degree of comfort.

11. Their warmer skin produces a greater rate of heat loss and the corresponding cooler feeling. Your skin temperature is not as great and the rate of loss is less—a more comfortable feeling.

12. The warm shower raises your skin temperature. The greater temperature difference between skin and air results in a greater rate of heat loss and a cooler feeling.

Reproduction Page 44

1. add 300 kilocalories

2. add 27.4 kilocalories

3. add 2160 kilocalories

4. remove 408 kilocalories

5. remove 536 kilocalories

6. add 53 kilocalories

7. remove 460 kilocalories

8. remove 1.41 kilocalories

9. add 1.59 kilocalories

10. add .428 kilocalories

Reproduction Page 46

1. Because water has such a high specific heat, it changes temperature more slowly than the surrounding air. The air loses heat to the cooler water during hot weather and gains heat from the warmer water as the season turns cooler.

2. The wet person loses heat through the vaporization of the water.

3. Water vapor gives up heat to the air as the water freezes into snow.

4. The rubber suit does not allow normal body cooling through evaporation of perspiration. As the body temperature continues to rise, more perspiration is put out in an attempt to cool the body. The excessive loss of fluid shows up as weight loss. (This process should only be used with appropriate supervision since too much fluid loss or overheating can be very dangerous.)

5. The radical cooling that produces hypothermia is due to the removal of heat by evaporation of the water on the clothing. (Also, insulation properties of most clothes decrease when the clothing is wet.)

6. Each kg of steam at 100°C has 540 k calories more heat to give up than water at the same temperature.

7. Boiling water is a constant temperature medium. If one adds heat too quickly, the heat vaporizes more water, while the temperature remains the same.

8. Potatoes have a relatively high specific heat compared to other foods. As a result, when some heat is lost the temperature change is not as great as it is for lower specific heat items on the plate.

9. The ignition temperature of paper is much higher than 100°C (the temperature of boiling water). Any paper in direct contact with the water will only reach the 100°C temperature.

10. Two factors operate here. The high specific heat of water allows for a considerable amount of heat transfer from water to room as the room temperature drops. This keeps the room warmer than it would be without the water. When the temperature reaches 0°C, an additional 80 kc/kg of heat goes to the cellar as the water begins to freeze.

11. Heating the water raises the kinetic energy of the molecules, so greater numbers of molecules have sufficient velocities to escape the liquid sample and become independent gas molecules.

12. Under normal atmospheric pressure, water undergoes a phase change at 100°C. Once this temperature is reached by adding heat, it will not increase. Any additional heat just produces more steam.

13. The ice cube removes more heat than the liquid due to the additional 80 kc/kg required to melt the ice.

14. Alcohol evaporates rapidly. The alcohol removes heat from the skin for this vaporization process thus cooling the skin.

15. The water removes 540 kc/kg from the contents as it evaporates.

16. Some of the water seeps through the pores and evaporates. The heat for this vaporization comes from the pot and thus cools the remaining contents.

Reproduction Page 48

1. Some of the water's gravitational potential energy (at the top of the water fall) is converted into molecular kinetic energy when the falling water strikes rocks at the bottom. This increases the average kinetic energy of the water, its temperature.

2. The work done in compressing the gas manifests itself as increased kinetic energy of the air molecules (increased temperature).

3. The spaces between the sections are to allow for expansion of the concrete when temperatures increase.

4. Heat released during the ignition causes the contents to expand and rupture the container. This produces the explosion.

5. The fingers are to allow for bridge expansion and contraction without opening up a gap between road and bridge. The rollers allow for free movement of the bridge during the expansion or contraction.

6. Because of the appreciable length of cable involved in a ski lift, considerable length changes occur due to thermal expansion and contraction. If the ends were fixed, they would be pulled toward each other during very cold spells; during warmer temperatures, the cable would sag due to expansion. The hanging weight moves up or down as the cable length changes maintaining proper tension.

7. The gas is usually cooler than the air on hot days because it is stored underground. As the gas warms up to air temperature, it expands, overflowing its tank.

8. Gas pumps measure volume. During cold weather, molecules are closer together. As a result, you get more molecules per gallon.

9. The lid is heated first and expands. This loosens the fit around the mouth of the jar.

10. The expansion or contraction of the aluminum produces movement of one piece of siding over another at the joints. This movement causes the noise you hear.

Reproduction Page 49

	$^4_2$He	$^6_3$Li	$^1_1$H	$^2_1$H	$^{107}_{47}$Ag	$^{208}_{82}$Pb	$^{238}_{92}$U
protons:	2	3	1	1	47	82	92
electrons:	2	3	1	1	47	82	92
neutrons:	2	3	0	1	60	126	146

Atomic Symbols

$^{16}_8$O

$^{4}_{2}$He

$^{226}_{88}$Ra

$^{59}_{28}$Ni

Reproduction Page 51

The minimum quantity of eggs is 6. The answer is based on 6 being the smallest quantity in the data. It checks since all the other egg purchases were multiples of 6, and the purchases are grouped with 6 being the minimum difference between them. The charge on one electron is 1.6×10^{-19}C.

Number of Electrons Gained or Lost

5

2

4

1

3

2

30

10

Reproduction Page 56

Isotope	Binding Energy Per Nucleon (Mev)
$^{2}_{1}$H	.605
$^{3}_{2}$He	1.92
$^{6}_{3}$Li	4.83
$^{7}_{3}$Li	5.17
$^{10}_{5}$B	5.93
$^{13}_{6}$C	6.95

$^{17}_{8}$O	7.24
$^{24}_{12}$Mg	7.76
$^{32}_{16}$S	7.96
$^{40}_{20}$Ca	8.04
$^{58}_{28}$Ni	8.12
$^{84}_{36}$Kr	8.22
$^{107}_{47}$Ag	7.98
$^{138}_{56}$Ba	8.14
$^{181}_{73}$Ta	7.95
$^{208}_{82}$Pb	7.33
$^{226}_{88}$Ra	7.17
$^{238}_{92}$U	7.04

Reproduction Page 58

Questions

1. Alpha and beta particles have a charge and are deflected by magnetic forces when they move through the field. Gamma radiation does not carry an electrical charge and is not deflected.

2. The charge on the beta particles is (−). Alphas have the opposite charge (+).

3. Although the *force* on an alpha particle is twice that on a beta particle because of charge differences (+ 2 versus − 1), the *acceleration* (deflection) is less on the much more massive alpha particle. Refer to $F = ma$ to illustrate this.

Reproduction Page 60

1. $^{222}_{86}$Rn $\rightarrow$ $^{4}_{2}$He + $^{218}_{84}$Po

2. $^{214}_{82}\text{Pb} \rightarrow\ ^{0}_{-1}\text{e} +\ ^{214}_{83}\text{Bi}$

3. $^{210}_{84}\text{Po} \rightarrow\ ^{4}_{2}\text{He} +\ ^{206}_{82}\text{Pb}$

4. $^{238}_{92}\text{U} \rightarrow\ ^{4}_{2}\text{He} +\ ^{234}_{90}\text{Th}$

5. $^{230}_{90}\text{Th} \rightarrow\ ^{4}_{2}\text{He} +\ ^{226}_{88}\text{Ra}$

6. $^{234}_{92}\text{U} \rightarrow\ ^{4}_{2}\text{He} +\ ^{230}_{90}\text{Th}$

7. $^{234}_{90}\text{Th} \rightarrow\ ^{0}_{-1}\text{e} +\ ^{234}_{91}\text{Pa}$

8. $^{210}_{83}\text{Bi} \rightarrow\ ^{0}_{-1}\text{e} +\ ^{210}_{84}\text{Po}$

9. $^{226}_{88}\text{Ra} \rightarrow\ ^{4}_{2}\text{He} +\ ^{222}_{86}\text{Rn}$

Reproduction Page 63

mass of U-235	235.0439 A.M.U
mass of neutron	1.0087 A.M.U.
Total:	236.0526 A.M.U.
mass of Ba 138	137.9050 A.M.U.
mass of Kr 95	94.9 A.M.U.
3 X mass of neutron	3.0261 A.M.U.
Total:	235.8 A.M.U.

mass difference = (236.0526 − 235.8) A.M.U. = .3 A.M.U.

.3 A.M.U. X 931 Mev./A.M.U. = 279 Mev.

Reproduction Page 64

Part	Function	Typical Materials
fuel	provides fissionable nuclei	uranium, plutonium
moderator	slows down neutrons	graphite, heavy water
control rods	absorb neutrons	boron, cadmium
coolant	transfers heat from reactor	water, carbon dioxide
shielding	contains radiation	lead, concrete

Reproduction Page 65

1. $^{238}_{92}U + ^{1}_{0}n \rightarrow ^{239}_{92}U$

2. $^{239}_{92}U \rightarrow ^{0}_{-1}e + ^{239}_{93}Np$

3. $^{239}_{93}Np \rightarrow ^{0}_{-1}e + ^{239}_{94}Pu$

Reproduction Page 67

1. b	10. c	19. b
2. c	11. d	20. b
3. c	12. a	21. a
4. d	13. b	22. b
5. c	14. c	23. b
6. a	15. c	24. c
7. c	16. d	25. a
8. b	17. a	26. c
9. d	18. c	27. a

Reproduction Page 68

1. speed   How fast the energy propagates; depends on the medium.

2. medium   That which the wave is traveling through.

3. pulse   A single, non repeated disturbance.

4. amplitude   The maximum displacement of a vibrating particle from its equilibrium position; see Reproduction Page 69.

5. frequency   The number of waves per unit time.

6. wavelength   The distance from one point on a wave to a point that is in phase on the next wave; see Reproduction Page 69.

7. period   The time for one complete wave to pass a point; the time for one complete oscilation.

8. phase   The position and motion of a part of a wave.

9. interference   The mutual effect (superposition of amplitudes) of two waves at the same point in a medium at the same time.

10. reflection   The turning back of a portion of a wave at the boundary between two media.

Reproduction Page 74

1.

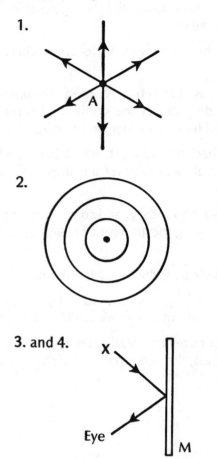

2.

3. and 4.

Eye

M

5. **virtual image**   An image which is formed in the eye; seen where rays or waves *appear* to originate.

   real image   An image which is formed by actual rays of light.

   reflection   The turning back of part of a wave at a boundary between two media.

   normal   A line perpendicular to a plane.

   plane (mirror)   A flat reflecting surface.

   incident ray   A ray of light going from a source toward a boundary.

Reproduction Page 77

1. Light from the part of the oar in the water bends away from the normal when it enters the air. This makes the bottom of the oar appear to be in a different location than it actually is.

2. The bending of light from the bottom causes the rays to appear to come from a location closer to the surface. This makes the depth appear less than it actually is.

3. Light rays from the sun, which would not otherwise get to the eye because of the horizon, are bent toward the normal when they slow down slightly upon encountering air. This bending allows the rays to get to the eye.

4. Because of refraction of light from the fish, they are not in the location where the eye sees them.

5. The water mirage is actually skylight, which has been refracted upon encountering the hotter air adjacent to the road. This bending causes the skylight to enter our eyes from below, as it would if it was reflected by some water on the road.

6. What they actually see is variably refracted background light, which is bent when it encounters the boundary between cooler air and warmer air above the heat source.

7. Light from the liquid is refracted at the glass air boundary, and some light appears to come from the region of the glass, thus making the amount of rootbeer appear greater than it actually is.

8. Variable atmospheric refraction of light from stars produces the twinkling.

9. Variable refraction of different frequencies of light (dispersion) by raindrops separates the various frequencies into the spectrum of colors we see in a rainbow.

10. Cheap glass surfaces are not flat and parallel but irregular. Various portions of light, representing an image passing through the glass, are refracted at different angles, distorting the image.

Reproduction Page 78

1. medium A

2. medium B

3. ray should be bent *toward* N

4. increases

5. remains the same

6. zero

7. no

8. and 9.

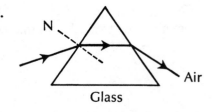

10. increases

Reproduction Page 81

Property	Wave	Particle	Explanation
1. rectilinear propagation	√	√	Both travel in straight lines.
2. reflection	√	√	Both make equal angles.
3. refraction	√	√	The speed depends on the medium for both.
4. diffraction	√		Particles don't bend around obstacles.
5. interference	√		No way to get two particles at the same point and have the effect be zero (complete destructive interference).
6. photoelectric emission		√	If light was a wave, brighter light would eject more electrons at greater energy. See Reproduction Page 80.

Reproduction Page 83

1.

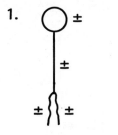

2.

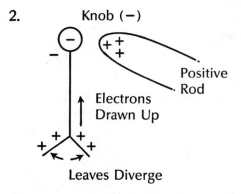

3. Electrons Come from Ground

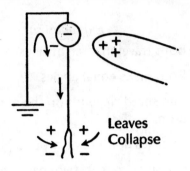

**Leaves
Collapse**

**Electroscope
Grounded**

4.

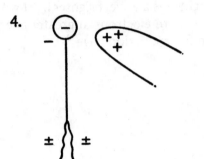

**Ground Path
Removed**

5.

When rod is removed, electrons
readjust and entire
electroscope shows net (−) change.

Reproduction Page 84

1. A (+) F indicates a force of repulsion. If Q_1 and Q_2 are both (+), a (+) F results; if Q_1 and Q_2 are both (−), a (+) F still results.

2. A (−) F indicates a force of attraction. The only way to get a (−) F is if one charge is (+) and the other is (−).

3. Values for k $\left(\times 10^9 \dfrac{Nm^2}{C^2} \right)$:

    paper 4.5
    paraffin 4.1

polyethylene 3.9
polystryene 3.6
hard rubber 3.2
mica 1.5
glass 1.1

4. If s doubles, F becomes $\frac{1}{4}$ as great.

If s triples, F becomes $\frac{1}{9}$ as great.

If s becomes $\frac{1}{2}$, F becomes four times as great.

Reproduction Page 85

The charge on the sphere is (+) because the lines of force point away.
Sphere B has the greater charge (line density is greater).

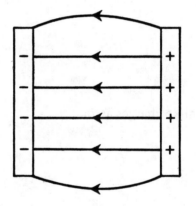

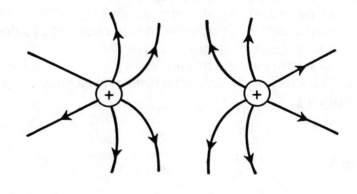

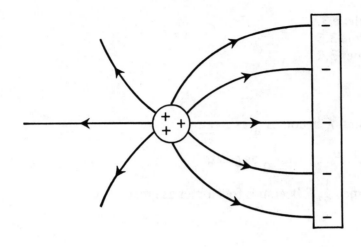

Reproduction Page 86

1. (−)

2. (+)

3. (+)

4. (−)

5. Like charges repel; unlike charges attract.

6. electrons

7. b

8. c

9. – 10. Examples of electrification (partial list):
   a. crackling of a comb going through hair
   b. sticking together of clothes when they come out of a dryer
   c. shocks when scuffing across a rug or tile
   d. shocks when sliding across seat covers
   e. balloons sticking to walls after being rubbed on hair
   f. lightning

Reproduction Page 87

1. a	6. c
2. b	7. a
3. a	8. b
4. b	9. b
5. b	10. c

Reproduction Page 88

1. The knob will be (−).
2. Electrons migrate upward toward the knob.
3. The leaves are diverged; their charge is (+).
4. (c)
5. Electrons flow from the electroscope to ground.
6. Leaves will be collapsed; their charge is neutral.
7. (d)
8. rod
9. (d)
10. (b)

Reproduction Page 89

1. positive
2. positive
3. positive
4. conductor
5. $\dfrac{Nm^2}{C^2}$
6. repulsive
7. $\dfrac{1}{4}$
8. A
9. (+)
10. (b)

Reproduction Page 94

1. 1.4×10^{-1}
2. $\dfrac{V}{A}$
3. A
4. 3
5. 12V
6. becomes $\dfrac{1}{2}$ as great, 1.5 amps.
7. top of R is (−); bottom is (+)
8. increases
9. become $\dfrac{1}{4}$ as great
10. decrease

Reproduction Page 95

1. d
2. c
3. b
4. c
5. b
6. c
7. c
8. c
9. a
10. a

Reproduction Page 100

1. 4 amperes
2. 32 watts
3. 48 watts
4. 2,400 joules
5. 1,440 joules

6. R_1
7. R_1
8. 20 volts
9. 2 amperes
10. 60 watts

Reproduction Page 101

Direction of Deflecting Force

1. upward
2. out of the page
3. out of the page
4. toward the right

Reproduction Page 103

1. A
2. b
3. B
4. d
5. decreases

6. b
7. b
8. b
9. c
10. The basic difference is in the connections between the coil and external circuit. (A.C. uses slip rings; D.C. uses a split ring commutator.)

Appendix C

Reproduction Pages

The pages that follow will help reproduce the exercises and other activities suggested in the text of this book. Each page is perforated to make removal from the book easy. Once removed, the page can be used in any of four ways:

1. For projection with an opaque projector. No further preparation is necessary if the page is to be used with an opaque projector. The page can simply be inserted in the projector for viewing by the whole class.

2. For projection with an overhead projector. The Reproduction Page must be converted into a transparency for use with an overhead projector. To produce the transparency, overlay the Reproduction Page with a blank transparency and run both through a copying machine.

3. For duplication with a spirit duplicator. A master can be made from the Reproduction Page by overlaying it with a special heat-sensitive spirit master and running both through a copying machine. The spirit master can then be used to reproduce 50–100 copies on paper.

4. For reproduction with a copying machine. Use the removed page as the "original" to make unlimited copies.

Please note that all material appearing on Reproduction Pages (as well as all other material in this book) is protected under the United States Copyright Law. Allyn and Bacon, Inc., grants readers the right to make multiple copies of reproduction pages for nonprofit educational use only. All other rights are reserved.

Name: _____   Section: _____

STUDENT NEEDS SURVEY

1. Why have you signed up to take physics?

2. What career(s) are you now considering?

3. List the most advanced math course you have completed and the grade you earned.

4. List your last two science courses and the grade in each.

5. What have you liked the most about science courses you have taken?

6. What have you liked the least?

7. What topics do you hope to learn about in physics?

8. List your out-of-class activities (hobbies, sports, special interests, leisure time activities).

Name: _____   Section: _____

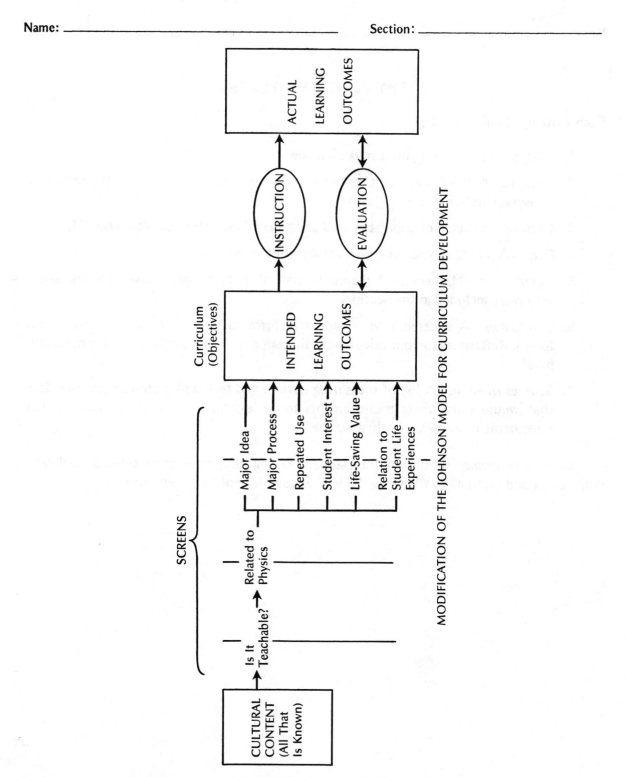

MODIFICATION OF THE JOHNSON MODEL FOR CURRICULUM DEVELOPMENT

Name: _____   Section: _____

PHYSICS LAB WRITE-UPS

Each write-up should include:

1. *Title*, your *name*, and your *partner's* name.

2. *Purpose.* A brief statement of what you are trying to find, verify, examine, measure, check, etc.

3. *Method.* A sketch of apparatus used and a brief description of what you did.

4. *Data.* A record of your observations and measurements.

5. *Calculations.* Mathematical manipulations of data to get what you are after; graphs are included in this section.

6. *Conclusion.* A statement, very similar in form to your "purpose," of what you found. References to your calculations that support your conclusion are appropriate here.

7. *Sources of error.* A list of measuring devices and techniques used to get your data that would cause these measurements to be less than 100 percent accurate. No measurement is ever perfectly accurate.

General guideline: Could another student taking physics at some other school read your report and understand what you did well enough to replicate your work?

Name: _____   Section: _____

SAMPLE LAB REPORT

1. Determination of Pi
   Bill Yurkewicz
   Partner: A. Einstein

2. *Purpose:* To determine a value of pi from measurements of the circumference and diameter of several circular shaped objects, using $C = (\text{pi}) \times D$.

3. *Method:*

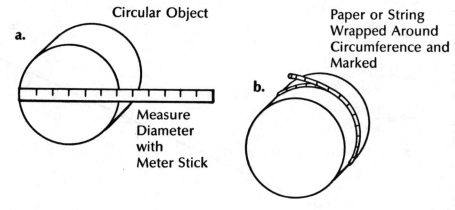

Circular Object

a.

Measure
Diameter
with
Meter Stick

Paper or String
Wrapped Around
Circumference and
Marked

b.

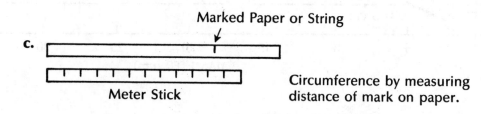

Marked Paper or String

c.

Meter Stick

Circumference by measuring
distance of mark on paper.

4. *Data:*

Diameter (cm)	Circumference (cm)
10.0	31.2
17.2	54.0
23.1	73.5
30.0	90.1
35.7	117.8

Diameter (cm)	Circumference (cm)
2.1	6.5
14.8	47.4

5. Calculations

equation for any straight line: $y = mx + b$

      ↓   ↓ ↓ ↓ is zero in this case

for this line: $C = \pi D$

therefore, the slope, *m*, is our value for π:

Calculation of slope:

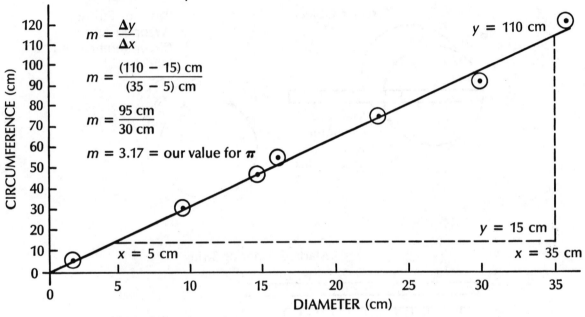

$$m = \frac{\Delta y}{\Delta x}$$

$$m = \frac{(110 - 15)\ cm}{(35 - 5)\ cm}$$

$$m = \frac{95\ cm}{30\ cm}$$

$$m = 3.17 = \text{our value for } \pi$$

6. *Conclusion:*   Our measured value for pi is 3.17.

7. *Sources of error:*
   a. Had to estimate meterstick readings of diameters.
   b. Had to estimate meterstick readings of circumference.
   c. Objects used were assumed to be perfect circles—probably their shape was only an approximation of a circle.

$$\% \text{ error} = \frac{\text{difference between measured and accepted value}}{\text{accepted value}} \times 100\%$$

$$\% \text{ error} = \frac{.03}{3.14} \times 100\%$$

$\% \text{ error} = .0095 \times 100\%$

$\% \text{ error} = .95\% \approx 1\%$ (anything around 10% or less is okay)

Name: _____   Section: _____

THE INTERNATIONAL SYSTEM OF UNITS (SI)

The International System of Units is a modernized version of the metric system. It provides a logical and interconnected framework for all measurements in science, industry, and commerce. Officially abbreviated SI, the system is built on a foundation of seven base units. All other SI units are derived from these. Multiples and submultiples are expressed in a decimal system.

Basic Units

Quantity	Unit	Symbol
length	meter	m
mass	kilogram	kg
time	second	s
electric current	ampere	A
temperature	kelvin	K
amount of a substance	mole	mol
luminous intensity	calenda	cd

Examples of Derived Units

Quantity	Name of Unit	Symbol	Expressions in Terms of Other SI Units
force	newton	N	$\dfrac{kg \cdot m}{s^2}$
speed			$\dfrac{m}{s}$
acceleration			$\dfrac{m}{s^2}$
impulse, momentum			$N \cdot s$ or $\dfrac{kg \cdot m}{s}$
work, energy	joule	J	$N \cdot m$ or $\dfrac{kg \cdot m^2}{s^2}$
power	watt	W	$\dfrac{J}{s}$
frequency	hertz	Hz	s^{-1}
charge	coulomb	C	$A \cdot s$
potential difference, e m f	volt	V	$\dfrac{J}{C}$
resistance	ohm	Ω	$\dfrac{V}{A}$
magnetic flux	weber	Wb	$V \cdot s$
magnetic field	telsa	T	$\dfrac{Wb}{m^2}$ or $\dfrac{N}{(A \cdot m)}$
electric field (E)			$\dfrac{V}{m}$ or $\dfrac{N}{C}$
radioactivity	becquerel	Bq	s^{-1}

Name: _____   Section: _____

A STUDENT'S GUIDE TO A SUCCESSFUL STUDY OF PHYSICS

Melinda Seaman

A methodical approach is essential to the study of any science. Foremost, a student should develop a positive attitude toward the subject of physics and attempt to do the work it involves with a sense of self-confidence. Since physics has many practical applications, it is useful to refer to these as one progresses through the course.

As new material is introduced during class, one should listen attentively, at least to grasp the fundamental concepts. Neat, organized notes of any formulas, diagrams, laws, explanations, and demonstrations are advantageous. I find that analogies are extremely helpful and often jot these down to reinforce ideas. Eventually one learns to discriminate the type of information to look for and note—ideas that will likely reappear on tests and in future chapters.

Good rapport is needed between the student and teacher. It is important to be assertive and ask questions pertaining not only to the immediate curriculum, but to related topics inspired by situations one might encounter in everyday life. To insure that I am accurately comprehending what is being discussed, I do not hesitate to ask the instructor to clarify certain ideas. It becomes evident through emphasis and repetition which points are most significant.

Homework assignments typically include reading pertinent sections in the textbook, responding to a number of questions, and solving mathematical problems. The method that seems most effective for me initially involves skimming over the chapter for context and reading to interpret the questions. Next I suggest re-reading the material for depth and understanding in preparation for answering the questions. In regard to problems, it is helpful to write down the given data to better suggest suitable equations; I also try to understand the context of what is being performed.

In regard to testing, my basic method for a successful performance is to employ my reasoning capabilities, rather than rote memorization. To prepare for a test, I suggest studying notes for a start, and then reading over the material in the text. In addition, previous homework papers and lab results should be covered. If a topical review sheet is provided by the teacher, it is useful to refer to it while studying, in order to determine the essence of the forthcoming test.

"Pop" quizzes provide an excellent opportunity to discover any of the concepts not yet understood, even if the quiz occurs at the expense of a poor mark. The possibility of a surprise quiz forces one to keep up with the presentation of new material and not get behind in trying to understand and learn it. It is wise to quickly skim class notes every night. During an actual exam, I try to reason out the questions, taking into account any basic formulas, principles, and theories.

When time is a factor, I try to initially glance at the test in its entirety, proceed to complete the test as quickly as possible, and then go back to check all my responses. After the paper has been corrected and the answers are being explained in class, I take notes on the majority of questions, including some of those on which I scored correctly. I find this method is immensely beneficial, particularly for future reference.

Lab experiments should be executed only after the purpose and procedure are completely understood. Precision will insure more accurate results upon which to base any conclusions. I suggest writing up the lab report as soon as the experiment is finished.

In closing, I have presented a brief outline suggesting various techniques that I have discovered to be very effective in attaining success in a physics course.

Name: _____   Section: _____

APPROXIMATE WEIGHTS OF THINGS IN NEWTONS

1 gram mass = .01N

1 kilogram mass = 10N

a bag of sugar = 20N

a female classmate = 400N

a male classmate = 600N

a pencil = .05N

a textbook = 12N

a car = 11,000N

Write down five other familiar objects and estimate their weights in newtons. Discuss your estimates with others in your group.

	Object	*Estimated Weight*
1.		
2.		
3.		
4.		
5.		

Name: _____   Section: _____

VECTORS AND SCALARS

DIRECTIONS: Indicate whether the following quantities are vector or scalar. Be prepared to support your choices in class.

1. a weight of 50N

2. 20 seconds of time

3. a mass of 10 kg

4. the length of your pencil

5. 50 kilowatt—hours of electric energy

6. the instructions on a treasure map

7. a frictional force

8. your age

Name: _____   Section: _____

GRAPHIC REPRESENTATION OF VECTORS

DIRECTION CONVENTION: Measure angles from the vertical upright of the axis in a clockwise direction.

Examples:

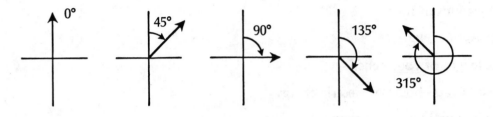

Problems:

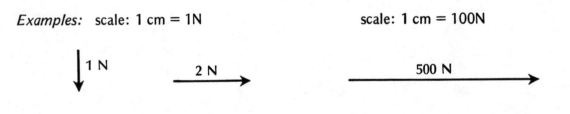

What is the direction of line A? _____

What is the direction of line B? _____

Magnitudes of forces are represented by an appropriate length line according to a predetermined scale.

Examples: scale: 1 cm = 1N   scale: 1 cm = 100N

Problems: If 1 cm = 10N, what is the magnitude of

⟶ ? ⟶ ?

Using the same scale, represent a force of 65N

On the back of this sheet, set up your own scales and represent force vectors of
(A) 5,000N at 30° (B) .0015N at 170°

Name: _____   Section: _____

TRIGONOMETRIC SOLUTION TO FIND THE RESULTANT
OF ANY TWO FORCES AT RIGHT ANGLES

Sample Problems:

Find the resultant of 100N at 90° and 150N at 180°.

   1. Sketch and label the two forces.

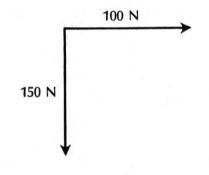

   2. Complete a parallelogram using the two forces as adjacent sides. The diagonal of this parallelogram (acting from the same point as the original forces) represents the resultant. Note that the diagonal divides the parallelogram into two congruent right triangles. Remember that the opposite sides of a parallelogram are equal.

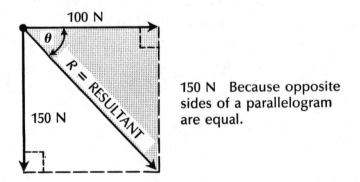

150 N   Because opposite sides of a parallelogram are equal.

Working with the shaded right triangle:

3. $\tan \theta = \dfrac{\text{opp.}}{\text{adj.}}$

   $\tan \theta = \dfrac{150N}{100N} = 1.5$

   from a trig. table: $\theta = 56.3°$

4. $\sin \theta = \dfrac{\text{opp.}}{\text{hyp.}}$

   $\sin \theta = \dfrac{150N}{R}$

   solving for R: $R = \dfrac{150N}{\sin \theta} = \dfrac{150N}{.833} = 180N$

5. Using the direction convention, the direction of R is $90° + 56.3° = 146.3°$

Problems:

Find the magnitude and direction of the resultant of:

1. 3N at 90° and 10N at 180°

2. 200N at 180° and 500N at 270°

Name: _____   Section: _____

GRAPHIC DETERMINATION OF THE RESULTANT OF ANY TWO FORCES

Example:

Find the resultant of 10N at 90° and 15N at 140°.

1. Choose an appropriate scale and construct an axis for direction measurements. Represent the two component forces to scale.

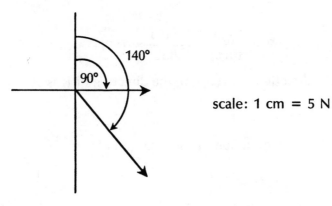

scale: 1 cm = 5 N

2. Complete the parallelogram around these two sides by drawing lines from the tip of one arrow and parallel to the other arrow. Draw in the diagonal which will represent the resultant to scale. This diagonal originates from the same point as the original two forces.

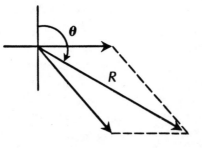

3. Measure the length of R and use your scale to convert this length to a force magnitude.

$$R = 4.5 \text{ cm since } 1 \text{ cm} = 5\text{N}, \ R = 22.5\text{N}$$

4. Measure angle θ with a protractor. It is 120°, therefore the *direction of R is 120°*.

Problems:

Find the resultant of the following pairs of forces, graphically.

1. 100N at 90° and 200N at 175°.

2. 50N at 180° and 20N at 30°.

Name: _____   Section: _____

VECTOR PROBLEMS

DIRECTIONS: Find the resultant for each of the following pairs of concurrent forces:

1. 50N at 45° and 75N at 100°.

2. 2,000N at 270° and 1,500N at 200°.

3. 4.7N at 10° and 7.5N at 150°.

4. 300N at 0° and 500N at 290°.

5. .05N at 180° and .15N at 100°.

Name: _____   Section: _____

COMPONENTS

DIRECTIONS: Identify the two components of each force. Consider the separate effects of each component.

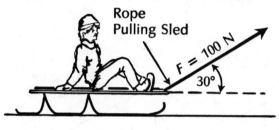

Rope
Pulling Sled

F = 100 N

30°

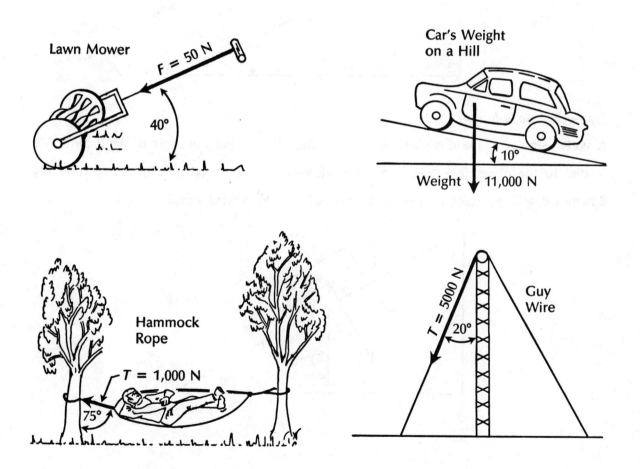

Lawn Mower

F = 50 N

40°

Car's Weight
on a Hill

10°

Weight 11,000 N

Hammock
Rope

T = 1,000 N

75°

T = 5000 N

20°

Guy
Wire

Name: _____   Section: _____

RESOLUTION OF A WEIGHT ON AN INCLINE

Problem:

Resolve the weight into two components, one parallel to the incline and one perpendicular to it.

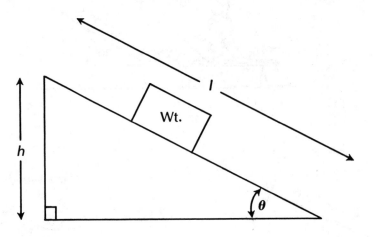

Trigonometric Solution:

A sketch similar to the one above is the first step. (Note that the angle of the incline, θ, is related to the dimensions: $\sin \theta = \dfrac{h}{l}$) Next, sketch in the weight vector acting vertically downward, and represent the two components. They are labeled x and y.

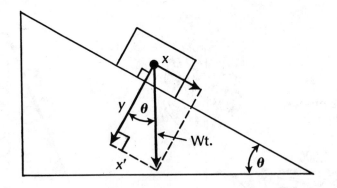

Complete the sketch by making the parallelogram around the weight vector (as the diagonal) with x and y as adjacent sides. The angle of the incline, θ, is also the angle between the weight and its y component. x^1, the side opposite x, is equal to x. We now have a right triangle in the force diagram, with the "known" weight as the hypotenuse, and x^1 and y as the other two sides.

$$\sin \theta = \frac{\text{opp.}}{\text{hyp.}} = \frac{x^1}{\text{wt.}}$$

and $x^1 = x = \text{wt.} \sin \theta$ (component parallel to incline)

$$\cos \theta = \frac{\text{adj.}}{\text{hyp.}} = \frac{y}{\text{wt.}}$$

and $y = \text{wt.} \cos \theta$ (component perpendicular to incline)

Graphic Solution

The construction is similar to the sketch in the trigonometric approach, except that all lines and angles are reproduced to scale. You will need two scales: one for a scale representation of the dimensions of the incline and a second scale for the force diagram. Once the force diagram is constructed by drawing in x and y around the weight vector, the respective lengths are measured and converted back into forces through the appropriate scale.

Name: _____ Section: _____

FRICTION LAB

A. The retarding force of friction, F_{fr}, depends mainly on two factors: μ, the nature of the surfaces in contact, and N, the normal force sandwiching the two surfaces together.

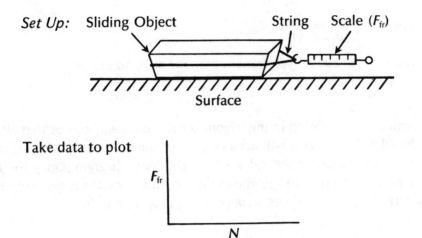

Set Up: Sliding Object   String   Scale (F_{fr})

Surface

Take data to plot

F_{fr}

N

N can be varied by adding weights to the object (N, in this case, is the total weight of the object.) Pull with a slow, steady motion.

Questions:

1. Theoretically, what shape should your graph have? What does this show?
2. Is the slope significant?
3. Calculate the coefficient of friction for each surface.

B. Repeat A but slide your object over a different surface from the lab table top. Plot data on the same graph.

Name: _____   Section: _____

FRICTION

DIRECTIONS: Discuss which variables are manipulated in order to produce a desired amount of frictional force in the following examples:

1. Snow skis have a special surface applied to the bottoms.

2. People often throw sand on icy walkways.

3. Spikes or cleats are often used in athletic competition.

4. For winter driving, some people place cement blocks in the trunks of their cars.

5. Machines use grease and oil.

6. Cross country skis use a special wax or a "fish scale" bottom. People can walk uphill quite easily with this type of ski.

7. It is difficult to walk on freshly waxed floors.

8. Roadsign: "Slippery when wet."

9. While sliding a heavy crate across a floor, someone yells, "Keep it going—don't stop!"

10. If you are stuck in mud with your car, it is best to gently apply the gas rather than spinning the tires rapidly.

11. When a car is stuck in snow, several people stand on the bumpers while trying to get it going.

DIRECTIONS: List several of your own examples:

Name: _____   Section: _____

THE INVERSE SQUARE LAW

Paint sprays radially away from the can in straight lines. Like gravity, the thickness or strength of the spray obeys the inverse square law.

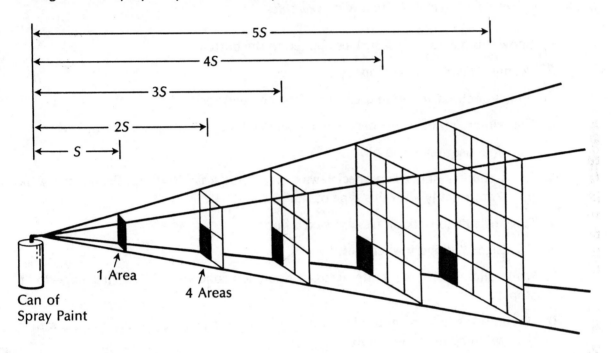

Distance	Number of Areas	Paint Thickness
S	1	1
2S	4	1/4
3S	9	1/9
4S	16	
5S		
⋮	⋮	⋮
10S		

If an object weighs 1N at the earth's surface, it will weigh $\frac{1}{4}$N when it is twice as far from the center because the gravitational pull is only $\frac{1}{4}$ as great. At three times the distance, it weighs $\frac{1}{9}$, and so on.

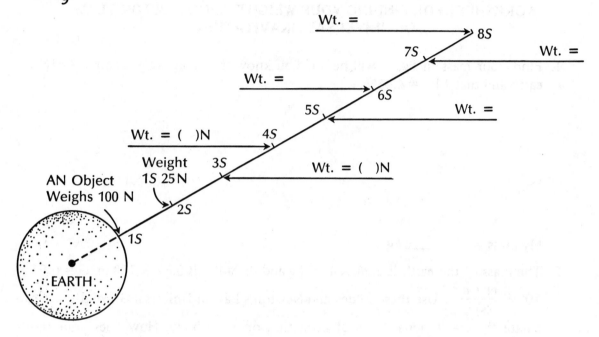

Name: _____   Section: _____

WORKSHEET FOR FINDING YOUR WEIGHT USING NEWTON'S LAW OF UNIVERSAL GRAVITATION

1. Find your mass in kg. It will help if you know that 1 kg weighs about 9.81N on earth and that 1 lb. = 4.45N.

    My mass = _____ kg

2. The mass of the earth is 5.96×10^{24} kg and its radius is 6.37×10^{6} m. $G = 6.67 \times 10^{-11} \frac{N \cdot m^2}{kg^2}$. Use these values and Newton's Law of Universal Gravitation to calculate the gravitational force of attraction on your body. How does your result compare with your "known" weight (in lbs.) as measured by a scale?

$$F = G\frac{m_1 m_2}{s^2}$$

Name: _____   Section: _____

FORCE TEST

I 1. List three common examples of forces and give the approximate magnitude of each in newtons.

II 1. Distinguish vector and scalar quantities. Give two examples of each quantity.

   2. Choose an appropriate scale, list it, and represent the following forces graphically:

   a. 10N at 70°
   b. 1500N at 250°

III 1. Determine the resultant of 20N at 0° and 35N at 90°, trigonometrically.

   2. Determine the resultant of 50N at 40° and 75N at 200° graphically.

IV 1. Resolve the weight into two components, one parallel to the incline and one perpendicular to it.

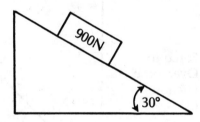

V 1. How can one tell if an object is in translational equilibrium or not by observing its motion?

   2. Find the tension in each of the ropes.

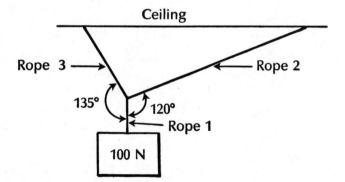

VI 1. If the object is sliding to the right, what is the magnitude and direction of the frictional force?

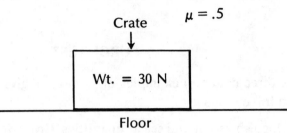

2. a. Describe one way in which the situation above could be altered in order to increase the frictional force.

    b. Describe one way to decrease the frictional force by changing the circumstances.

3. This graph is the result of a lab on friction. The data was obtained by measuring the force needed to overcome friction versus a varying normal force. Calculate the coefficient of friction for the surfaces.

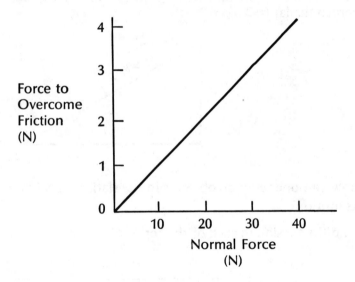

VII   1. The mass shown in the diagram weighs 90N on the earth's surface. How much will it weigh if it is moved to two earth radii above the surface of the planet? Show your reasoning.

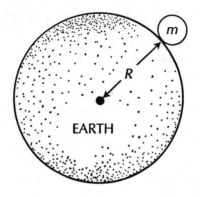

2. Two masses isolated in space.

$$G = \frac{6.67 \times 10^{-11}\text{N} \cdot m^2}{\text{kg}^2}$$

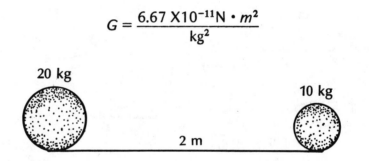

   a. What is the direction of the gravitational force on the 20 kg mass? On the 10 kg mass?

   b. What is the magnitude of the gravitational force between the two masses?

Name: _____   Section: _____

SPEED AND VELOCITY

DIRECTIONS: This is a scene of a harbor taken from a helicopter above. A number of boats are moving over the water.

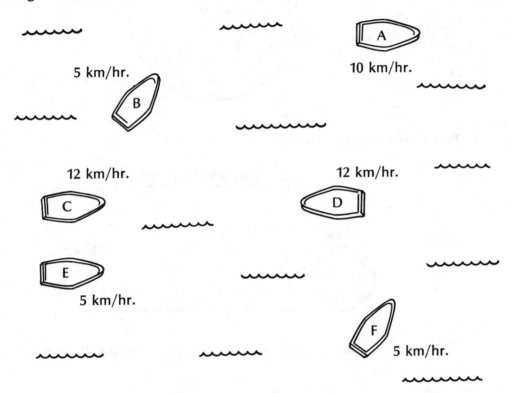

Which boats are moving at the same speed?

Which boats are moving at the same velocity?

Name: _____   Section: _____

DERIVATION OF A FORMULA FOR THE DISTANCE TRAVELED
BY A UNIFORMLY ACCELERATING OBJECT

1. $\bar{s} = \bar{v}_{ave.} t$

   The displacement, $\bar{s}$, covered by any moving object, is given by equation (1), where $\bar{v}_{ave.}$ is the average velocity and t is the time of travel. An average is the sum of the things to be averaged divided by the number in the sample. In this case, with two velocities, $\bar{v}_i$ and $\bar{v}_f$ (an initial and final velocity), this becomes $\bar{v}_{ave.} = \dfrac{\bar{v}_i + \bar{v}_f}{2}$. Substituting in equation (1) we get:

2. $\bar{s} = \left[\dfrac{\bar{v}_i + \bar{v}_f}{2} \right] t$

   From the definitional equation for acceleration, $\bar{a} = \dfrac{\bar{v}_f - \bar{v}_i}{t}$, we can solve for an expression for $\bar{v}_f$: $\bar{v}_f = \bar{a}t + \bar{v}_i$. Substituting this in equation (2):

3. $\bar{s} = \left[\dfrac{\bar{v}_i + (\bar{a}t + \bar{v}_i)}{2} \right] t$

   Multiplying by the t outside the bracket:

$$\bar{s} = \frac{\bar{v}_i t + \bar{a}t^2 + \bar{v}_i t}{2}$$

Combining $\bar{v}_i t$'s:

$$\bar{s} = \frac{2\bar{v}_i t + \bar{a}t^2}{2}$$

Performing the indicated division by 2:

$$\boxed{\bar{s} = \bar{v}_i t + \frac{1}{2}\bar{a}t^2}$$

Name: _____   Section: _____

MOTION PROBLEMS

DIRECTIONS: Solve the following problems on separate paper (Use $g = 9.8 \frac{m}{s^2}$ for the acceleration due to gravity)

1. A woman jogs a 1,000 meter course in 480 seconds. What is her average speed? Assuming she maintains this speed, how far can she run in one hour?

2. A car starts from rest and reaches a speed of 25 $\frac{m}{s}$ in 8 seconds. What was its acceleration? How far did it travel during the acceleration?

3. A rock is dropped from a bridge and falls freely to the water below in 1.5 seconds. How high is the bridge? How fast was the rock going when it hit the water?

4. How long does it take for a freely falling object to fall 100 meters from rest? How fast is it going as it passes the 100 meter mark? What is its speed one second after it crosses the mark?

5. A man throws a baseball upwards. Three seconds later, it hits the ground. How high did it go? How fast was it moving when it first left the man's hand?

Name: _____   Section: _____

STEPS FOR PROBLEM SOLVING IN PHYSICS

1. Read the problem carefully. Make sure you understand all the terms used.

2. Produce a sketch of the situation described. Label all the quantities given on your sketch.

3. Carefully make a list of all the quantities given in the problem using an appropriate letter symbol and setting it equal to the value given.

$$\text{Ex.: } \bar{v}_f = 4 \, \frac{m}{s}$$

$$t = 5 \text{ s}$$

4. Add to the list of "givens" any other quantities that may be determined from the description in the problem but which are not specifically stated.

$$\text{Ex.: } \bar{a} = \bar{g} = 9.8 \, \frac{m}{s^2} \text{ (a falling object)}$$

$$\bar{v}_i = 0 \text{ (it started from rest)}$$

5. Finally, indicate on this list the symbol for the variable (s) to be determined with a question mark.

$$\text{Ex.: } \bar{s} = ?$$

6. Now inspect the list and try to find the basic relationships among the variables. Write down these equation(s) in standard form.

7. Solve the equations for the unknowns; then plug in your data. Be sure to include the units for each quantity in the formulas. Remember, subcalculations are often needed to arrive at values to use in the final calculation.

8. Inspect your final solution. Do the units as determined make sense for the quantity? Look at the magnitude of your answer. Is it reasonable for the situation described? If the answer to these questions is yes, your result is probably correct. If not, first check your math and then repeat steps 1–8.

Name: _____   Section: _____

GRAPHIC REPRESENTATION OF MOTION

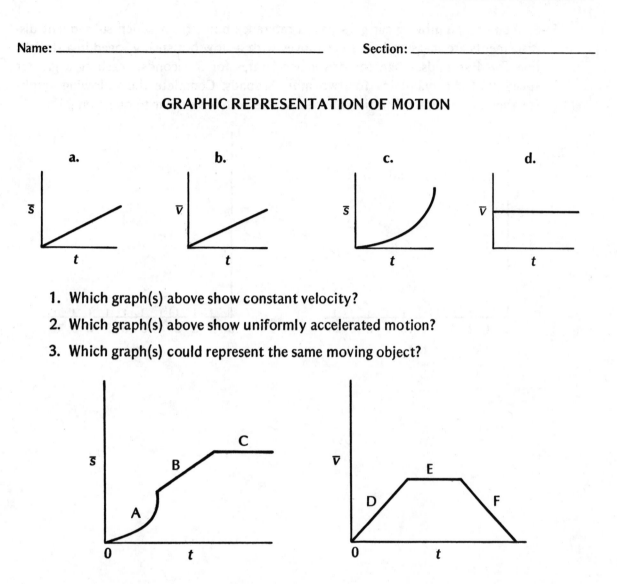

1. Which graph(s) above show constant velocity?

2. Which graph(s) above show uniformly accelerated motion?

3. Which graph(s) could represent the same moving object?

4. Describe the motion displayed by the moving objects that produced the above graphs for each indicated letter segment of the graph.

5.-6. At $t = 0$, a moving car goes past a reference point from which subsequent displacements are measured. The car moves with a slow but steady speed in a straight line for 4 seconds. Then the driver accelerates for 3 seconds, reaching a greater speed that she maintains for two more seconds. Complete the following graphs for the nine seconds of motion of the car (use sketches similar to question #4):

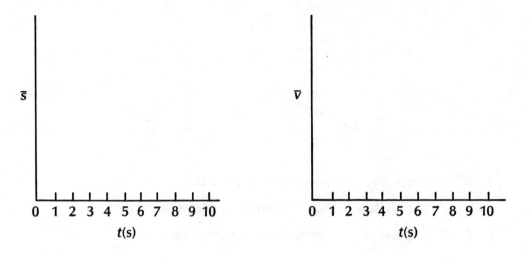

Name: _____ Section: _____

Score: _____

KINEMATICS QUIZ

1. An object travels at $2 \frac{m}{s}$. Three seconds later it is going at $8 \frac{m}{s}$. What acceleration did it experience?

_____

2. The acceleration due to gravity is $9.8 \frac{m}{s^2}$. How fast will an object dropped from rest be traveling after 3 seconds of fall?

_____

3. How far will the object (#2) fall during the 3 second fall?

_____

4. When a 10N rock is dropped, it accelerates at $9.8 \frac{m}{s^2}$. How much will a 5N rock accelerate when it is dropped?

_____

5. Which quantity doesn't belong?
   a. force
   b. time
   c. velocity
   d. acceleration

_____

6. How many seconds does it take for an object to fall 19.6 m if it starts from rest?

_____

7. Which term does *not* apply to "terminal velocity"?
   a. weight
   b. air friction
   c. acceleration
   d. constant velocity

   _____

8. On another planet, an object dropped from rest falls 10 meters in 2 seconds. What is the acceleration due to gravity on that planet?

   _____

9. What shape would a distance versus time graph have for a freely falling object?

   _____

10. Which statement is true for the motion represented by the graph?
    a. it is falling freely
    b. the forces on the object are balanced
    c. it is accelerating
    d. it is decelerating

   _____

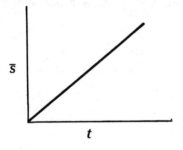

Name: _____   Section: _____

DERIVATION OF IMPULSE–MOMENTUM RELATIONSHIP

Newton's 2nd law: $\overline{F} = m\overline{a}$

    $\overline{F}$—net force on object

    m—mass of object

    $\overline{a}$—acceleration produced

Substituting for $\overline{a}$ from its definition; $\overline{a} = \dfrac{\Delta \overline{v}}{\Delta t}$, we get:

$$\overline{F} = m\,\frac{\Delta \overline{v}}{\Delta t}$$

    $\Delta \overline{v}$—change in object's velocity

    Δt—time in which the velocity change happened

Multiplying both sides by Δt:

$$\overline{F}\Delta t = m\Delta \overline{v}$$

If the mass is constant, this is the same as:

$$\boxed{\overline{F}\Delta t = \Delta m\overline{v}}$$

    $m\overline{v}$—momentum of object

    $\Delta m\overline{v}$—the *change* in momentum

    $\overline{F}\Delta t$—IMPULSE, or the net force on the object multiplied by how long it acts

In words, the equation reads:

IMPULSE = CHANGE IN MOMENTUM

Check the *units:*

$$\overline{F}\Delta t = \Delta m\overline{v}$$

$$N \cdot s = kg \cdot \frac{m}{s}$$

But $1N = 1 \frac{kg \cdot m}{s^2}$ by definition, so we will substitute that for the N

$$\frac{kg \cdot m}{s^2} \cdot s = kg \cdot \frac{m}{s}$$

The second s in the left hand side combines with the s^2 in the denomenator, and we get:

$$kg \cdot \frac{m}{s} = kg \cdot \frac{m}{s} \quad \text{The units are equal.}$$

Name: _____   Section: _____

FORCES ACTING ON A CAR AS IT MOVES

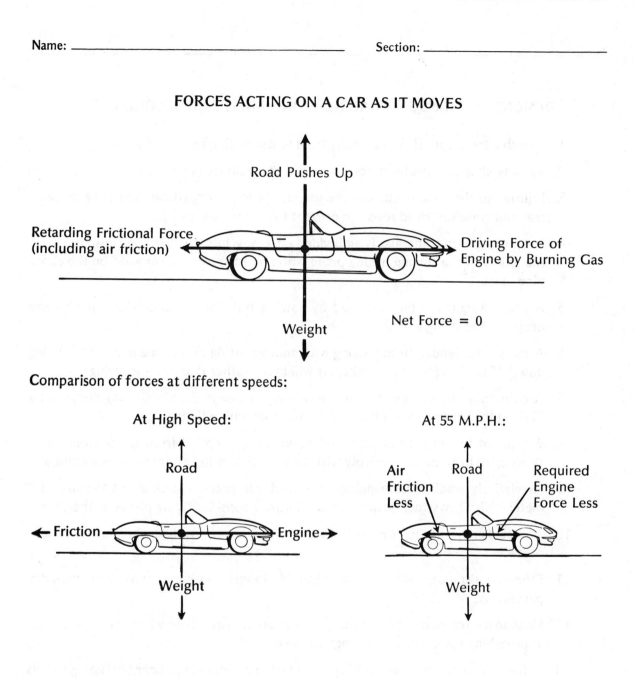

Road Pushes Up

Retarding Frictional Force
(including air friction)

Driving Force of
Engine by Burning Gas

Weight

Net Force = 0

Comparison of forces at different speeds:

At High Speed:

Road

← Friction

Engine →

Weight

At 55 M.P.H.:

Air
Friction
Less

Road

Required
Engine
Force Less

Weight

Name: _____   Section: _____

DEMONSTRATIONS SHOWING NEWTON'S FIRST AND SECOND LAWS

1. Snatch a tablecloth (handkerchief) from underneath a beaker of water.

2. Subway strap hangers lurch forward when the train stops suddenly.

3. Injuries to the neck occur to a person sitting in a stopped car that experiences a rear end collision. Head rests can prevent this injury somewhat.

4. In splitting wood, the axe is embedded part way into the log. To finish the split, the axe with the cutting blade up and wood on top strikes downward on the chopping block.

5. A heavy weight can be supported by a string, but if the mass is raised up a bit and dropped, the string will break.

6. A mass is suspended from a string with another string tied to the mass and hanging down. If the lower string is jerked, it will break rather than the top string.

7. A coin on a piece of cardboard over a glass can be made to fall into the glass by flicking the cardboard out from under the coin with a finger.

8. A stack of five or six flat pieces of wood can be unpiled from the bottom up by striking the bottom piece sharply with a meter stick, using a pool player's technique.

9. A relatively small mass hanging by a cord will break a stick about the size of a meter stick when struck with a swing. (*Caution:* consider flying pieces of the stick.)

10. An accident victim is "thrown" through the front windshield when his car hits an obstacle.

11. Stopping distances for cars are considerably longer on slippery pavements than dry pavements.

12. Most space travel will be "coasting." Rockets are fired only when leaving a planet, approaching for landing, or changing course.

13. A football coach teaches his players to tackle a running opponent by going for his ankles rather than the opponent's middle.

Name: _____   Section: _____

CIRCULAR MOTION

DIRECTIONS: Discuss the following situations in terms of ideas related to centripetal force and circular motion:

1. Turns on racetracks are banked inward.

2. An earth satellite will stay in orbit at some distance from the earth only if it is going at the right speed.

3. If a satellite is going faster than the required orbiting speed, it will leave its orbit.

4. If a satellite slows down, it will fall to the earth.

5. It is difficult to make a sharp turn if a car is going very fast.

6. A small sports car can negotiate a winding road easier than a larger car.

7. A centrifuge is used as a separater in lab.

8. A spin dry washing machine in operation.

9. A scale attached with string to a mass shows a greater reading when the mass is swinging than when it is stationary.

10. A small bucket full of water can be swung in a vertical circle without the water spilling out.

11. Astronauts could experience variable g forces in a human centrifuge before manned rocket launches were tried.

12. Riding a bike without a rear fender through a puddle produces a spray of water down the rider's back.

Name: _____   Section: _____

NEWTON'S THIRD LAW

DIRECTIONS: Each situation involves the concept of equal and opposite forces acting in pairs. Describe what exerts the action and reaction force in each case, what each force acts on, the direction of each force, and the effects of each force.

1. A shotgun "kicks."

2. The operation of a jet engine.

3. The operation of a rocket engine.

4. Walking.

5. A sprinter on the track team coming out of the starting blocks at the beginning of a race.

6. An object falls.

7. A car speeding out of a gravel parking lot often sends a spray of stones backward.

8. A cannon recoils when fired.

9. A propeller driving a boat.

10. A balloon flies around if released as the air rushes out.

11. A rotating lawn sprinkler.

12. The end of a hose will move around on the ground as water comes out.

Name: _____   Section: _____

IMPULSE–CHANGE IN MOMENTUM

DIRECTIONS: Discuss the following phenomena in terms of impulse and change in momentum ideas.

1. A bullet shot into a piece of wood is deformed when extracted from the wood, but a bullet fired into a deep tube of water can be retrieved intact.

2. A car slowing to a stop from a high speed is no problem, but when that car hits a barrier at a high speed, it is badly damaged.

3. It is said that falling off a high building is no problem; it's the sudden stop that kills you.

4. A catcher's mit has a lot of cushion in it.

5. A trapeze artist falls into a net and is not injured. But if she did not have the net, she would be seriously injured.

6. Insurance companies give a special "bumper discount" on insurance rates for cars that have bumpers designed to move slightly on impact.

7. When going off a diving board, a person doing a head first dive completes the dive with no problem, but the same person would suffer some pain if he did a "belly whopper."

8. A car equipped with a small engine takes longer to accelerate to a certain speed than a similar car with a larger engine.

9. During slippery road conditions, drivers are advised to make changes in speed more slowly.

10. Airports have had to make their runways longer to accomodate larger planes.

Name: _____   Section: _____

DYNAMICS TEST

1. Inertia is
   a. a force
   b. a way masses behave
   c. an acceleration
   d. an impulse

2. Newton's first law is true when forces are
   a. balanced
   b. very small
   c. unbalanced
   d. very large

3. Which is an example of Newton's first law?
   a. a ball being swung in a circular path on a string
   b. a train coming to a stop
   c. a dragster accelerating
   d. a car traveling at 55 m.p.h.

4. Which has more inertia?
   a. a 1 kg mass
   b. a 10 kg mass
   c. it depends on the motion of the masses
   d. both the 1 kg and 10 kg masses have the same amount

5. The amount of inertia possessed by an object can be determined by measuring its
   a. speed
   b. velocity
   c. acceleration
   d. mass

II 1. A "newton" is equal to a

   a. $kg \cdot \dfrac{m}{s}$

   b. $kg \cdot \dfrac{m}{s^2}$

   c. kg

   d. $\dfrac{m}{s}$

2. If 3N of unbalanced force acts on a 5 kg mass, its acceleration will be

   a. $15 \dfrac{m}{s^2}$

   b. $5 \dfrac{m}{s^2}$

   c. $1.67 \dfrac{m}{s^2}$

   d. $.6 \dfrac{m}{s^2}$

3. A 5 kg mass weighs about _____N at the earth's surface
   a. 50
   b. .5
   c. 2
   d. 10

4. A certain force gives a 10 kg mass an acceleration of $5 \dfrac{m}{s^2}$. The same force will accelerate a 20 kg mass at

   a. $10 \dfrac{m}{s^2}$

   b. $5 \dfrac{m}{s^2}$

   c. $2.5 \dfrac{m}{s^2}$

   d. $50 \dfrac{m}{s^2}$

5. A 2 kg mass is swinging in a 2 m circle at the end of a string. It has a speed of $3 \frac{m}{s}$. How great is the centripetal force?

   a. 3N
   b. 6N
   c. 9N
   d. 18N

6. What is the centripetal acceleration of the mass in question II.5.?

   a. $1.5 \frac{m}{s^2}$

   b. $1 \frac{m}{s^2}$

   c. $9 \frac{m}{s^2}$

   d. $4.5 \frac{m}{s^2}$

III 1. A jet engine produces a force of 2,000N accelerating propellant out of the exhaust. What thrust does the engine produce?

   a. 1,000N
   b. 2,000N
   c. 3,000N
   d. 4,000N

2. A 5N object rests on a table top. The table top exerts a force on the object

   a. greater than 5N
   b. less than 5N
   c. equal to 5N
   d. of zero N

3. If the "action" is produced by your hand striking downward on a table, the "reaction" is exerted

   a. upward by the table
   b. upward by your hand
   c. downward on your hand
   d. downward on the table

4. In terms of Newton's third law, a car cannot accelerate as rapidly on icy pavement as it can on dry roads because

   a. the action is not equal to the reaction
   b. the tires cannot exert as great an action force
   c. the reaction is the spinning of the wheels
   d. the reaction force cannot be produced

IV 1. Which has the least momentum?

   a. a freight train at rest
   b. an electron going at half the speed of light
   c. a bowling ball going down an alley
   d. a car going at 55 m.p.h.

2. A 5 kg mass, initially at rest, is set in motion with a velocity of $2 \frac{m}{s}$. What impulse did it receive?

   a. $5N \cdot s$
   b. $.4N \cdot s$
   c. $2.5N \cdot s$
   d. $10N \cdot s$

3.–6. A compressed spring is placed between two masses initially at rest on a frictionless surface. The spring is allowed to expand pushing both masses. One mass of 5 kg moves to the right at $3 \frac{m}{s}$. The other mass of 2 kg moves to the left.

3. What is the momentum of the 5 kg mass?

   a. $2.5 \text{ kg} \cdot \frac{m}{s}$

   b. $1.7 \text{ kg} \cdot \frac{m}{s}$

   c. $6 \text{ kg} \cdot \frac{m}{s}$

   d. $15 \text{ kg} \cdot \frac{m}{s}$

4. If the spring expanded in .5 s, what average force did it exert on the 5 kg mass?

   a. 15N
   b. 30N
   c. 7.5N
   d. 10N

5. What velocity will the 2 kg mass have?

 a. $15 \frac{m}{s}$

 b. $30 \frac{m}{s}$

 c. $2.5 \frac{m}{s}$

 d. $7.5 \frac{m}{s}$

6. After the spring expands, the total momentum of the system will be

 a. $15 \text{ kg} \cdot \frac{m}{s}$

 b. $30 \text{ kg} \cdot \frac{m}{s}$

 c. $60 \text{ kg} \cdot \frac{m}{s}$

 d. $0 \text{ kg} \cdot \frac{m}{s}$

Name: _____   Section: _____

MACHINE PRINCIPLES

DIRECTIONS: Each of the descriptions below refer to mechanical arrangements for changing the form of work. Each uses principles of simple machines like those discussed in class. In each case, identify the simple machine principle employed and indicate how the work form is changed; that is, does the machine multiply force or distance to produce its desired effect? Labeled diagrams showing the forces, points of application, and respective distances will be helpful in your explanation.

1. a nut cracker

2. a mountain road

3. a block and tackle system

4. a door knob

5. a wedge for splitting wood

6. a ramp

7. the gear system of a 10 speed bicycle

8. a wrench

9. the location of a handle on a door

10. the muscular-skeletal system of the human arm when throwing a ball

11. a golf club in use

12. peeling an apple with a knife

13. the rope and wheel system attached to the boom of a sailboat

14. a screw

Name: _____   Section: _____

SOME ALTERNATE ARRANGEMENTS FOR WORK TRANSFORMATION WITH SIMPLE MACHINES

Lever systems:

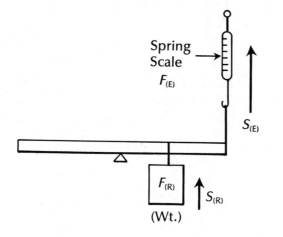
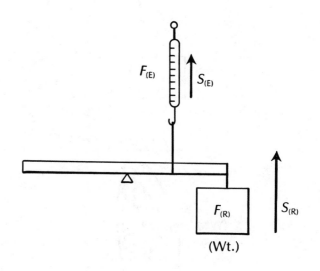

Pulleys:

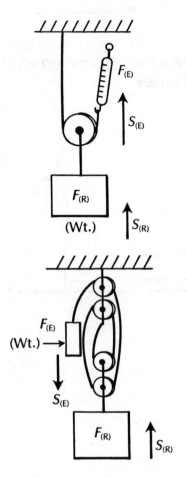

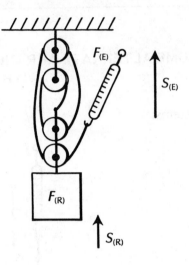

Inclined planes:

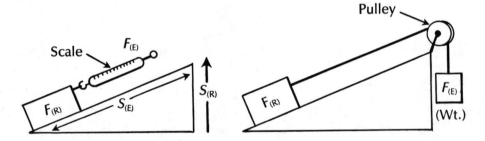

Name: _____   Section: _____

AREA UNDER A FORCE VERSUS DISTANCE CURVE

When a force of 1N acts through a distance of 1 m, 1 joule of work is done. The graph would look like this:

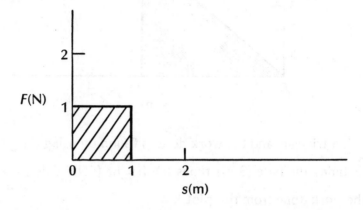

Note that the shaded portion is a rectangle. The area of this rectangle is the product of its length (*s*) times width (*F*). If we calculate this area, it is the same as calculating the work (the product of force times distance); therefore, the *area under the curve is equal to the work done.*

How much work was done when this curve was produced?

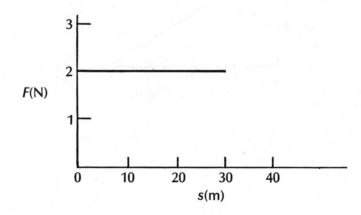

When the force doing the work varies with distance the same relationship holds, but the geometric shape is different. Suppose a force varies regularly from 0 to 5N over a distance of 3 m. The graph would look like this:

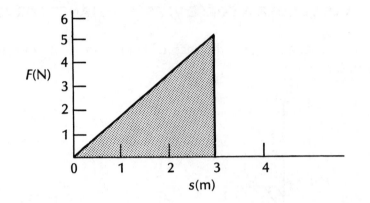

The shaded area is a triangle, and the work done is found by using the geometry for the area of a triangle: $\frac{1}{2}$ times the base (3 m) times the height (5N). This works out to 7.5 joules of work. Find the work done from this plot:

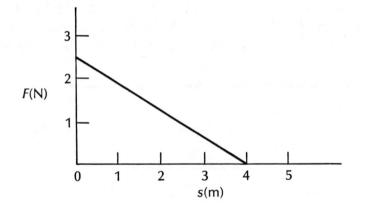

For forces that vary regularly through several values, reduce the total area to subareas of regular geometric shapes and add them up to find the total work.

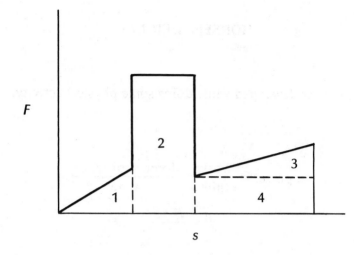

The work done is equal to the total area that is the sum of triangle 1, rectangle 2, triangle 3, and rectangle 4.

Find the total work for these plots:

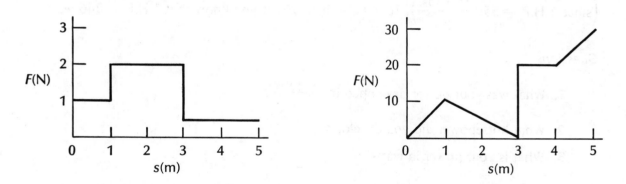

Name: _____   Section: _____

HORSEPOWER LAB

Purpose:

To measure the horsepower developed while doing some physical activity.

*Method:**

$$\text{power} = \frac{\text{work}}{\text{time}} = \frac{\text{force} \times \text{distance}}{\text{time}}$$

$$P = \frac{F \cdot s}{t}$$

For this lab, measure the force exerted, F, the distance moved, and the time required, t, while doing some activity. (F is in lbs., s in feet, t in seconds.) Your first calculation will give you your power in $\frac{\text{ft.} \cdot \text{lbs.}}{s}$. To get your horsepower, H.P., divide your result by 550 $\left(\text{since 1 H.P.} = 550 \frac{\text{ft.} \cdot \text{lbs.}}{s}\right)$. It will also help you if you know that 1 H.P. = 746 watts.

Questions:

1. What was your power developed in $\frac{\text{ft.} \cdot \text{lbs.}}{s}$?

2. What horsepower did you develop?

3. What is your power in watts?

*Techniques for measurement will be discussed in lab.

Name: _____   Section: _____

EXPRESSION FOR KINETIC ENERGY

Diagram:

Object of mass, *m*, some height above a table top, *h*. In this position, the object has gravitational potential energy, $PE_g = mgh$, where *g* is the acceleration due to gravity.

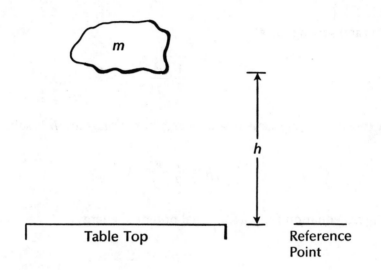

As the object falls, its potential energy is converted into energy due to motion, kinetic energy. This energy is dependent on the mass of the object and its velocity, *v*. This velocity at any instant is determined as follows:

$$g = \frac{v_f - v_i}{t}$$ If dropped from rest, $v_i = 0$,

and $$g = \frac{v_f}{t}$$ v_f will equal the velocity just before the object hits the table, call it *v*.

solving for *v*: $v = gt$ (1)

(the distance formula): $s = \frac{1}{2} gt^2$ (2)

$$t = \sqrt{2 \frac{s}{g}}$$ (3)

t is expressed as a relationship to s by equation (2). Solving this for t, we get equation (3). Substituting this value in equation (1), we get:

$$v = g\sqrt{\frac{2s}{g}}$$

Squaring both sides:

$$v^2 = g^2 \cdot \frac{2s}{g}$$

Combining terms and solving for s:

$$s = \frac{1}{2}\frac{v^2}{g}$$

Since s in this expression is the same quantity as h in the diagram, h is substituted for s:

$$h = \frac{1}{2}\frac{v^2}{g}$$

Now use the original equation for gravitational potential energy:

$$PE = mgh$$

and substitute the above expression for h:

$$E = mg\frac{v^2}{2g}$$

Combining terms we have an expression for the energy of motion just before the object hits the table, the kinetic energy:

$$KE = \frac{1}{2}\,m\,v^2$$

Using standard SI units and substituting:

$$KE = (\text{kg})\left(\frac{\text{m}}{\text{s}}\right)^2$$

$$KE = \text{kg} \cdot \frac{\text{m}^2}{\text{s}^2}$$

$$KE = \text{kg} \cdot \frac{\text{m}}{\text{s}^2} \cdot \text{m}$$

since $1\text{N} = 1\ \text{kg} \cdot \dfrac{\text{m}}{\text{s}^2}$:

$$KE = \text{N} \cdot \text{m}$$

$$KE = \text{joules}$$

Name: _____   Section: _____

ENERGY PROBLEMS

DIRECTIONS: Solve the following problems using energy relations and conservation:

1. A girl's mass is 60.5 kg. If she climbs a flight of stairs 5 m high, how much potential energy has she acquired?

2. A boy is jogging at 1.5 $\frac{m}{s}$. If his mass is 72.5 kg, what is his kinetic energy?

3. An object is thrown vertically upward with a velocity of 10 $\frac{m}{s}$. How high will it rise?

4. A mass is dropped from rest and falls freely to the ground, a distance of 20 meters. How fast is it going when it hits?

5. A 10 kg mass is at the top of a frictionless incline that is 3 meters high and 10 meters long. It slides down this incline. How fast is it going at the bottom?

6. A 5 kg cart starts from rest at point A and goes over the course shown. For *each* labeled point (A, B, C, and D), calculate the potential energy, the kinetic energy, and the speed of the cart.

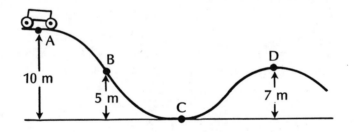

Name: _____   Section: _____

ENERGY TEST

$$\left(g = 9.8 \, \frac{m}{s^2}\right)$$

1. The same units can be used to measure
   a. power and acceleration
   b. work and energy
   c. force and distance
   d. power and energy

2. Which units don't belong?
   a. joules
   b. watts
   c. $kg \cdot \dfrac{m^2}{s^2}$
   d. $nt \cdot m$

3. To measure the potential energy acquired by an object raised from the floor to a table top, the minimum equipment needed is: (mark all correct options)
   a. meter stick
   b. stop watch
   c. spring scale
   d. protractor

4. Kilowatt hours could be converted into
   a. newtons
   b. joules
   c. $\dfrac{m}{s^2}$
   d. watts

5. An object thrown vertically upwards will rise until
   a. *KE* becomes O
   b. *PE* becomes O
   c. both *PE* and *KE* reach a maximum value
   d. total energy reaches a minimum

6. Which is *not* an example of potential energy?
   a. a match
   b. a car going along a road
   c. a stretched spring
   d. a bent stick

7. The shaded area under this graph represents
   a. work
   b. power
   c. velocity
   d. acceleration

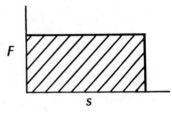

8. In circular motion the centripetal force doesn't do work because
   a. there is an equal centrifugal reaction
   b. the object doesn't move
   c. the object doesn't get closer to the center
   d. the object tends to go in a straight line

9. A 10 kg object is raised 5 m upwards. The power involved is
   a. 50 watts
   b. 49.1 watts
   c. 0 watts
   d. insufficient information to answer

10. Joules =
   a. $kg \cdot \dfrac{m^2}{s^2}$

   b. $kg \cdot \dfrac{m}{s}$

   c. $\dfrac{watts}{s}$

   d. $nt \cdot m^2$

11. If an object's speed is doubled, its *KE*
    a. becomes $\frac{1}{2}$ the original valve
    b. doubles
    c. quadruples
    d. is unchanged

12. A 2 kilowatt motor does a certain amount of work in 600 s. A 6 kilowatt motor will do the same amount of work in
    a. 1200 s
    b. 1000 s
    c. 200 s
    d. 100 s

13. A 2N object has 12 joules of gravitational potential energy. How high above the zero reference point is it?
    a. 24 m
    b. 16 m
    c. 120 m
    d. 6 m

14. An object is 19.6 m above a table top. It is dropped. Just before it hits the table, its velocity will be about
    a. $28.9 \frac{m}{s}$
    b. $9.8 \frac{m}{s}$
    c. $19.6 \frac{m}{s}$
    d. insufficient information

15. Neglect friction. How much work is done to move the weight to the top of the incline?
    a. 50 J
    b. 20 J
    c. 15 J
    d. 10 J

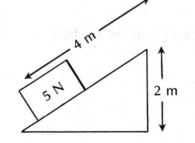

(16–19) a = increases; b = decreases; c = remains same

16. As an object slides down a frictionless incline, its *KE* _____

17. As an object slides down a frictionless incline its *PE* _____

18. As an object slides down a frictionless incline, its total mechanical energy _____

19. If twice as much time is taken to do twice as much work, the power involved _____

(20–25) A certain amount of work, *w*, is done in moving a mass vertically upward a distance, *h*. This work is done in a certain amount of time, *t*.

20. The potential energy at this height is
  a. w
  b. $\dfrac{w}{t}$
  c. $w \times h$
  d. $\dfrac{1}{2} w^2$

21. The kinetic energy at this height is
  a. $\dfrac{1}{2} w$
  b. 0
  c. $\dfrac{w}{2}$
  d. $w h$

22. The potential energy half way down (as the object falls) is
  a. $\dfrac{1}{2} w$
  b. 0
  c. $w h$
  d. $\dfrac{1}{2} w h$

23. The kinetic energy half way down (as the object falls) is
  a. $\dfrac{1}{2} w$
  b. 0
  c. $w h$
  d. $\dfrac{1}{2} w h$

24. The power developed in moving the mass up was

 a. $\dfrac{w}{t^2}$

 b. $t \times w$

 c. $w \times \dfrac{h}{t}$

 d. $\dfrac{w}{t}$

25. The *KE* just before it hits the bottom is

 a. w

 b. 0

 c. $\dfrac{1}{2}\, w\, h$

 d. $\dfrac{1}{2}\, w$

(26–30)

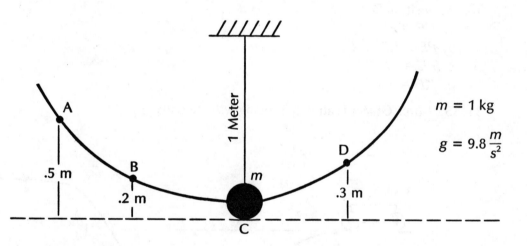

Mass $m = 1$ kg is suspended from the end of a 1 m string as shown. Assume no air friction or friction at pivot point.

26. When the mass is in position C and not moving, the force, in newtons exerted by the string on the mass, is

 a. 0

 b. 4.9N upward

 c. 9.8N downward

 d. 9.8N upward

27. When the mass is in position A, its potential energy is
    a. 0
    b. 4.9 J
    c. 9.8 J
    d. 19.6 J

28. If the mass is released from point A and is allowed to swing, its *KE* at point C is
    a. 0
    b. 4.9 J
    c. 9.8 J
    d. 19.6 J

29. At which position is the total mechanical energy the greatest?
    a. A
    b. C
    c. D
    d. same at all points

30. At position D:
    a. *KE > PE*
    b. *PE > KE*
    c. *PE = KE*
    d. *KE = 0*

31-35. *Note:* Object is already moving with velocity, v_1

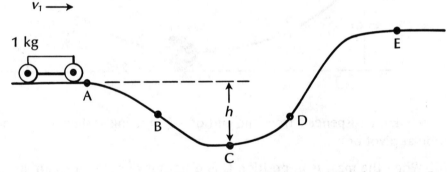

Diagram of a 1 kg cart sliding along a frictionless track from A to E.

31. At which two points will the kinetic energy of the cart be the same?
    a. A and B
    b. A and C
    c. B and D
    d. B and E

32. At which two points will the gravitational potential energies be the same?
    a. A and B
    b. A and C
    c. D and B
    d. B and E

33. The kinetic energy of the cart will be the greatest at point
    a. A
    b. B
    c. C
    d. D

34. Which expression best represents the *KE* of the cart at point C?
    a. mgh

    b. $mgh - \dfrac{mv_1^2}{2}$

    c. $\dfrac{mv_1^2}{2} - mgh$

    d. $\dfrac{mv_1^2}{2} - mgh$

35. The velocity of the cart will be least at point
    a. A
    b. B
    c. C
    d. E

Name: _____   Section: _____

HEAT TRANSFER-SENSATION

DIRECTIONS: Explain the following in terms of ideas presented in class.

1. When walking barefoot around the house, a girl notices that the tile floor feels colder than carpeted portions.

2. After sunbathing on a beach, the water in a lake feels very cold upon entry.

3. When the sunbather (in #2) asks people who have been in swimming for a time, "How is the water?", the swimmers respond (truthfully), "It's fine—once you get in!"

4. A person who is not ill can detect if you have a fever by placing his hand on your forehead.

5. You can't tell if you have a fever by feeling your own forehead.

6. After coming indoors in the winter time, the room feels very warm at first—later it does not feel as warm.

7. Water in lakes does not feel as cold at night as it did during the daytime.

8. Areas sheltered from the wind feel warmer than windy places, even though the air temperature is the same.

9. Experienced outdoors people know the value of keeping their socks and footwear dry. They remain comfortable during cold weather while a person with wet feet is chilled.

10. People put on extra clothing in cold weather and remove clothing during warm weather.

11. Visitors to your house who keep their homes very warm in winter notice that it is cooler when they arrive, while you feel very comfortable at the cooler temperature.

12. You feel cooler after taking a warm shower during hot weather.

Name: _____   Section: _____

TEMPERATURE SCALES

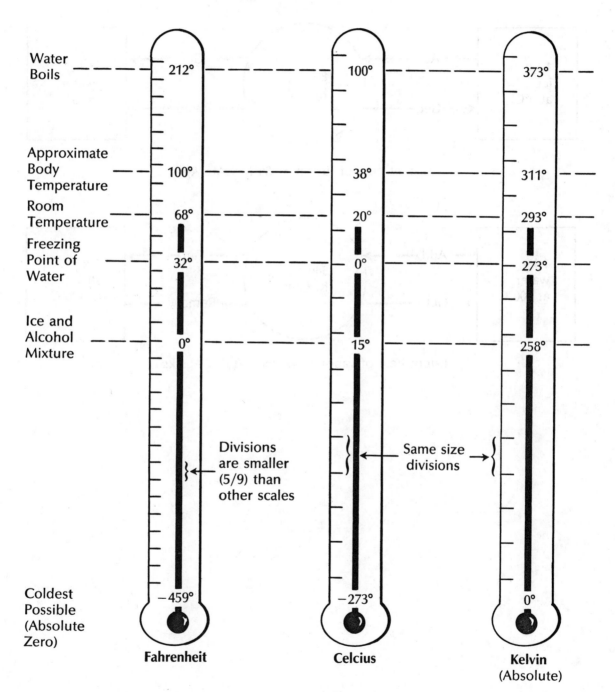

Water Boils — 212° / 100° / 373°

Approximate Body Temperature — 100° / 38° / 311°

Room Temperature — 68° / 20° / 293°

Freezing Point of Water — 32° / 0° / 273°

Ice and Alcohol Mixture — 0° / 15° / 258°

Divisions are smaller (5/9) than other scales

Same size divisions

Coldest Possible (Absolute Zero) — −459° / −273° / 0°

Fahrenheit   Celcius   Kelvin (Absolute)

Name: _____   Section: _____

LATENT HEATS FOR WATER

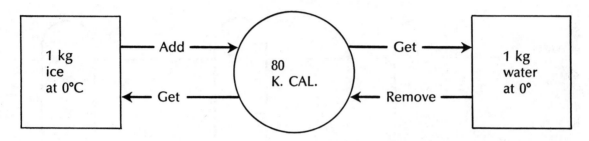

Latent heat of fusion = 80 K. CAL./kg

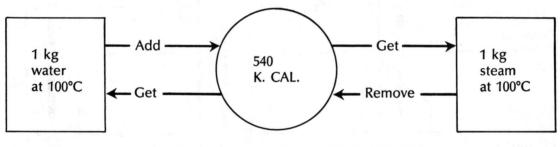

Latent heat of vaporization = 540 K. CAL./kg

Name: _____   Section: _____

TABLE OF HEAT CONSTANTS

Material	Specific Heat $\left(\frac{K.C.}{kg°C}\right)$	Melting Point (°C)	Boiling Point (°C)	Heat of Fusion $\left(\frac{K.C.}{kg}\right)$	Heat of Vaporization $\left(\frac{K.C.}{kg}\right)$
Alcohol	.581	−115	78.5	24.9	204
Aluminum (20°C)	.214	660	2467	94	2520
Liquid Ammonia	1.125	− 77.7	−33.4	108	327
Brass	.0917	900			
Copper	.0924	1083	2595	49	1150
Glass	.161				
Iron	.1075	1535	3000	7.89	1600
Lead	.0305	328	1744	5.47	207
Mercury	.0333	− 38.87	356.6	2.82	70.6
Silver	.0562	961	2212	26	565
Tungsten	.0322	3410	5927	43	
Water	1		100		540
Ice	.53	0		80	
Steam	.48				
Zinc	.0922	419	907	23	420

Name: _____   Section: _____

HEAT CALCULATIONS

DIRECTIONS: For each problem, calculate the amount of heat needed to produce the effect described. Note whether the process requires heat to be added *or* removed:

1. Warm 3 kg of water from its freezing point to its boiling point.

2. Melt 5 kg of lead at 328°C.

3. Vaporize 4 kg of water at 100°C.

4. Condense 2 kg of alcohol vapor at 78.5°C.

5. Cool a 7.5 kg brass sample from 800°C to 20°C.

6. Warm a piece of ice having a mass of 10 kg from −10°C to its melting point.

7. Solidify 20 kg of zinc at 419°C.

8. Cool a .5 kg piece of silver from 100°C to 50°C.

9. Increase the temperature of .025 kg tungsten from 20°C to 2,000°C.

10. Warm an aluminum calorimeter cup having a mass of .025 kg from 20°C to the boiling temperature of water.

Name: _____   Section: _____

GUIDE TO SETTING UP SOLUTIONS TO HEAT EXCHANGE PROBLEMS

Step 1. Follow the standard procedure of reading the problem and listing "knowns" and "unknowns."

Step 2. Set up an equation setting Q Lost = Q Gained.

Step 3. Identify which items will lose heat and which will gain that heat. List them under the appropriate sides of the equation from Step 2.

Step 4. Below Step 3, identify the heating effects produced when each item loses or gains heat.

Step 5. Represent each heat effect with the appropriate expression, adding each effect on either side of your equation.

Step 6. Isolate the unknown(s) algebraically, substitute known values, and complete the solution.

Sample Problem

A laboratory experiment to find the specific heat of a metal sample used the following data. What was the specific heat of the metal?:

Step 1. mass of calorimeter, $m(c) = 1.60$ kg

specific heat of calorimeter, $c(c) = .093 \frac{kc}{kg°C}$

mass of water, $m(w) = .225$ kg

specific heat of water $c(w) = \frac{1kc}{kg°C}$

mass of metal $m(m) = .185$ kg

initial temperature of water and calorimeter, $T(iw)$, and $T(ic) = 18°C$

initial temperature of metal, $T(im) = 99.5°C$

final temperature of mixture $T(f) = 23.5°C$

specific heat of metal, $c(m) = ?$

Step 2. Q Lost $= Q$ Gained

Step 3.   metal sample $=$ water $+$ calorimeter

Step 4.   metal cools $=$ water warms $+$ calorimeter warms

Step 5. $m(m)\, c(m)\, \Delta T(m) = m(w)\, c(w)\, \Delta T(w) + m(c)\, c(c)\, \Delta T(c)$

Step 6. $c(m) = \dfrac{m(w)\, c(w)\, \Delta T(w) + m(c)\, c(c)\, \Delta T(c)}{m(m)\, \Delta T(m)}$

$$c(m) = \frac{(.225\text{ kg})(1\text{ kc/kg}^\circ\text{C})(23.5^\circ\text{C} - 18^\circ\text{C}) + (.160\text{ kg})(.093\text{ kc/kg}^\circ\text{C})(23.5^\circ\text{C} - 18^\circ\text{C})}{(.185\text{ kg})(99.5^\circ\text{C} - 23.5^\circ\text{C})}$$

$$c(m) = .094\ \frac{kc}{kg^\circ C}$$

Name: _____   Section: _____

HEAT PHENOMENA

DIRECTIONS: Explain the following phenomena in terms of concepts discussed in class:

1. Air temperatures near large bodies of water are cooler in hot weather and more moderate during cold seasons.

2. A person dripping wet after swimming is cold, while another person also in a bathing suit but not wet is not chilly.

3. The air temperature sometimes rises during a snowstorm.

4. Wrestling team members will sometimes run in a rubber sweat suit to lose weight.

5. Hypothermia often follows when a hiker's clothing gets wet.

6. Steam produces a more severe burn than water at 100°C.

7. Boiling water is used as a cooking medium.

8. The baked potatoe will still be hot when other food on your plate is cold from sitting for a time.

9. If you place a paper cup full of water in the coals of a campfire, the water will eventually boil but the paper will not catch fire. Try it!

10. Gardeners will place a large tub of water in their cold cellars to keep the food from freezing during cold nights.

11. Water will evaporate from a dish more rapidly if the water is heated.

12. Even poor cooks can't "burn water."

13. An ice cube will cool a drink more effectively than an equal amount of ice water, even though both are at 0°C.

14. Alcohol feels cool to the skin.

15. Hikers often dip their cloth covered canteens in water to keep the contents cooler.

16. Water in southwestern areas is stored in porous pots to keep it cool.

Name: _____   Section: _____

MATERIALS

DIRECTIONS: What do the following things have in common?

1. storm windows

2. cellulose fibers

3. thermal underwear

4. fiberglas batts

5. styrofoam

6. urea-formaldehyde foam

7. down-filled jackets

8. thermal pane windows

9. "fish net" underwear

10. snow covering the ground

11. sweaters with a nylon shell over the top

12. quilts and quilted clothing

Name: _____   Section: _____

WORK, HEAT AND EXPANSION

DIRECTIONS: Explain the following phenomena in terms of concepts studied in class:

1. The water at the bottom of a waterfall will be slightly warmer than it was at the top.

2. The tube of a bicycle pump gets very warm while pumping up a tire.

3. Concrete roadways and sidewalks are poured in separate sections rather than in one continuous length.

4. The explosion of a bomb or firecracker.

5. Bridges are connected to adjacent roadbeds by intermeshing steel "fingers" and are supported on rollers.

6. The pulley wheel at the end of a ski lift is not attached firmly to the ground. Tension is maintained in the cable by attaching this wheel to a very heavy hanging weight.

7. Gas will overflow out of your car's tank after it has been filled on a hot day.

8. You get more energy for your money when you purchase gasoline during very cold weather rather than during summer heat.

9. People often loosen jar covers by holding the lid under hot water.

10. You can hear the aluminum siding on houses make noise when the air temperature is changing.

Name: _____   Section: _____

ATOMIC SYMBOLS

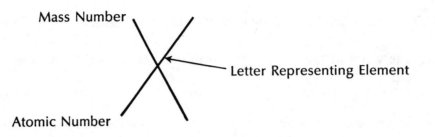

Atomic number: The charge on the nucleus, in elementary charges. Since protons in the nucleus each have a charge of +1, this gives the number of protons. Because atoms as a whole are usually neutral and electrons have a charge of −1, the number of protons also indicates the number of electrons associated with the atom. Identity of the element depends on atomic number.

Mass number: The mass of the nucleus, to the nearest whole number, in A.M.U.s. Since both protons and neutrons have a mass of about 1 A.M.U. each, this gives the total number of the protons plus neutrons in the nucleus. Find the number of neutrons by subtracting the number of protons (atomic number) from the mass number.

Example:

This is the symbol for oxygen − 18: $^{18}_{8}O$

The atomic number is 8, which identifies this atom as oxygen. It has 8 protons in its nucleus and an equal number, 8, of orbital electrons.

The mass number is 18, which is the mass of the nucleus, to the nearest whole number, in A.M.U.s—there are a total of 18 nucleons (protons + neutrons). 8 of these 18 are protons (atomic number), leaving 10 neutrons.

DIRECTIONS: For each of the symbols listed, tell the number of protons, electrons, and neutrons associated with the atom.

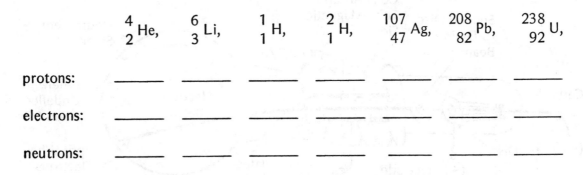

$${}^{4}_{2}He, \quad {}^{6}_{3}Li, \quad {}^{1}_{1}H, \quad {}^{2}_{1}H, \quad {}^{107}_{47}Ag, \quad {}^{208}_{82}Pb, \quad {}^{238}_{92}U,$$

protons: _____ _____ _____ _____ _____ _____ _____

electrons: _____ _____ _____ _____ _____ _____ _____

neutrons: _____ _____ _____ _____ _____ _____ _____

DIRECTIONS: Write the atomic symbol for each of the following atoms. You will need a periodic table to determine the appropriate letter to use.

	Number of Protons	Number of Electrons	Number of Neutrons	Symbol
A.	8	8	8	_____
B.	2	2	2	_____
C.	88	88	138	_____
D.	28	28	31	_____

Name: _____   Section: _____

J. J. THOMSON'S DETERMINATION OF THE CHARGE
TO MASS RATIO OF AN ELECTRON

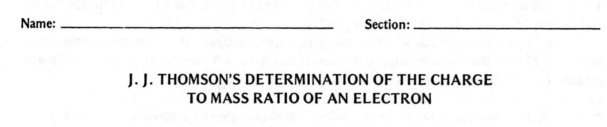

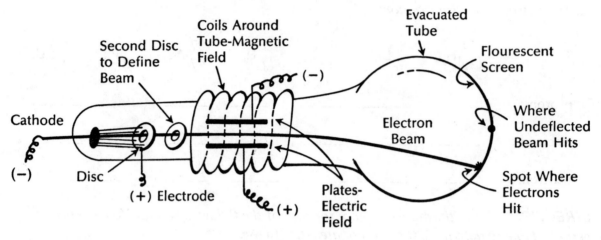

A high voltage between the electrodes at the left produces a beam of electrons that is further defined by the second slotted disc. This beam produces a spot of light where it hits the fluorescent coated screen on the right. The beam is deflected by the electric field between the charged plates and also by the magnetic field due to the coils.

When only the magnetic field, B, is turned on, electrons having a charge q and speed v experience a perpendicular deflecting force, $q\,v\,B$. The deflection would be in a nearly circular arc of radius, r. The electrons of mass, m, experience a centripetal force, $\dfrac{mv^2}{r}$, which is provided by the magnetic field so:

$$q\,v\,B = \frac{mv^2}{r}$$

and

$$\frac{q}{m} = \frac{v}{Br}$$

B is calculated from the coil geometry and current through them. r is found from the displacement of the beam. Thomson found v by arranging the electric and magnetic deflection in opposite directions and adjusting the fields to cancel each other's effects. This produced a straight line beam:

$$E q = q v B$$

where E is the electric field intensity.

Solving: $v = \dfrac{E}{B}$. E is calculated from the plate separation and voltage. This makes all the terms in $\dfrac{q}{m} = \dfrac{v}{Br}$ known and the ratio is determined. The presently accepted value for the charge to mass ratio is 1.76×10^{11} coulombs/kilogram.

Name: _____   Section: _____

THE MILLIKAN OIL DROP EXPERIMENT

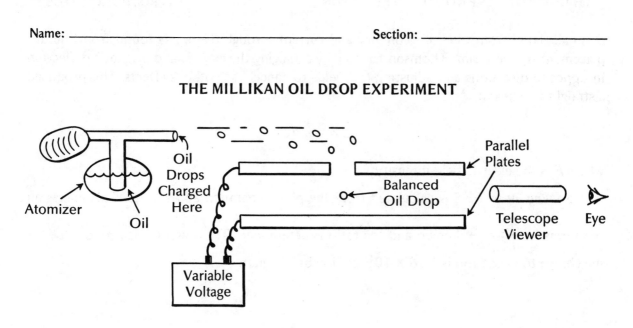

Millikan measured the charge on oil drops by balancing the weight of the drop with an upward electrical force:

$$wt. = F \text{ (electrical)}$$

$$mg = qE \qquad m = \text{mass of drop}$$

$$q = \frac{mg}{E} \qquad g = \text{acceleration due to gravity}$$

$$E = \text{electric field strength}$$

$$q = \text{charge on drop}$$

Millikan found that the charges on the oil drops were always a whole number multiple of the smallest charge, which he identified as the charge on one electron—the elementary charge.

Analog

Suppose a store was having a sale on eggs and you want to determine the smallest quantity of eggs that this store will sell you. In order to determine the quantity that eggs are sold in, you stand in front of the store and ask shoppers how many eggs they have in their cart as they exit. Suppose your record looks like this after many trials.

Shopper	Number of Eggs
1	12
2	36
3	6
4	54
5	24
6	60
7	432

Can you figure out the minimum quantity in which this store will sell eggs?

_____

(Check your answer like Millikan did.)

Here are some data representative of Millikan's measured charges on oil drops. What is the charge on one electron? Check your answer by completing the table.

Charge on one electron = _____

Charge on Oil Drop, q ($\times 10^{-19}$ C)	Number of Electrons Gained or Lost
8.0	_____
3.2	_____
6.4	_____
1.6	_____
4.8	_____
3.2	_____
48.0	_____
16.0	_____

Name: _____   Section: _____

RUTHERFORD SCATTERING EXPERIMENT

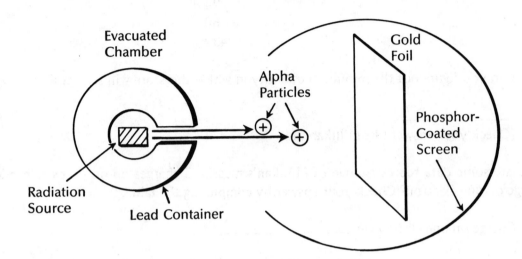

Observations

Conclusions

Name: _____   Section: _____

MASS SPECTROGRAPH

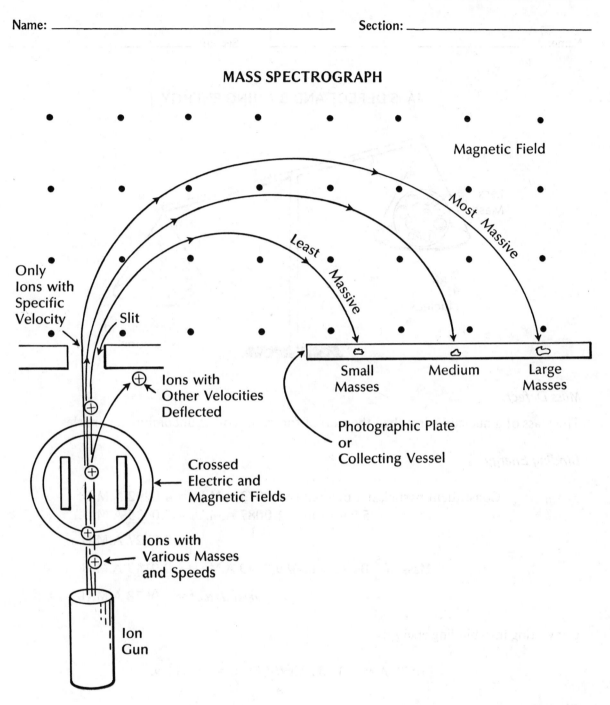

Name: _____   Section: _____

MASS DEFECT AND BINDING ENERGY

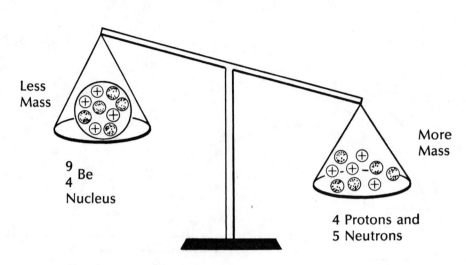

Mass Defect

The mass of a nucleus is less than the sum of the masses of its uncombined particles

Binding Energy

$$\text{Constituent particles: 4 protons @ 1.0073 A.M.U.} = 4.0292 \text{ A.M.U.}$$
$$\text{5 neutrons @ 1.0087 A.M.U.} = \underline{5.0435} \text{ A.M.U.}$$
$$9.0727 \text{ A.M.U.}$$
$$\text{Mass of } {}^{9}_{4}\text{Be nucleus @ 9.0149 A.M.U.} - \underline{9.0149} \text{ A.M.U.}$$
$$\textit{mass defect} = .0578 \text{ A.M.U.}$$

Converting into binding energy:

$$(.0578 \text{ A.M.U.}) \; 931 \text{ Mev/A.M.U.} = 53.8 \text{ Mev.}$$

Binding energy per nucleon (there are 9 − 4 protons and 5 neutrons):

$$53.8 \text{ Mev/9 nucleons} = 5.98 \text{ Mev/Nucleon}$$

Name: _____   Section: _____

DERIVATION OF MASS–ENERGY CONVERSION FACTOR

1 A.M.U. = 931 Mev

All mass-energy conversions are described by Einstein's famous equation, $E = mc^2$, where m is the mass converted into energy, E. c is the speed of light. Since 1 A.M.U. = 1.66 × 10^{-27} kg, substitute this value in the equation:

$$E = mc^2$$

$$E = (1.66 \times 10^{-27} \text{ kg}) \left(3 \times 10^8 \frac{m}{s}\right)^2$$

$$E = (1.66 \times 10^{-27} \text{ kg}) \left(9 \times 10^{16} \frac{m^2}{s^2}\right)$$

$$E = 14.94 \times 10^{-11} \text{ kg} \frac{m^2}{s^2}$$

$$E = 1.49 \times 10^{-10} \text{ joules}$$

since 1 Mev = 1.6 × 10^{-13} joules:

$$E = 1.49 \times 10^{-10} \text{ joules} \frac{(1 \text{ Mev})}{(1.6 \times 10^{-13} \text{ joules})}$$

$$E = 931 \text{ Mev}$$

Thus for every A.M.U. of mass converted into energy, 931 Mev result:

1 A.M.U. = 931 Mev

Name: _____   Section: _____

BINDING ENERGY

Isotope	Mass of Nucleus (A.M.U.)	Binding Energy Per Nucleon (Mev)
$_{1}^{2}H$	2.0147	_____
$_{2}^{3}He$	3.0171	_____
$_{3}^{6}Li$	6.0169	_____
$_{3}^{7}Li$	7.0178	_____
$_{5}^{10}B$	10.0163	_____
$_{6}^{13}C$	13.0077	_____
$_{8}^{17}O$	17.0045	_____
$_{12}^{24}Mg$	23.9919	_____
$_{16}^{32}S$	31.9823	_____
$_{20}^{40}Ca$	39.9745	_____

Isotope	Mass of Nucleus (A.M.U.)	Binding Energy Per Nucleon (Mev)
$^{58}_{28}$Ni	57.959	_____
$^{84}_{36}$Kr	83.938	_____
$^{107}_{47}$Ag	106.948	_____
$^{138}_{56}$Ba	137.916	_____
$^{181}_{73}$Ta	180.928	_____
$^{208}_{82}$Pb	208.057	_____
$^{226}_{88}$Ra	226.10	_____
$^{238}_{92}$U	238.14	_____

Name: _____   Section: _____

RADIATION DETECTION DEVICES

Electroscope Ions created by the radiation cause this device to discharge more rapidly near a radiation source.

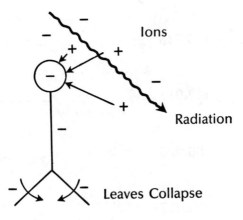

Ionization Chamber Radiation produces ions in gas of chamber. These ions are then attracted to the electrodes.

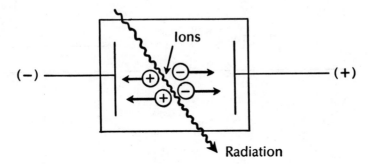

Geiger-Müller Tube   Ions produced by radiation cause an avalanche to build up because of the high potential on the electrodes.

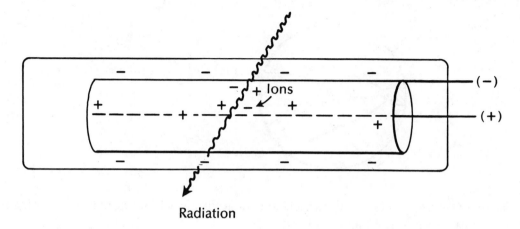

Radiation

Spark Chamber   Voltage is applied to the electrodes, which produces a spark along the ionized trail of the radiation.

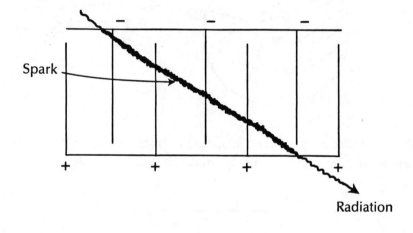

Radiation

Cloud Chamber Ionizing effect of radiation causes condensation of a vapor that produces visible tracks.

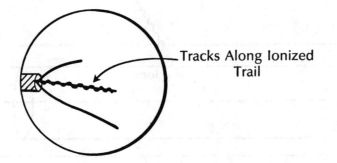

Tracks Along Ionized Trail

Bubble Chamber Tracks of particles become visible when liquid boils forming bubble paths around the ions produced.

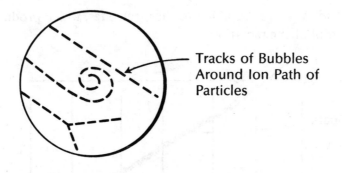

Tracks of Bubbles Around Ion Path of Particles

Solid State Tracks are produced in some solids (mica, glass, plastics) by charged nuclear particles. Etching with acid helps make these tracks visible with an electron microscope.

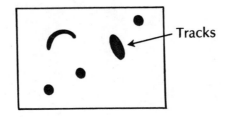

Tracks

Junction Detector Passage of a charged particle ionizes a region of the P-type base and produces an output signal.

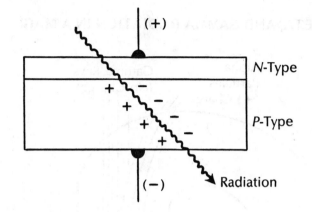

Spinthariscope and Scintillation Counter Subatomic particles hit a fluorescent screen and produce light. This scintillation can be viewed directly or changed to electricity with a photomultiplier tube.

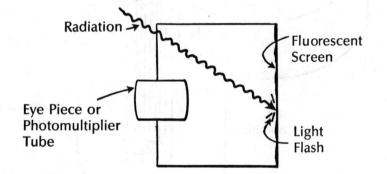

Photographic Emulsions Chemical changes in the photographic emulsion produced by passing radiation become visible when the film is developed.

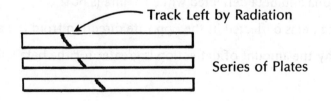

Name: _____   Section: _____

ALPHA, BETA, AND GAMMA RADIATION IN A MAGNETIC FIELD

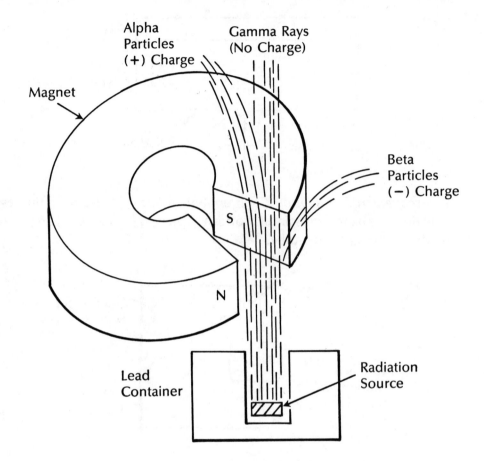

Questions:

1. Why are alpha and beta deflected while gamma is not?

2. Why are the betas deflected in the opposite direction from the alphas?

3. Explain why the amount of deflection is greater for the beta particles.

Name: _____   Section: _____

SUBATOMIC PARTICLES

Particle	Symbol	Charge	Mass (AMU)
neutron	$^{1}_{0}n$	0	1
proton	$^{1}_{1}H$	+1	1
beta	$^{0}_{-1}e$	−1	0
alpha	$^{4}_{2}He$	+2	4
positron	$^{0}_{+1}e$	+1	0
gamma ray	γ	0	0

Name: _____   Section: _____

NUCLEAR EQUATIONS

Complete the equations for:

1. $^{222}_{86}$ Rn emits an alpha particle

2. $^{214}_{82}$ Pb emits beta

3. $^{210}_{84}$ Po emits alpha

4. $^{238}_{92}$ U emits alpha

5. $^{230}_{90}$ Th emits alpha

6. $^{234}_{92}$ U emits alpha

7. $^{234}_{90}$ Th emits beta

8. $^{210}_{83}$ Bi emits beta

9. $^{226}_{88}$ Ra emits alpha

Name: _____   Section: _____

TALLY SHEET FOR COIN FLIP

Number	Wager	Amount	Won (+)	or	Lost (−)	Net Profit
1	$1.00		_____		_____	_____
2			_____		_____	_____
3			_____		_____	_____
4			_____		_____	_____
5			_____		_____	_____
6			_____		_____	_____
7			_____		_____	_____
8			_____		_____	_____
9			_____		_____	_____
10			_____		_____	_____
11			_____		_____	_____
12			_____		_____	_____
13			_____		_____	_____
14			_____		_____	_____
15			_____		_____	_____
16			_____		_____	_____
17			_____		_____	_____
18			_____		_____	_____
19			_____		_____	_____
20			_____		_____	_____
21			_____		_____	_____
22			_____		_____	_____
23			_____		_____	_____
24			_____		_____	_____

Number	Wager	Amount	Won (+)	or	Lost (	Net Profit
25			_____		_____	_____
26			_____		_____	_____
27			_____		_____	_____
28			_____		_____	_____
29			_____		_____	_____
30			_____		_____	_____
31			_____		_____	_____
32			_____		_____	_____
33			_____		_____	_____
34			_____		_____	_____
35			_____		_____	_____
36			_____		_____	_____
37			_____		_____	_____
38			_____		_____	_____
39			_____		_____	_____
40			_____		_____	_____
41			_____		_____	_____
42			_____		_____	_____
43			_____		_____	_____
44			_____		_____	_____
45			_____		_____	_____
46			_____		_____	_____
47			_____		_____	_____
48			_____		_____	_____
49			_____		_____	_____
50			_____		_____	_____
51			_____		_____	_____
52			_____		_____	_____

Number	Wager	Amount	Won (+)	or	Lost (−)	Net Profit
53			————		————	————
54			————		————	————
55			————		————	————
56			————		————	————
57			————		————	————
58			————		————	————
59			————		————	————
60			————		————	————
61			————		————	————
62			————		————	————
63			————		————	————
64			————		————	————
65			————		————	————
66			————		————	————
67			————		————	————
68			————		————	————
69			————		————	————
70			————		————	————
71			————		————	————
72			————		————	————
73			————		————	————
74			————		————	————
75			————		————	————
76			————		————	————
77			————		————	————
78			————		————	————
79			————		————	————
80			————		————	————

TALLY SHEET FOR COIN FLIP

Number	Wager	Amount	Won (+)	or	Lost (−)	Net Profit
81			_____		_____	_____
82			_____		_____	_____
83			_____		_____	_____
84			_____		_____	_____
85			_____		_____	_____
86			_____		_____	_____
87			_____		_____	_____
88			_____		_____	_____
89			_____		_____	_____
90			_____		_____	_____
91			_____		_____	_____
92			_____		_____	_____
93			_____		_____	_____
94			_____		_____	_____
95			_____		_____	_____
96			_____		_____	_____
97			_____		_____	_____
98			_____		_____	_____
99			_____		_____	_____
100			_____		_____	_____

Total number of wins: _____

Total number of losses: _____

Name: _____   Section: _____

FISSION OF URANIUM-235

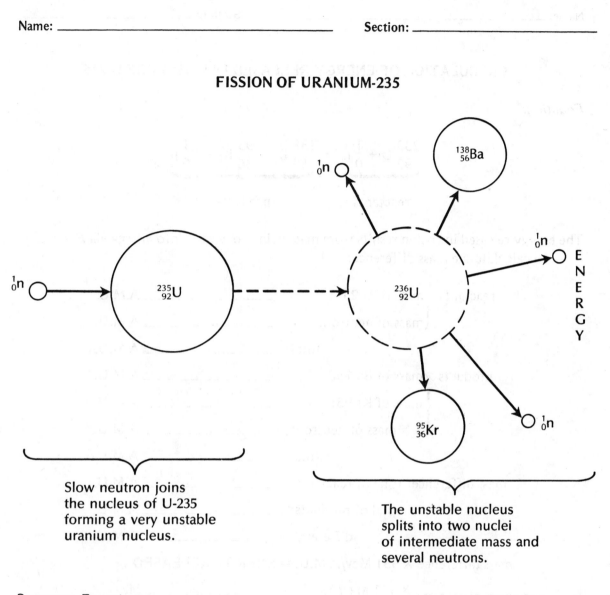

Slow neutron joins the nucleus of U-235 forming a very unstable uranium nucleus.

The unstable nucleus splits into two nuclei of intermediate mass and several neutrons.

Summary Equation:

$$^{235}_{92}U + ^{1}_{0}n \rightarrow ^{138}_{56}Ba + ^{95}_{36}Kr + 3^{1}_{0}n + energy$$

Name: _____   Section: _____

CALCULATION OF ENERGY RELEASED IN FISSION OF U-235

Equation:

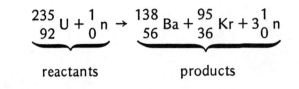

$$\underbrace{{}^{235}_{92}U + {}^{1}_{0}n}_{\text{reactants}} \rightarrow \underbrace{{}^{138}_{56}Ba + {}^{95}_{36}Kr + 3{}^{1}_{0}n}_{\text{products}}$$

The energy released in fission results from mass being converted into energy via $E = mc^2$.
To calculate the mass difference:

reactants { mass of U-235:   _____ A.M.U.

mass of neutron: _____ A.M.U.

total   _____ A.M.U.

products { mass of Ba 138:   _____ A.M.U.

mass of Kr 95:   _____ A.M.U.

3 X mass of neutron: _____ A.M.U.

total   _____ A.M.U.

mass difference: total of reactants: _____ A.M.U.

− total of products: _____ A.M.U.

difference = _____ A.M.U.

mass difference X 931 Mev/A.M.U. = ENERGY RELEASED

_____ X 931 Mev/A.M.U. = _____ Mev

Name: _____   Section: _____

NUCLEAR REACTORS FOR ELECTRICITY

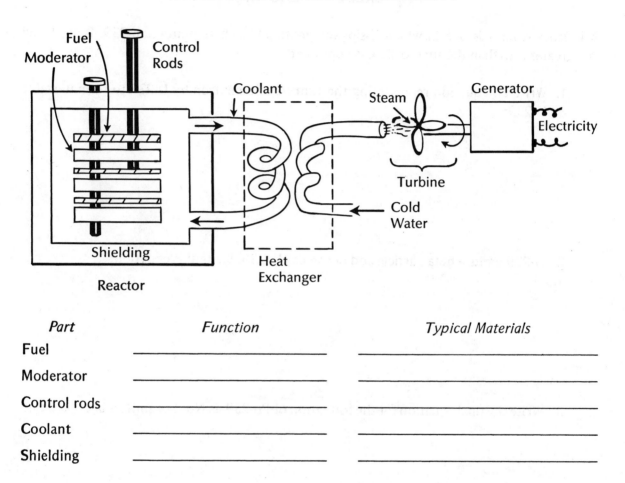

Part	Function	Typical Materials
Fuel	_____	_____
Moderator	_____	_____
Control rods	_____	_____
Coolant	_____	_____
Shielding	_____	_____

Name: _____   Section: _____

BREEDER REACTOR

A breeder reactor is one in which fissionable material, such as plutonium-239, is produced at a greater rate than the fuel, U-235, is consumed.

1. Write an equation representing the capture of a neutron by U-238 to form unstable U-239:

2. U-239 emits a beta particle and becomes Np-239. Write this equation:

3. Write the final equation for the formation of Pu-239 as Np-239 emits a beta particle:

Name: _____   Section: _____

FUSION PROCESSES

Fusion   A reaction where light nuclei combine to form a nucleus of greater mass. In this process, the total mass of the products is less than the reactants, the difference in mass accounting for the energy liberated via $E = mc^2$.

Some laboratory fusion reactions:

$$\,_{1}^{2}\text{H} + \,_{1}^{2}\text{H} \rightarrow \,_{1}^{3}\text{H} + \,_{1}^{1}\text{H} + 4 \text{ Mev}$$

$$\,_{1}^{2}\text{H} + \,_{1}^{2}\text{H} \rightarrow \,_{2}^{3}\text{He} + \,_{0}^{1}\text{n} + 3.3 \text{ Mev}$$

$$\,_{1}^{2}\text{H} + \,_{1}^{3}\text{H} \rightarrow \,_{2}^{4}\text{He} + \,_{0}^{1}\text{n} + 17.6 \text{ Mev}$$

$$\,_{1}^{2}\text{H} + \,_{2}^{3}\text{He} \rightarrow \,_{2}^{4}\text{He} + \,_{1}^{1}\text{H} + 18.3 \text{ Mev}$$

Summary of the processes on stars:

$$4\,_{1}^{1}\text{H} \rightarrow \,_{2}^{4}\text{He} + 2\,_{+1}^{0}\text{e} + 26 \text{ Mev}$$

Thermonuclear bomb:

$$\,_{3}^{6}\text{Li}\,_{1}^{2}\text{H} \rightarrow 2\,_{2}^{4}\text{He} + 22.4 \text{ Mev}$$

Name: _____ Section: _____

UNIT TEST ON NUCLEAR ENERGY

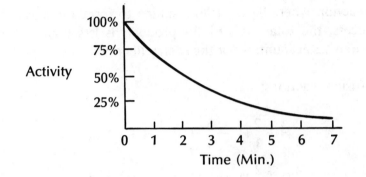

1. The half life of the radioactive sample plotted is about:

   a. 1 min.
   b. 2 min.
   c. 4 min.
   d. 7 min.

2. If twice as much material was used in #1, the half life would:

   a. increase
   b. decrease
   c. remain the same

3. If the sample is 25 percent radioactive, how long has it been sitting around?

   a. 1 min.
   b. 2 min.
   c. 4 min.
   d. 7 min.

4. Ba 137 m has a half life of 2.6 min. How would its decay curve shape compare with one for C^{14}?

   a. Ba would be straighter
   b. Ba curve would have more fluctuations
   c. Ba would be parabolic
   d. same general shape

5.

$$^{222}_{86}\text{Rn} \rightarrow {}^{218}_{84}\text{Po} + {}^{4}_{2}\text{He} \qquad {}^{222}_{86}\text{Rn} = 222.0165 \text{ A.M.U.}$$

$$^{218}_{84}\text{Po} = 218.0079 \text{ A.M.U.}$$

$$^{4}_{2}\text{He} = 4.0026 \text{ A.M.U.}$$

$$1 \text{ A.M.U.} = 931 \text{ Mev}$$

The energy released in this reaction is about:
a. 931 Mev
b. 4 Mev
c. 6 Mev
d. 222 Mev

(6–8)

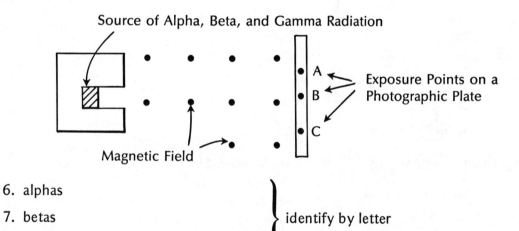

Source of Alpha, Beta, and Gamma Radiation

A, B, C — Exposure Points on a Photographic Plate

Magnetic Field

6. alphas

7. betas   } identify by letter

8. gammas

9. Which of the following does not use the ionization property of radiation in detecting it?

a. cloud chamber
b. bubble chamber
c. Geiger-Müller tube
d. photographic emulsion

10. Which is the most penetrating form of radiation?

    a. alpha
    b. beta
    c. gamma
    d. cathode ray

11. $^{222}_{86}Rn \rightarrow \; ^{218}_{84}Po + \left[\quad\quad\quad \right]$

    What should be in the bracket?

    a. $^{0}_{-1}e$

    b. $^{1}_{0}n$

    c. positron
    d. alpha particle

12. $^{214}_{82}Pb \rightarrow \; ^{214}_{83}Bi + \left[\quad\quad\quad \right]$

    a. $^{0}_{-1}e$

    b. $^{1}_{0}n$

    c. positron
    d. alpha particle

13. The half life of $^{226}_{88}Ra$ is 1620 years. How much of a 2 kg sample will be left after 3240 years?

    a. .25 kg
    b. .5 kg
    c. 1 kg
    d. 1.5 kg

14. Which of these processes would provide the most energy if equal amounts of fuel are considered?

    a. radioactive decomposition
    b. fission
    c. fusion
    d. chemical combination

15. The function of a moderator in a nuclear reactor is to:
    a. control speed of fissions
    b. slow reaction
    c. slow neutrons
    d. cool the reactor

16. Control rods must have the ability to:
    a. slow neutrons
    b. speed up fission
    c. remove U-235 from the reaction
    d. absorb neutrons

17. In order for hydrogen to fuse into helium:
    a. high temperature and pressure are needed
    b. critical mass is needed
    c. slow neutrons are needed
    d. all of the above are needed

DIRECTIONS: (18–27): Use this code   *a = increases*
                                        b = decreases
                                        c = remains the same

18. As the strength of a magnetic field increases, the effect it has on a gamma ray
    _____.

19. As the length of a control rod inside a working nuclear reactor increases, the rate
    of the reaction _____.

20. As a radioactive substance emits an alpha particle, its atomic number _____.

21. As a radioactive substance emits a beta particle, its atomic number _____.

22. As a U-235 captures a neutron, its stability _____.

23. From a series of different radioactive isotopes, as the activity of an isotope in-
    creases, its half life _____.

24. As a sample of Pb^{-214} decays radioactively, the half life of the Pb^{-214} sample
    _____.

25. As the mass "lost" in a nuclear reaction increases, the energy released from that
    reaction _____.

26. As heat and pressure are applied to a radioisotope, its half life _____.

27. In uncontrolled fission of U-235, the number of neutrons involved _____.

Name: _____   Section: _____

WAVE VOCABULARY

DIRECTIONS: Define and/or describe the following terms as they relate to waves. Use sketches and examples to aid your descriptions.

1. speed _____
   _____

2. medium _____
   _____

3. pulse _____
   _____

4. amplitude _____
   _____

5. frequency _____
   _____

6. wavelength _____
   _____

7. period _____
   _____

8. phase _____
   _____

9. interference _____
   _____

10. reflection _____
    _____

Name: _____   Section: _____

WAVE REPRESENTATIONS

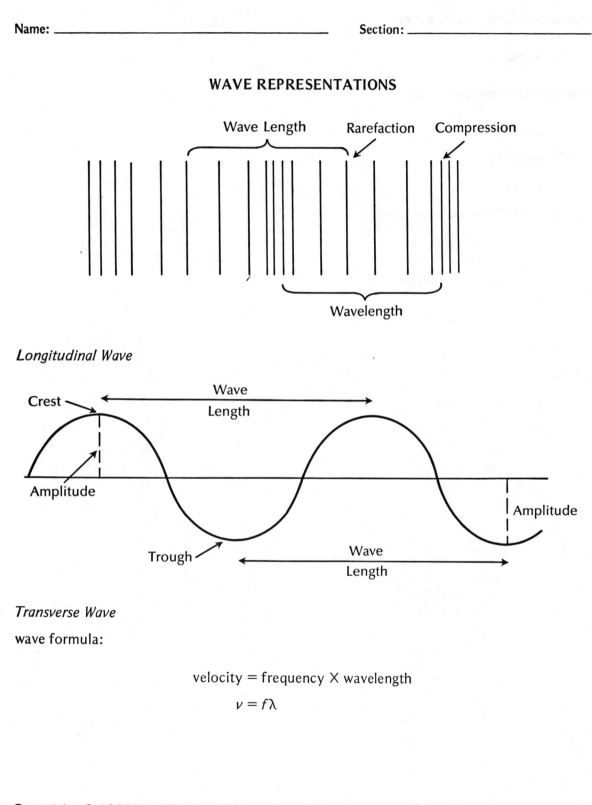

Longitudinal Wave

Transverse Wave

wave formula:

$$\text{velocity} = \text{frequency} \times \text{wavelength}$$

$$v = f\lambda$$

Examples of longitudinal waves:

    1. sound

Examples of transverse waves:

    1. light

    2. gamma rays

    3. x-rays

    4. electrical waves

Name: _____   Section: _____

$$v = f \times \lambda$$

Purpose

To cheek the above equation by measuring all the variables and seeing if v, velocity, is equal to frequency times wavelength.

Method

First, see if you can get both a full and half waves in the slinky at a particular tension. When you can, you're ready to start getting data.

Velocity determination Measure the length of the stretched spring. This is distance, d. Send a pulse down the spring and time it, t. Repeat the timing two more times getting t_2 and t_3. Use the distance divided by the average of the three times to get the velocity, $v = \dfrac{d}{t_{ave.}}$. If times are very short, let the pulse reflect from the far end and time the round trip. In this case, your distance will be $2d$.

Wavelength measures This is determined from the distance, d, and the wave pattern.

When you have this pattern, the wavelength is equal to d.

When you have this pattern, the wavelength is equal to twice d, $2d$.

Frequency While maintaining each of the above patterns, count ten complete wiggles. Record the time, t, in seconds. The frequency is ten divided by t, $f = \dfrac{10}{t}$.

By keeping the tension constant, you can get two f and λ measures for each v measured.

$$v = f \times \lambda$$

Data Table for $v = f\lambda$ lab:

	Distance, d (or $2d$, if reflected) t_1 t_2 t_3	$v^* = d/t_{ave.}$ (or $v = 2d/t_{ave.}$) (if reflected)	Wave Length, (d, or $2d$)	Time for 10 Oscillations	$f = 10/t$	$f \times \lambda$ **
$\frac{1}{2}$ wave						
Full wave	Keep same tension and v will be the same as above					
Change tension and repeat:						
$\frac{1}{2}$ wave						
Full wave	Keep the same tension and v will be the same					

In each case, compare the v (*) against $f \times \lambda$ (**). They should, ideally, be equal.

Name: _____   Section: _____

DIRECTIONS: Write the names of students who can see each other in the boxes that ap-proximate their location in the room. Represent light rays from the "seen" pupil to the mir-ror and then to the person doing the seeing.

REFLECTION

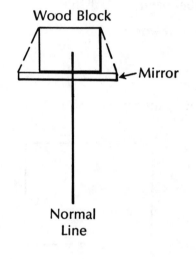

Wood Block

←Mirror

Normal
Line

_____ _____ _____ _____ _____

_____ _____ _____ _____ _____

_____ _____ _____ _____ _____

_____ _____ _____ _____ _____

_____ _____ _____ _____ _____

_____ _____ _____ _____ _____

Name: _____   Section: _____

IMAGE IN A PLANE MIRROR I

Equipment

1 sheet of paper	1 piece of cardboard
1 mirror	1 pin
1 rubber band	1 ruler
1 block of wood	

Directions

1. Draw line M across your paper:

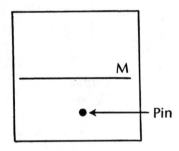

2. Stick the pin through the paper into the piece of cardboard roughly in the position shown.

3. Block up the mirror with the rubber band and place it with its front surface on line M. During this exercise, the mirror can be slid along M to see rays at wide angles, but the front surface should always be on line M.

4. With your eyes at paper level, look at the image of the pin in the mirror. Note its general location.

5. Take the ruler. With one eye, sight along the ruler at the image of the pin. Do this as far to the left of the actual pin as you can. When your ruler is lined up, draw a line along its edge. Draw an arrow on the line pointing toward your eye, since this represents a ray of light coming into your eye.

6. Repeat this process from different positions on either side of the pin. Your paper should look like this when you are finished.

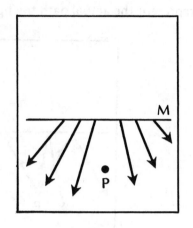

7. The rest of this exercise can now be done from the lines you have drawn.

8. The lines you have drawn represent rays of light from the pin that have been reflected toward your eye. But you see the image of the pin *behind* the mirror. Extend each of your sight lines as dotted lines beyond M until they intersect. Label the point of intersection P^1. This is where you saw the image. Measure and compare the position of P^1—with respect to the sides of the paper and M—with the location of P (the pin)—with respect to M and the sides of the paper. How do the locations compare?

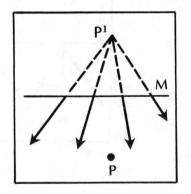

9. Actual path of the light: The solid lines you drew represent light rays that originated at P, hit the mirror at various points, and came into your eye. Draw solid lines with arrows toward M from P to where each of your lines leaves the mirror. Your solid lines now represent the actual path the light rays took.

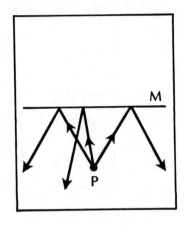

10. At *each* reflection point draw a normal to M; label each incident angle *i*, and each reflected angle *r*. Does the law of reflection hold?

11. How would this diagram look if the wave fronts were drawn in (besides messy)?

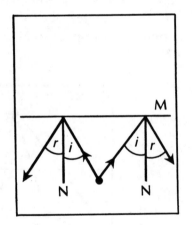

Name: _____   Section: _____

PLANE MIRROR IMAGE II

Equipment

(same as Exercise I)

It should be apparent from Exercise I that *any two rays* are sufficient to locate the image of a point.

1. Set up your equipment similar to Exercise I, *except* draw an uneven triangle in the bottom half of your paper. Label its points A, B, C.

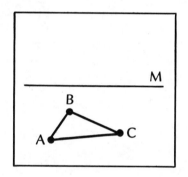

2. Place the pin at point A. Sight at the image from the right, then the left side of the pin. Draw arrows on your sight lines. Label the lines a_1 and a_2.

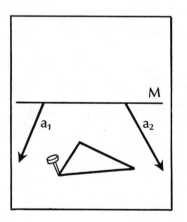

3. Repeat with the pin at B and then C.

4. As in Exercise I, extend a_1 and a_2 until they cross. Label this A^1. Do likewise for b_1 and b_2 and c_1 and c_2, to locate B^1 and C^1. Connect these points to construct the image of your triangle.

5. For each of your 6 sight lines (a_1, a_2, b_1, b_2, c_1, and c_2), do steps #9 and #10 from Instruction Sheet I.

6. Compare image and actual triangle locations with respect to left and right and line M.

Name: _____   Section: _____

REFLECTION QUIZ

1. The dot A represents a "point source" of light. Draw in representations of the rays of light from the source.

      •   •
      A   B

2. Dot B is also a point score. Draw in representations of the "wave fronts."

3. Draw the path (ray) that light from X must follow to get to the eye. (M is a mirror)

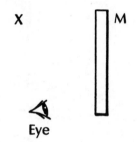

4. Draw where the eye will "see" point X.

Define:

5. virtual image _____

   _____

6. real image _____

   _____

7. reflection _____

   _____

8. normal _____

_____

9. plane (mirror) _____

_____

10. incident ray _____

_____

Name: _____   Section: _____

RAY DIAGRAMS FOR LENSES

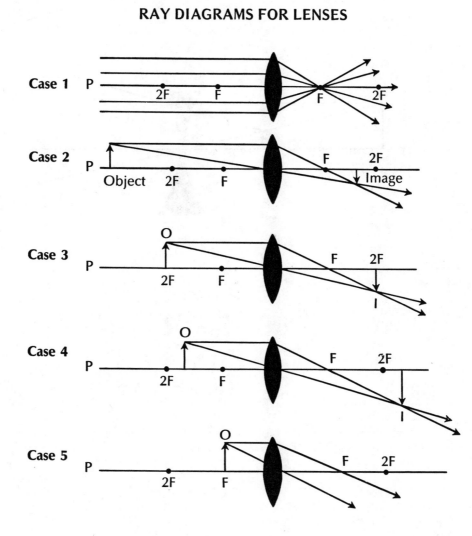

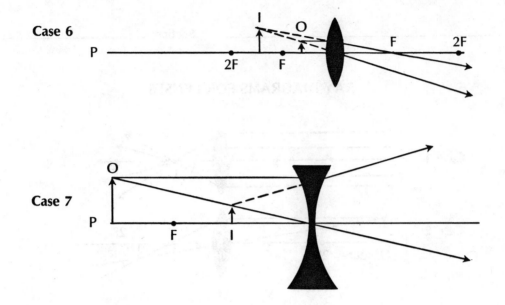

Name: _____   Section: _____

LENSES LAB SHEET

Case	Object Location	Convert to cm.	Distance You Placed Object	Predicted Image Position	Convert to cm.	Actual Image Dist.	√ if agree	Type Image	√ if agree	Inverted or not	√ if agree	Larger or Smaller	√ if agree	Comment
I	across room	∞	∞	at F	—	(your F)	—	real	—	—	—	dot		
II	farther than 2 F			between F and 2 F				real		inverted		smaller		
III	at 2 F			at 2 F				real		inverted		same size		
IV	between F and 2 F			farther than 2 F				real		inverted		larger		
V	at F			no image	—	—		—		—		—		
VI	closer than F			behind lens	behind lens	in front or behind?		virtual		upright		larger		
VII	behind concave lens			behind lens	behind lens	in front or behind?		virtual		upright		smaller		

Name: _____   Section: _____

REFRACTION

DIRECTIONS: Explain the way in which refraction affects the situations described below. Be thorough in your presentation. Diagrams often will help make a clearer explanation.

1. An oar appears bent when it is placed in the water.

2. Streams and swimming pools are actually deeper than they appear to be.

3. You can see the sun before it is actually above the horizon.

4. "As easy as shooting fish in a barrel" might not be all that easy.

5. We often see a mirage of water on a highway some distance ahead of us.

6. People say they can "see the heat" above hot surfaces.

7. Root beer mugs are not as full of soda as they appear to be.

8. Stars "twinkle."

9. The production of a rainbow.

10. Scenes viewed through a piece of cheap glass are distorted.

Name: _____   Section: _____

REFRACTION QUIZ

Medium A

$n = 1.2$

Medium B

$n = 2.0$

1. In which medium does light travel faster? _____

2. Which medium has the greater optical density? _____

3. Draw the path of light in medium B.

4. As angle i increases, angle r would _____ .

5. As angle i increases, the relative index of refraction between A and B _____ _____ .

6. If angle $i = 0$, angle r would equal _____ .

7. Could light originating in medium A be totally internally reflected? _____

_____

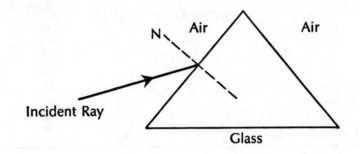

8.–9. Trace the path of the incident light ray *through* the glass triangle.

10. As the light leaves the glass, its velocity _____.

Name: _____   Section: _____

YOUNG'S DOUBLE SLIT EXPERIMENT

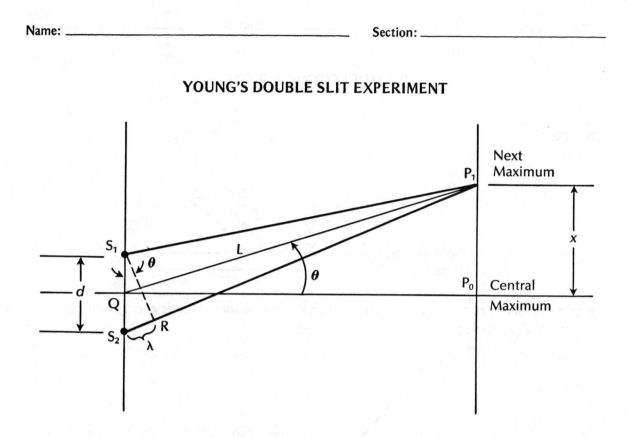

In this diagram, L is the distance from the center of the two slits to P_1, the point where the bright line of light appears on the screen. P_0 is the central bright line and x is the distance from the central bright line to P_1.

The distance between the two slits is measurable and is marked d. The distance from the central line to the bright line of reinforcement is x. The distance from S_2 to P_1 is one wavelength longer than the distance from S_1 to P_1, so in right triangle $S_2 S_1 R$ the base, $S_2 R$, equals the wavelength, λ. This triangle is similar to triangle $P_1 P_0 Q$ (corresponding sides are mutually perpendicular). Therefore, since the ratios of corresponding sides of similar triangles are equal,

$$\frac{x}{L} = \frac{\lambda}{d}$$

and from this:

$$\lambda = \frac{xd}{L}$$

Name: _____   Section: _____

PHOTOELECTRIC EFFECT

The effect:

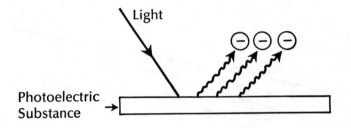

certain number of photo electrons (current) emitted with some kinetic energy (voltage)
   If red light is used:

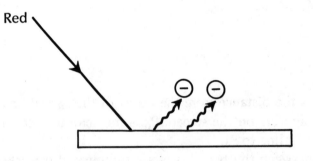

brighter red produces more electrons (current), but the energy per electron (voltage) is the same:

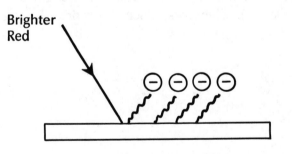

Blue light has a frequency greater than red ($E = hf$). If blue light is used:

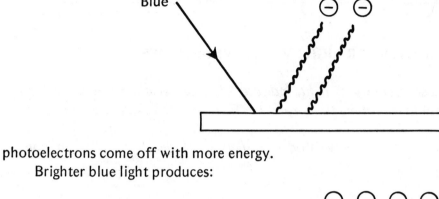

Blue

photoelectrons come off with more energy.

Brighter blue light produces:

Bright
Blue

more electrons at the same energy.

If we let a quantum of light (a photon) be represented by a drawing, then the size of the energy bundle depends on the frequency, because $E = hf$ and the brightness determines the number of bundles. In the diagrams above:

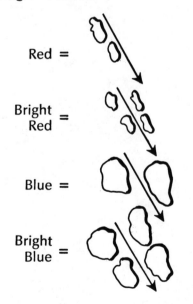

Red =

Bright
Red =

Blue =

Bright
Blue =

Name: _____   Section: _____

MODELS FOR LIGHT VERSUS PROPERTIES

DIRECTIONS: After each property of light, indicate (√) whether a wave model, a particle model, or both are useful in describing that property. Then go on to explain your choices.

Property	Wave Model	Particle Model	Explanation
1. rectilinear propogation	_____	_____	_____
2. reflection	_____	_____	_____
3. refraction	_____	_____	_____
4. diffraction	_____	_____	_____
5. interference	_____	_____	_____
6. photoelectric emission	_____	_____	_____

Name:_____   Section: _____

DERIVATION OF THE PARTICLE-WAVE EQUATION

Around 1924, Louis de Broglie suggested the particle-wave nature of light might indicate that in every mechanical system, waves are associated with particles. By using Einstein's equation for mass-energy equivalency, $E = mc^2$, where m is the mass of a particle in motion and $E = hf$, the energy of a photon, DeBroglie considered the energy of a photon to be equal to that of a moving particle:

$$E = E$$

setting both equations equal to each other:

$$hf = mc^2$$

divide by c:

$$\frac{hf}{c} = mc$$

substitute for $c = f\lambda$ (wave equation)

$$\frac{hf}{f\lambda} = mc$$

fs cancel:

$$\frac{h\cancel{f}}{\cancel{f}\lambda} = mc$$

$$\frac{h}{\lambda} = mc$$

solving for λ:

$$\lambda = \frac{h}{mc}$$

The wavelength, λ, of a photon is expressed in terms of its momentum, *mc*. Perhaps the wavelength of any particle of velocity, *v*, may be expressed in terms of its momentum:

$$\lambda = \frac{h}{mv}$$

Name: _____   Section: _____

CHARGING A LEAF ELECTROSCOPE PERMANENTLY BY INDUCTION

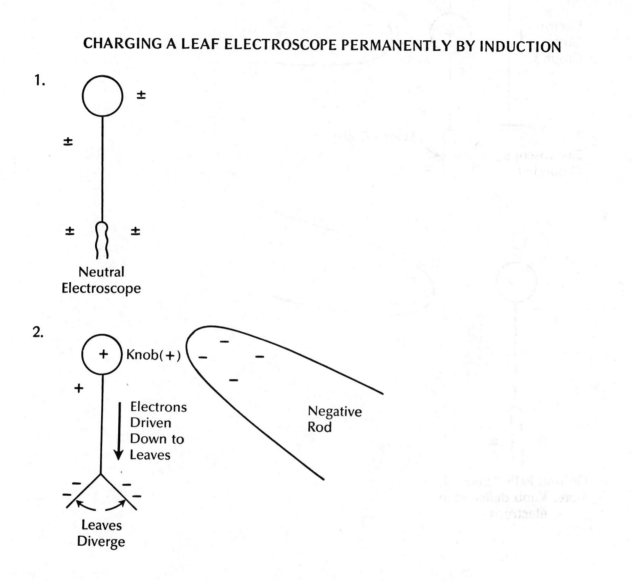

1.

Neutral
Electroscope

2.

Knob(+)

Electrons
Driven
Down to
Leaves

Negative
Rod

Leaves
Diverge

3.

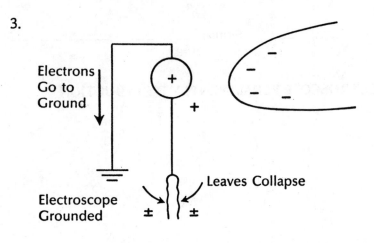

Electrons
Go to
Ground

Leaves Collapse

Electroscope
Grounded

4.

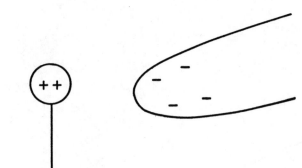

Ground Path Removed
Note: Knob deficient in
electrons

5.

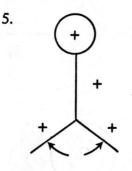

When rod is removed, electrons
readjust and entire electroscope
shows net (+) charge.
±

DIRECTIONS: *Below, do a similar series of diagrams to show the steps necessary to produce a net (−) charge on an electroscope by induction. Start at step (1). Step (2) will use a positively charged rod:*

Name: _____   Section: _____

COULOMB'S LAW OF ELECTROSTATICS

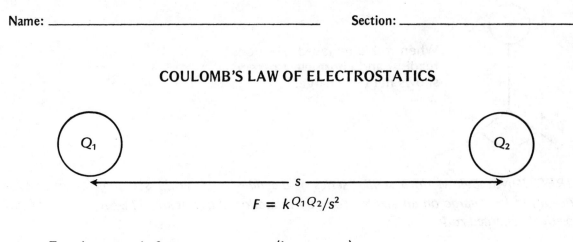

$$F = k Q_1 Q_2 / s^2$$

F = electrostatic force   (in newtons)

Q_1 = charge on one conductor   (in coulombs)

Q_2 = charge on the other conductor   (in coulombs)

k = proportionality constant which depends on the medium separating the charges $\left(\text{for air, } k = 9 \times 10^9 \text{N} \dfrac{\text{m}^2}{\text{c}^2}\right)$

s = distance between centers of conductors (in meters)

Questions

1. Explain the significance of a solution that has a $+F$ and how it is dependent on the sign of the charges.

2. What does a $-F$ solution imply? Why?

3. Look up values for k other than the one for air.

4. What happens when the two charges are moved twice as far apart? Three times as far? Half as far?

Name: _____ Section: _____

LINES OF FORCE

Electric fields are represented by lines of force. These lines represent the direction of electrical force on a (+) charge at a point in the field. The density of the lines (closeness) is used to describe the relative strength of the field.

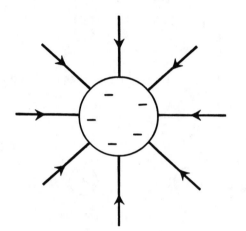

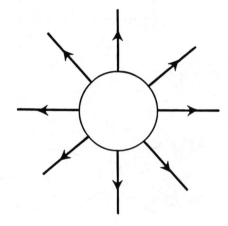

Example

What is the charge on this sphere? _____

Which sphere has the greater charge? Why? _____

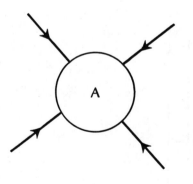

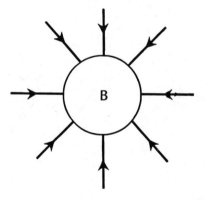

When several charges are contributing to a net field, one must determine the resultant force on a (+) test charge in order to determine the lines of force in the region around the conductors:

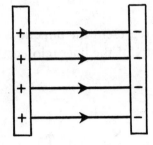

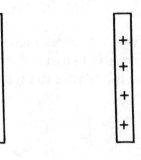

Example　　　　　　　　　　　　　　　　　　Draw in the lines of force.

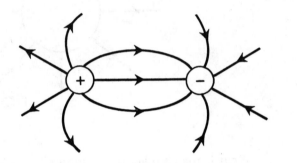

Example　　　　　　　　　　　　　　　　　　Draw in the lines of force.

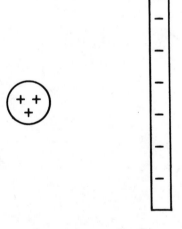

Draw in the lines of force.

Name: _____   Section: _____

ELECTROSTATICS QUIZ I

1. A hard rubber rod is rubbed with fur. What kind of charge does the rod get?
   _____

2. The fur? _____

3. A glass rod is rubbed with silk. What kind of charge does the rod get? _____

4. The silk? _____

5. State the law of electrostatics: _____
   _____

6. Electrical charge is produced by transfering mainly _____.

7. The theoretical source of all electrical phenomena is the _____.
   a. molecule
   b. atom
   c. solid state
   d. wave model

8. "Static" means _____.
   a. a spark
   b. lightning
   c. non-moving
   d. a and b

9–10. List 2 examples in which electrification occurs:
   a. _____
   _____
   b. _____
   _____

Name: _____   Section: _____

ELECTROSTATICS QUIZ II

DIRECTIONS 1–10: Answer (a) if what is referred to has a positive charge, (b) for negative charge, and (c) for neutral.

1. Fur, after it has been rubbed with a rubber rod. _____

2. Silk, after being rubbed with a glass rod. _____

3. Leaves of an electroscope when a (+) rod is brought near. _____

4. Leaves of an electroscope after being charged by conduction with a (−) rod. _____

5. Dome of a Van de Graaff generator when operating. _____

6. The earth. _____

7. An ion formed by an intense electric field while a conductor is discharging. _____

8. The conducting ball of an electroscope after being charged by conduction with a (−) rod. _____

9. The conducting ball of an electroscope while it is being charged by induction with a (+) rod. _____

10. The inside of Faraday's ice pail after it is given a (+) charge. _____

Name: _____   Section: _____

ELECTROSTATICS QUIZ III

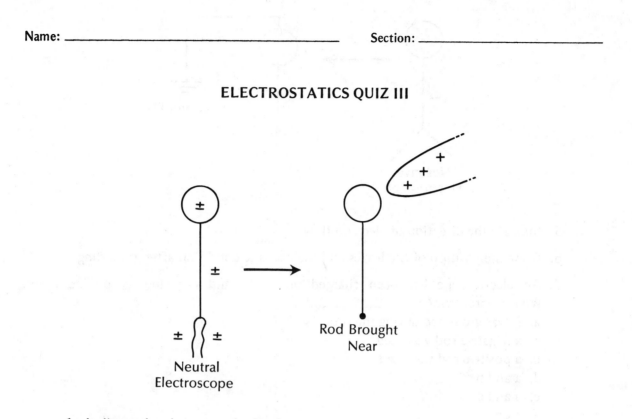

1. Indicate the charge on the knob.

2. Indicate the direction of charge flow in the electroscope.

3. Indicate the position and charge on the leaves.

4. If the rod in the above diagram is made of glass, it was probably rubbed with
   _____

   a. cat's fur
   b. wood
   c. silk
   d. rubber

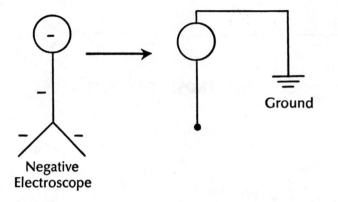

Ground

Negative
Electroscope

5. Indicate the direction of electron flow.

6. Draw the position of the leaves and their charge condition after grounding.

7. An electroscope has been charged positively and permanently by induction. What is (are) true? _____
   a. it was grounded during the process
   b. a negative rod was used
   c. a positive rod was used
   d. a and b
   e. a and c
   f. c only

8. In producing a charge on a rubber rod with fur, the electrons of the _____ _____ are the more tightly held to their atoms.

9. Which has the most free electrons? _____
   a. rubber
   b. glass
   c. silk
   d. gold

10. A negatively charged rod attracts a neutral piece of paper because _____
    a. charges attract neutral bodies
    b. the rod temporarily charges the paper
    c. insulators are attracted by charges
    d. the charge on the rod is very strong

Name: _____   Section: _____

ELECTROSTATICS QUIZ IV

1. An object that has a deficiency of electrons has a _____ charge.

2. If a positively charged pith ball is repelled by an object, the object has a _____ _____ charge.

3. If the leaves of a negatively charged electroscope converge as an object is brought near, the object has a _____ charge.

4. A _____ has more "free" electrons than an insulator.

5. What are the SI units for k in Coulomb's law? _____

6. If F in Coulomb's law is (+), the force is _____ .

7. If two charges are moved twice as far apart, the electrostatic force between them becomes _____ .

8. What sphere has the greater charge? _____

9. What sign charge is on both spheres? _____

10. A positive charge is placed half-way between spheres A and B. In which direction will it move? _____
    a. toward A
    b. toward B
    c. it will not move
    d. vertically

Name: _____   Section: _____

CURRENT, VOLTAGE AND RESISTANCE IN A SIMPLE CIRCUIT

Definitions

current → rate of charge transfer

$$I = \frac{Q}{t}$$

$$ampere = \frac{coulomb}{second}$$

voltage → energy per charge

$$V = \frac{E}{Q}$$

$$volt = \frac{joule}{coulomb}$$

resistance → opposition to current

$$R = \frac{V}{I}$$

$$ohm = \frac{volt}{ampere}$$

Water Analog for a Simple Circuit

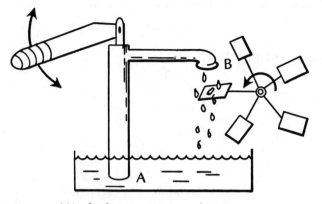

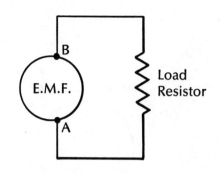

Work done on water by pump
increases potential energy
from A to B. Falling water
converts its potential energy
into work by turning paddle wheel.

E.M.F. increases energy of
charges from A to B.
Potential energy of
charges does work
in the load resistor.

Name: _____   Section: _____

POTENTIAL DIFFERENCE

Neutral Conductor

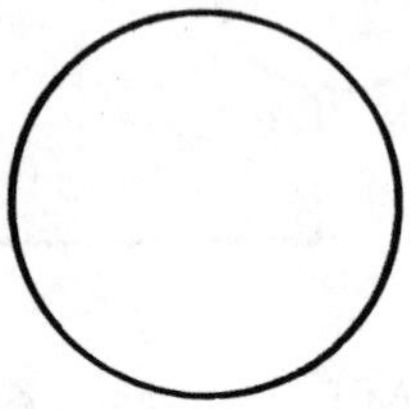

⊖¹
Electron
at Ground

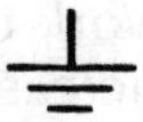

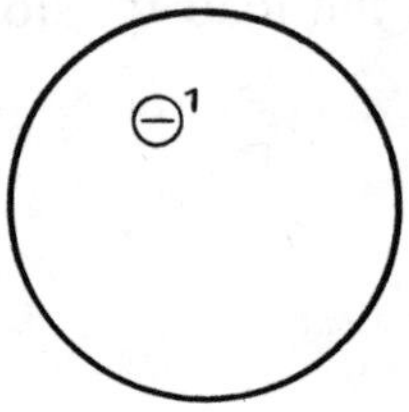

⊖¹ #1 electron moved onto
conductor making it (−)

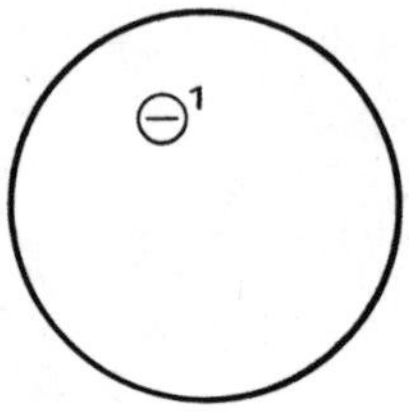

⊖¹ #2 electron will be
repelled by #1, so a
force is needed to
overcome the repulsion
and place #2 on the
conductor.

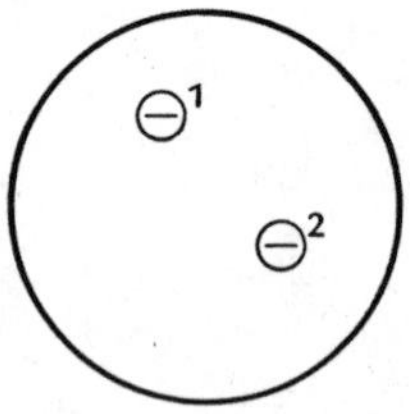

⊖²

⊖¹   Work was done on
⊖²   charge #2 to get it from
ground on the
conductor. Now charges
1 and 2 have more
potential energy on the
conductor than they did
at ground — a potential
difference exists.

⊖³

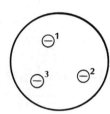

Work is done by the force needed to move #3 from A to B so there is a potential difference between these points.

As more amd more charges are placed on the conductor, the work required increases because of greater repulsive forces. The difference in potential for any charge on the sphere (compared to ground) increases as a result of this process.

Name: _____   Section: _____

OHM'S LAW LAB

Purpose

To answer the following questions:

1. Is the $\frac{E}{I}$ ratio for a circuit constant?

2. Is this ratio different for different circuits?

3. Is this ratio equal to what we call the "resistance" in that circuit? $\left(\frac{E}{I} = R?\right)$

Method

for #1: take values of E and I for a circuit and plot

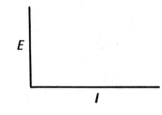

for #2: repeat method #1 for two "different" circuits (use a different load resistor)

for #3: calculate each of the slopes of your two lines; $m = \frac{\Delta y}{\Delta x} = \frac{\Delta E}{\Delta I} = R$, according to Ohm, and compare these slopes to the known value of the resistance in each circuit.

Circuit

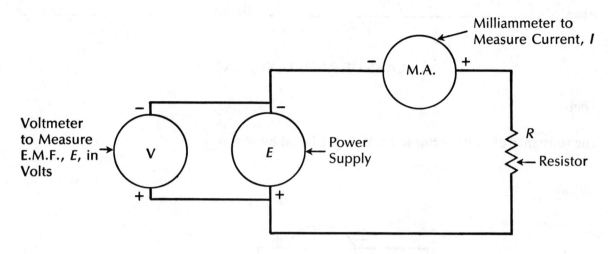

Name: _____   Section: _____

LAWS OF RESISTANCE LAB

Theory

The resistance of a conductor-like wire is predicted by $R = \rho \dfrac{l}{A}$

Circuit

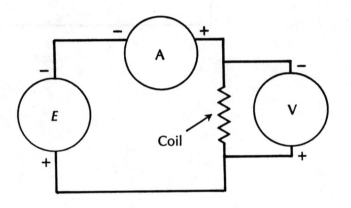

R resistance in Ω

ρ resistivity (depends on type of material and temp.)

l length of conductor

A cross sectional area of wire (thickness)

Purpose

To check the effect of each of the variables in the above formula qualitively (R found by voltmeter-ammeter method)

1. **Effect of l:** Take data to plot (should be a straight line if, in fact, $R \propto l$)

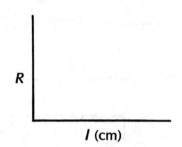

l (cm)

2. **Effect of A:** Compare two different guage wires (#28 and #30) (#30 has a cross-sectional area less than #29). How does R vary with cross-sectional area?

3. **Effect of ρ:** Compare R of 2,000 cm of copper with R of 200 cm nickel-silver.

Note: the R of 200 cm nickel-silver must be multiplied by 10 in order to make it comparable to 2,000 cm nickel-silver for comparison with the copper. How does R vary with ρ?

$$\rho \text{ of Cu} = 1.7 \times 10^{-6} \ \Omega \text{ cm}$$

$$\rho \text{ of NiAg} = 49 \times 10^{-6} \ \Omega \text{ cm}$$

Name: _____   Section: _____

CURRENT ELECTRICITY QUIZ I

1. If 2.8 × 10⁻⁷ coulombs of charge passes a point in a circuit in 2.0 × 10⁻⁶ seconds, the current is _____ amperes.

2. What are the S.I. units for the ohm? _____

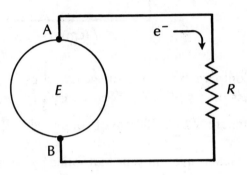

3. Which is the negative terminal? _____

4. If E = 12 V and R = 4 ohms, the current in the circuit is _____ amps.

5. What is the potential drop across R? _____

6. If R is replaced with a resistor having twice the resistance, the current _____ _____.

7. Label the high potential end of the resistor (−) and the low potential end (+).

8. As the length of a wire increases, its resistance _____.

9. If the cross sectional *radius* of a wire is doubled, its resistance will _____ _____.

10. If nickel silver wire replaces copper wire in an electric circuit, the current in that circuit will _____.

Name: _____   Section: _____

CURRENT ELECTRICITY QUIZ II

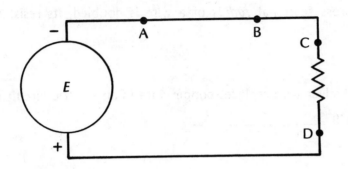

1. An ammeter measures
   a. charge/volt
   b. charge
   c. potential difference
   d. charge/time

2. A voltmeter measures
   a. charge/volt
   b. charge
   c. potential difference
   d. charge/time

3. An ammeter should be connected in the circuit between points
   a. C and D
   b. A and B
   c. A and D
   d. none of these

4. The high potential end of a voltmeter across the resistance should be connected
   to point
   a. A
   b. B
   c. C
   d. D

5. If 2 amps of current is measured _____ coulombs of charge flow each second
   a. 1
   b. 2
   c. 1.6×10^{-19}
   d. 4

6. A 10 volt E.M.F. increases the energy of each coulomb of charge it handles by
   a. 2 volts
   b. 10 volts
   c. 10 joules
   d. 10 amps

7. If a 10 volt potential drop is measured when 2 amps of current is used, the size of the resistor is
   a. 10 Ω
   b. 2 Ω
   c. 5 Ω
   d. 20 Ω

8. One ohm is equal to
   a. N − m
   b. $\frac{C}{s}$
   c. volt/amp
   d. $N - \frac{m^2}{C^2}$

9. A voltmeter has
   a. high
   b. low
   c. variable resistance

10. Current will flow in the circuit at the top of the page from
    a. A to B to C to D
    b. D to C to B to A
    c. first (a), then (b)

Name: _____   Section: _____

CURRENT, VOLTAGE AND RESISTANCE IN SERIES CIRCUITS

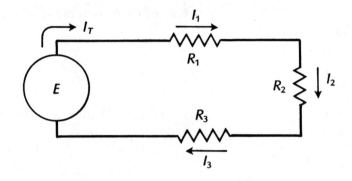

Current. Since there is only one pathway through the circuit, the current through any portion of the path is the same:

$$\boxed{I_T = I_1 = I_2 = I_3}$$

Resistance. The current is resisted by the resistance in R_1, then R_2, and then R_3, so the total resistance, R_T, in this circuit is the sum of the individual resistances:

$$\boxed{R_T = R_1 + R_2 + R_3}$$

Voltage. Ohm's law states that the resistance in any part of a circuit is equal to the voltage divided by the current. If we use the resistance relationship from above:

$$R_T = R_1 + R_2 + R_3$$

and substitute from Ohm's law:

$$\frac{E}{I_T} = \frac{V_1}{I_1} + \frac{V_2}{I_2} + \frac{V_3}{I_3}$$

but $I_T = I_1 = I_2 = I_3$ and therefore:

$$\boxed{E = V_1 + V_2 + V_3}$$

The E.M.F. impressed across a series circuit divides among the individual resistances in the circuit so that the sum of the voltage drops (V_1, V_2, and V_3) equals the E.M.F. (E).

Name: _____   Section: _____

CURRENT, VOLTAGE AND RESISTANCE IN PARALLEL CIRCUITS

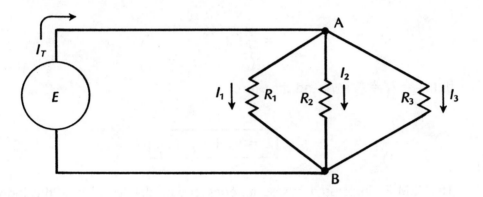

Current. The total current in the circuit, I_T, divides at point A, a portion of it going through each branch, I_1, I_2, and I_3 before recombining again at point B:

$$\boxed{I_T = I_1 + I_2 + I_3}$$

Voltage. Each resistance connects the same two points in the circuit, A and B, so the potential difference (voltage drop) across each resistor is the same. Any energy carrying charge migrates through only one resistor in this circuit, so:

$$\boxed{E = V_1 = V_2 = V_3}$$

Resistance. From Ohm's law, the current in a circuit or any portion of a circuit is equal to the voltage divided by the resistance. Using the current relationships for parallel connections:

$$I_T = I_1 + I_2 + I_3$$

and substituting via Ohm's law:

$$\frac{E}{R_T} = \frac{V_1}{R_1} + \frac{V_2}{R_2} + \frac{V_3}{R_3}$$

but: $E = V_1 = V_2 = V_3$ so:

$$\boxed{\frac{1}{R_T} = \frac{1}{R_1} + \frac{1}{R_2} + \frac{1}{R_3}}$$

As the number of parallel branches increases, the overall resistance of the circuit, R_T, decreases.

Name: _____   Section: _____

SERIES CIRCUITS

Key aspect: only *one* current *path* from high to low potential. Circuit diagram of *two resistors in series (meters included):*

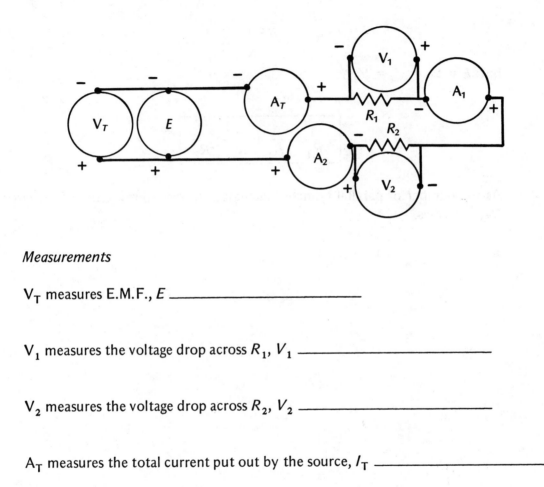

Measurements

V_T measures E.M.F., E _____

V_1 measures the voltage drop across R_1, V_1 _____

V_2 measures the voltage drop across R_2, V_2 _____

A_T measures the total current put out by the source, I_T _____

A_1 measures the current through R_1, I_1 _____

A_2 measures the current through R_2, I_2 _____

Color codes show the value of R_1 and R_2 R_1 _____

R_2 _____

Calculations

1. Does $E = V_1 + V_2$?

2. Does $I_T = I_1 = I_2$? } Cardinal rules for series circuits

3. Does $R_T^* = R_1 + R_2$?

   *($E = I_T R_T$), Solve for value of R_T

   Does Ohm's law hold true for each part of the circuit?

4. Does $V_1 = I_1 R_1$?

5. Does $V_2 = I_2 R_2$?

Name: _____   Section: _____

PARALLEL CIRCUITS

Key aspect: alternate paths for current from high to low potential. Circuit diagram of *two resistors in parallel* (meters included):

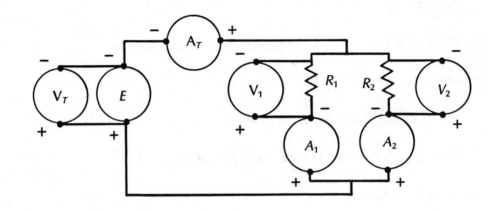

Measurements

V_T measures the E.M.F., E _____

V_1 measures the voltage drop across R_1, V_1 _____

V_2 measures the voltage drop across R_2, V_2 _____

A_T measures the current (total) put out by the source I_T _____

A_1 measures the current through R_1, I_1 _____

A_2 measures the current through R_2, I_2 _____

Color codes give R_1 and R_2, R_1 _____

R_2 _____

Calculations

Does:

1. $E = V_1 = V_2$?

2. $I_T = I_1 + I_2$?

$\left.\begin{array}{l}\end{array}\right\}$ Cardinal rules for parallel circuits

3. $\dfrac{1}{R_T^*} = \dfrac{1}{R_1} + \dfrac{1}{R_2}$?

   *($E = I_T R_T$), Solve for value of R_T

Does Ohm's law hold true for each part of the circuit? Does:

4. $V_1 = I_1 R_1$?

5. $V_2 = I_2 R_2$?

Name: _____   Section: _____

POWER AND ENERGY QUIZ

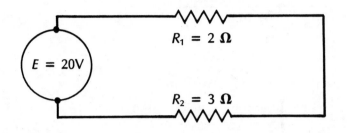

(1–5)

1. The current in this circuit is _____

2. What is the power dissipated in R_1? _____

3. What is the power dissipated in R_2? _____

4. If the circuit operates for 30 seconds, how much energy is provided by the source?

   _____

5. How much energy is dissipated in R_2 in 30 seconds? _____

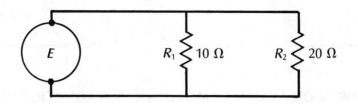

(6–10)

6. Which resistor has more current in it? _____

7. Which one dissipates more power? _____

8. After 30 seconds of operation, R_2 has used 600 joules of energy. What is the circuit E.M.F.? _____

9. What is the current in R_1? _____

10. What is the power output of the E.M.F.? _____

Name: _____   Section: _____

FORCE ON A CHARGE MOVING IN A MAGNETIC FIELD

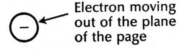

Electron moving out of the plane of the page

Use Ampere's left-hand rule to draw the flux lines associated with this moving electron.

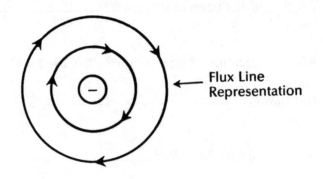

Flux Line Representation

Suppose this electron moves through a magnetic field as shown:

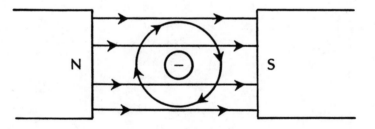

Note that *above* the charge, its flux lines and the ones due to the magnetic field are in the same direction—producing a strong resultant field in that region. Below the charge, its flux lines are opposite in direction to those of the magnets—producing a weaker resultant field. The charge experiences a deflecting force from stronger to weaker regions—downward in this example.

Predict the direction of the deflecting force in the following cases. In each instance figure out the direction of the flux lines associated with the movement of the charge. Combine that field with the flux lines due to the magnet, determine strong and weak regions of the resultant field based on similarity and oppositeness of flux line directions, then predict the deflecting force direction:

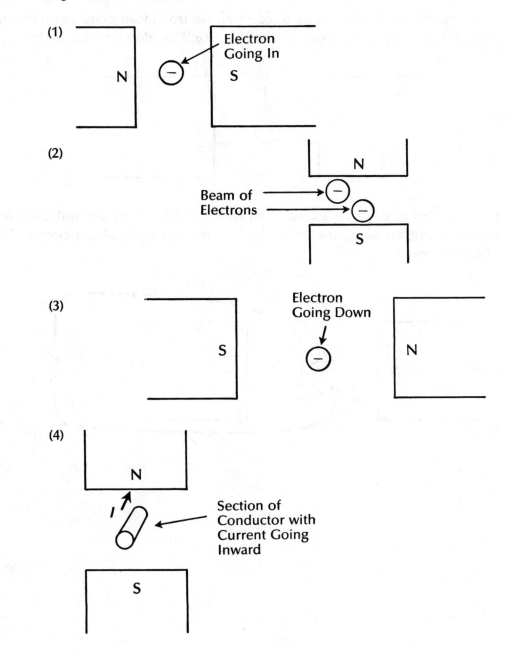

Name: _____   Section: _____

INDUCED CURRENTS

You can now predict that the deflecting force on an electron moving downward through a magnetic field as shown is in to the plane of the page (see Reproduction Page 101):

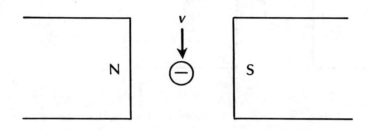

If this charge happens to be inside a conductor, then the deflecting force will cause it and other electrons to migrate along the conductor and through a completed circuit. This is called an induced current.

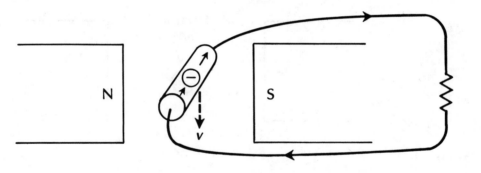

Lenz's law states that the direction of the induced current is such that its magnetic effect opposes the motion inducing the current. In our example, the direction of the induced current in the section of conductor shown is in to the plane of the page; the direction of the motion inducing it is downward. If we draw in the flux lines associated with the induced current:

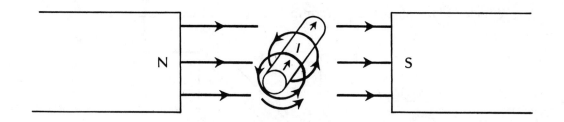

Combining this magnetic effect with the permanent magnetic field, the resultant field below the conductor is strong, while the resultant field above the conductor is weak. This tends to deflect the conductor upward. This upward force is the opposition to the downward motion of the conductor that is inducing the current in the first place—thus exemplifying Lenz's statement.

Name: _____   Section: _____

INDUCTION AND FIELDS QUIZ

1. Which end becomes the (−) terminal? _____

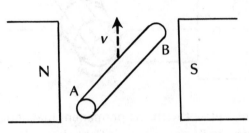

2. According to Lenz, the magnetic force on the conductor is directed _____
   a. up
   b. down
   c. right
   d. left

3. Which end is the N. pole? _____

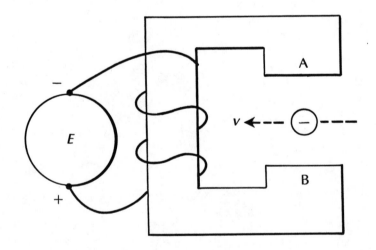

4. The direction of the force on the electron is _____
   a. up
   b. left
   c. in
   d. out

5. As the speed of an operating motor increases, the current drawn _____

   _____ .

6. When current goes through the two wires as shown, the wires will _____
   a. attract
   b. repel
   c. show no effect

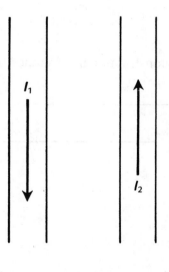

7. The current in the coil of a D.C. generator travels _____
   a. in one direction
   b. in both directions

8. Where is the field the strongest? _____
    a. on top
    b. bottom
    c. left
    d. right

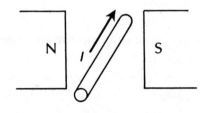

9. In which direction will the conductor tend to move? _____
    a. left
    b. right
    c. up
    d. down

10. What is the basic constructional difference between an A.C. and a D.C. generator?

_____

_____

Appendix D

Feedback Form

Your comments about this book will be very helpful to us in planning other books in the *Guidebook for Teaching* Series and in making revisions in *A Guidebook for Teaching Physics*. Please tear out the form that appears on the following page and use it to let me know your reactions to *A Guidebook for Teaching Physics*. The author promises a personal reply. Mail the form to:

William Yurkewicz, Jr.
c/o Longwood Division
Allyn and Bacon, Inc.
7 Wells Avenue
Newton, Massachusetts 02159

Your school: _____
Address: _____
City and state: _____
Date: _____

William Yurkewicz, Jr.
c/o Longwood Division
Allyn and Bacon, Inc.
7 Wells Avenue
Newton, Massachusetts 02159

Dear Bill:

My name is _____ and I want to tell you what
I thought of your book *A Guidebook for Teaching Physics*. I liked certain things about the
book, including: _____

_____

_____

_____

I do, however, feel that the book could be improved in the following ways: _____

_____

_____

_____

There were some other things I wish the book had included, such as: _____

_____

_____

_____

Here is something that happened in my class when I used an idea from your book: _____

_____

_____

_____

[optional] : Enclosed is an alternate learning activity that has worked well with my classes. You may wish to include it in future revisions. _____

_____

_____

_____

_____

_____

Sincerely yours,

_____